T0319277

# THE FUTURE OF CHINESE MANUFACTURING

# THE FUTURE OF CHINESE MANUFACTURING

Employment and Labour Challenges

**TACHIA CHIN**
*Professor, School of Management,
Hangzhou Dianzi University,
Hangzhou, China*

**CHRIS ROWLEY**
*Kellogg College, University of Oxford and
Cass Business School, City, University of London
Griffith Business School and Griffith Asia Institute,
Griffith University, Australia Institute of Asia and
Pacific Studies, Nottingham University, UK*

ELSEVIER

Elsevier
Radarweg 29, PO Box 211, 1000 AE Amsterdam, Netherlands
The Boulevard, Langford Lane, Kidlington, Oxford OX5 1GB, United Kingdom
50 Hampshire Street, 5th Floor, Cambridge, MA 02139, United States

**Notices**
Knowledge and best practice in this field are constantly changing. As new research and experience
broaden our understanding, changes in research methods, professional practices, or medical treatment
may become necessary.

Practitioners and researchers must always rely on their own experience and knowledge in evaluating and
using any information, methods, compounds, or experiments described herein. In using such information
or methods they should be mindful of their own safety and the safety of others, including parties for
whom they have a professional responsibility.

To the fullest extent of the law, neither the Publisher nor the authors, contributors, or editors, assume any
liability for any injury and/or damage to persons or property as a matter of products liability, negligence or
otherwise, or from any use or operation of any methods, products, instructions, or ideas contained in the
material herein.

**Library of Congress Cataloging-in-Publication Data**
A catalog record for this book is available from the Library of Congress

**British Library Cataloguing-in-Publication Data**
A catalogue record for this book is available from the British Library

ISBN: 978-0-08-101108-9

For information on all Elsevier publications
visit our website at https://www.elsevier.com/books-and-journals

Working together
to grow libraries in
developing countries

www.elsevier.com • www.bookaid.org

*Publisher:* Glyn Jones
*Acquisition Editor:* Glyn Jones
*Editorial Project Manager:* Charlotte Rowley
*Production Project Manager:* Sreejith Viswanathan
*Cover Designer:* Greg Harris

Typeset by SPi Global, India

# CONTENTS

*Foreword*                                                                                   *vii*

1. **Introduction: China's Manufacturing: Labour Challenges Ahead**          **1**
   1.1 Introduction                                                                           1
   1.2 Structure of the Book                                                                  2
   1.3 Conclusion                                                                             3

2. **Challenges for Manufacturing in China**                                      **5**
   2.1 Introduction                                                                           5
   2.2 Development History of China's Auto Manufacturing                                      6
   2.3 Policy Support for Own-Brand Car Production: Panacea or Placebo?                       10
   2.4 Conclusion                                                                            23
   Appendix                                                                                  23

3. **FDI Manufacturers and Their Upgrading Strategies**                          **25**
   3.1 Introduction                                                                          25
   3.2 Upgrading Strategies by Singapore/FDI OEMs in China                                   26
   3.3 Upgrading to OBM by an Entrepreneurial British OEM in China                           44
   3.4 Conclusion                                                                            58

4. **Branding in Reverse Internationalization: Evidence From
   Local Entrepreneurial OEMs**                                                   **61**
   4.1 Introduction                                                                          61
   4.2 Reverse Internationalization by Chinese Global Start-UP OEMs                          62
   4.3 Entrepreneurial Orientation–Performance Relationships in Reverse
       Internationalization by Chinese Global Start-Up OEMs: Social Networks
       and Strategic Flexibility                                                             83
   4.4 Conclusion                                                                           107

5. **A Yin–Yang Harmony Cognition to Employer–Employee
   Relationships**                                                                **109**
   5.1 Introduction                                                                         109
   5.2 Harmony and OCB in Chinese Organizations                                             110
   5.3 Harmony as a Means to Enhance Affective Commitment
       in Chinese Organizations                                                             132
   5.4 Conclusion                                                                           150

**6. Labour Dispute and Conflict Resolution: A Yin–Yang Harmony View**                                              **153**

    **6.1** Introduction                                                      153

    **6.2** Understanding Labour Conflicts in Chinese Manufacturing:
        A Yin–Yang Harmony Perspective                                156

    **6.3** Conclusion                                                       188

**7. Cross-Cultural Management: A Globalized Production Network**         **191**

    **7.1** Introduction                                                     191

    **7.2** Cross-Cultural Knowledge Transfer in a Chinese Manufacturing MNE:
        The Role of Translation                                       192

    **7.3** Conclusion                                                       215

    **Appendix:** Interview questions                                        216

**8. Conclusion: Reflection**                                            **217**

*References*                                                             *221*

*Index*                                                                  *239*

# FOREWORD

For decades, China has been the world's manufacturing hub employing the largest labour force, and it still is. However, the increasing urbanization and the necessary upgrades to the international standards of employment have pushed an unprecedented yet continuous transformation of China's manufacturing sector that requires a much deeper investigation. In this book, Prof. Chin and Prof. Rowley provide a variety of precious and factual materials that bring new insights into relevant issues, particularly regarding the importance of building a harmonious culture to resolve labour disputes. It is a must read for all who seek to gain a better understanding of the ongoing transformation and corresponding labour challenges happening in the Chinese context.

RICHARD TSUEI, Ph.D,
Vice President
Guanxgxi Wuzhou Zhongheng Group Co., Ltd.
China

While the development of automation, Internet of things as well as artificial intelligence added to 'things' have fundamentally changed China's manufacturing landscape, the skillsets required nowadays are becoming more and more difficult to acquire by the mass of Chinese workers available. Prof. Chin and Prof. Rowley have made a remarkable effort in weaving together representative stories and significant evidence that disclose fresh and critical information on relevant issues—this book presents a comprehensive analysis of the evolution course, emerging trend as well as the future prospect of the Chinese manufacturing sector.

CHANG CHAI TAN,
Chairman
Spindex Industries Ltd.
Singapore

CHAPTER ONE

# Introduction: China's Manufacturing: Labour Challenges Ahead

## 1.1 INTRODUCTION

Along with the 2008 financial crisis, the 2010 Euro zone debt crisis, and the 2015 Brexit 'yes' vote, the world's economic and political situation has become more volatile and unpredictable, while global manufacturing industries are facing a new round of restructuring. Given that a viable manufacturing sector constitutes the cornerstone for a nation's social and economic growth, to sustain national competitiveness in this new era riddled with uncertainties, several of the top manufacturing countries have proposed strategies at the state level: the United States proclaimed a reindustrialization and manufacturing renaissance strategy in 2010; Germany advocated a new concept of *Industry 4.0* in 2013; and the United Kingdom called for economic 'rebalancing' with the resurgence of manufacturing.

China is no exception to this developmental trend. The government has also proclaimed the *Made in China 2025* initiative, encouraging local manufacturing firms to upgrade themselves from the traditional labour-intensive to a modern high-tech, innovation-driven, and service-oriented manufacturing industry. In other words, moving towards higher value-added domains is the guiding direction of China's manufacturing transition.

However, this upgrading and transformation process has and will inevitably bring forth new and complex labour- and employment-related challenges for China's manufacturing as traditional jobs requiring low pay, manual dexterity, and physical skills are disappearing, coinciding with the appearance of more labour shortages, high-tech, and knowledge-intensive job opportunities. Yet the current manufacturing workforce in China is mainly composed of poorly educated migrant workers, many of whom come from poverty-stricken rural areas. Hence, it is not easy for these workers to upgrade their skills in adaptation to new job specifications and

*The Future of Chinese Manufacturing*
https://doi.org/10.1016/B978-0-08-101108-9.00001-X

qualifications, particularly for those who are aged or have spent more than 10 years in similar positions. This situation sometimes creates a dilemma for companies. Old staff need retraining to meet new work standards while young migrant workers do not see manufacturing jobs as a good career choice as more and more such jobs will be replaced by machines.

In this vein, in recent years, manufacturing employment in China has been confronted with severe labour-related issues, such as high turnover rates, difficulties in recruiting young people, and shortages of skilled workers. While labour strikes, mass layoffs, and downsizing are deemed as a common business practice in Chinese manufacturing, the conflicts between production workers and management have become one of the major concerns that requires greater attention and deeper investigation (Chin & Liu, 2015). Hence, our book aims to elucidate the employment and human resource (HR)-related challenges that the Chinese manufacturing industry is facing in the new era of economic transformation.

## 1.2 STRUCTURE OF THE BOOK

In Chapter 2, using the auto manufacturing industry as an example, our book begins with an overview of the historical development of the Chinese manufacturing industry over the past three decades. It then introduces an empirical study that illustrates the role of the government as the most crucial 'invisible hand' in influencing goal orientation towards the creation of own brands among manufacturing firms in China.

In Chapter 3, three cases that focus on Singapore-, Taiwan-, and British-invested companies in China demonstrate how foreign manufacturers from different home countries cope with changes in the Chinese market and make strategic options when carrying out upgrading along global value chains (GVCs). In addition to addressing the contributions of foreign investment to the growth of Chinese manufacturing, this chapter also highlights the importance of acquiring institutional resources to compete in China.

In Chapter 4, two empirical studies are presented to introduce a typical, yet still under-researched, type of global start-up manufacturer emerging from China. Facing the recent global industrial and economic restructuring, such firms could not continue to rely on the export-oriented growth model of the past three decades to sustain profits. Hence, this chapter addresses a prominent 'reverse internationalization phenomenon', delineating why and how these Chinese entrepreneurial manufacturers are striving to transform their focus from international competition to local markets.

In Chapter 5, two studies are introduced to elucidate how Chinese harmonious culture—which is decoded and interpreted by *Yijing*'s eight-trigram model (Fung, 1997)—affects manufacturing employees' attitude and behaviour at work. While China to date still has more than 100 million production workers, many of whom are recruited by the foreign-invested enterprises (FIEs), this chapter explores what fosters an attitude of openness to see the wisdom ingrained in Chinese harmonious culture and, most importantly, to link it with HR practices during the transition from a transitional labour-intensive and export-driven system to a modern service-oriented and innovation-driven manufacturing system.

In Chapter 6, from an emic Yin–Yang harmony perspective, we present a unique, indigenous circled 5C (conflict–clash–communication–compromise–consensus) model for helping to possibly resolve labour conflicts in China's manufacturing sector. While more and more Chinese manufacturers shut down their local factories and shift production lines to other regions with cheap labour, it is expected that the number of labour dispute cases and work activism will possibly continue to increase. This chapter helps to deepen our understanding of how to tackle labour conflicts in China's socialist market economy system.

In Chapter 7, considering the ongoing trend to build geographically dispersed manufacturing bases for cost advantages, cross-cultural management and corresponding language and translation-related issues are raising harsh challenges for Chinese manufacturers. To better describe this phenomenon, we introduce a research that proposes a novel, indigenous model delineating the dynamic and vital role of translation as a boundary-spanning tool in cross-border knowledge transfer within the intra-organizational networks of Chinese manufacturing firms.

In Chapter 8, we first make a brief summary of this book and then examine the prospect of future employment in China's manufacturing.

## 1.3 CONCLUSION

Overall, the overarching aim of our book is to delve into the root causes of relevant issues in China's economy today in a more comprehensive and contextualized way. We present several studies built upon the Chinese context to elucidate the distinctive growth patterns and models of Chinese manufacturing relative to those of the developed economies in the West.

In addition, it is worth noting that owing to the uniqueness of China's socialist market system, culture, and rich history, its manufacturing-led economic miracle and the above-mentioned labour-related issues cannot be fully explained or solved by the rationales underpinning Western business theories and practices (Chin & Liu, 2017; Redding, 2016; Rowley & Oh, 2016). Hence, in our book, to truly embody the cultural idiosyncrasy of Chinese employees, we employ a unique 'Yin–Yang Harmony' perspective to discuss labour–management relations that could better make sense, decode, and contextualize the phenomena that may be indigenous to China's manufacturing industry.

In sum, we aim to provide relevant theory, research, evidence, and practical insight and impacts for twin audiences: first, for academics globally to both expand and teach with; and second, for business and management practitioners and policymakers. Too often, for both 'camps', these domains are seen and treated as somewhat irrelevant to each other and sealed. We hope to break that seal.

# CHAPTER TWO

# Challenges for Manufacturing in China

## 2.1 INTRODUCTION

### 2.1.1 Labour Challenges of China's Manufacturing Industry

With one-fifth of the world's workforce (Chin, 2015), China has taken advantage of its cheap labour to become the world's factory—such as providing low-end, labour-intensive production services, that is, original equipment manufacturing (OEM) to mature-market clients. This has helped to achieve stunning growth in the past three decades (Child & Rodrigues, 2005; Chin, Liu, & Yang, 2016; Warner, 2015). The manufacturing sector has attracted huge foreign direct investment (FDI), making tremendous contributions to the gross domestic product (GDP), still accounting for 40.9% of total GDP (US$ 10.4 trillion) in 2015 (National Bureau of Statistics of China, 2017).

However, the new labour contract law was promulgated by the Chinese government, which began to raise labour costs in 2008. The fluctuation of the RMB exchange rate was among the factors diminishing the original cost advantages in the Chinese manufacturing. To tackle the resultant enormous cost pressure, many large multinational corporations (MNCs), such as Panasonic, Philips, and Seagate, increased their automation levels and also shifted their production bases from coastal to inland cities of China or to other developing countries with lower wages, such as India, Vietnam, and Indonesia. For example, the Yue Yuan Group, listed on the Hong Kong Stock Exchange, is the world's largest footwear manufacturer. It set up its first manufacturing facilities in China in 1988, mainly providing OEM services for global brands such as Nike, Adidas, New Balance, Puma, Converse, etc. It once had >10 plants with around 175,000 workers but now has only five factories with about 40,000 employees in China. The Yue Yuan Group has vastly expanded its production lines in Vietnam and Indonesia since 2009, its factories accounting for 64% of its total output in 2015.[1]

Despite the above phenomenon signifying a new trend of shifting production capacity from China to other countries with cheaper workforces among OEM firms, China still has the largest manufacturing companies and factories in the world and continues to be the United States biggest trading partner for manufacturing goods. The information of the development history of China's manufacturing sector over the past three decades is provided to the readers in the following sections. The development history of China's auto industry is described in the next section, followed by recent study of the effect of policy support on own-brand innovation in China's auto industry. The concepts of the GVC and three corresponding upgrading terms are explained in the conclusion.

## 2.2 DEVELOPMENT HISTORY OF CHINA'S AUTO MANUFACTURING

### 2.2.1 Employment Dilemma

Before introducing our research on the growth story of the Chinese auto industry, we use Fig. 2.1 to provide readers with a clear picture and better understanding of the significance of the labour-related issues facing China's manufacturing. The histogram shows the contribution proportions of the manufacturing sector to total GDP (see values on the right side), while the

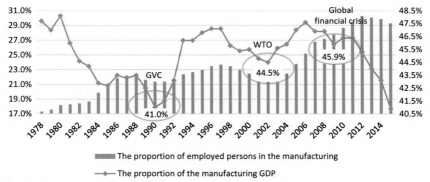

**Fig. 2.1** Employment versus GDP in China's manufacturing.

---

[1] http://www.yueyuen.com/index.php/en/

curve indicates the proportion of the manufacturing employment to the total employment from 1978 to 2015 in China (see the values on the left side).

A closer examination of Fig. 2.1 suggests three key turning points (V curves):

**(1)** About 1990: The key event explaining the trend from fall to rise was the emergence of GVCs that enabled low-end, labour-intensive manufacturers in China to serve as OEM suppliers for advanced economy MNCs whereby the Chinese manufacturing industry gained quick access to export markets and began to boom.

**(2)** About 2002: The key event explaining this turning point was China joining the World Trade Organization (WTO) in 2001 whereby the government agreed to reduce trade barriers, such as import tariffs, and provide export tax exemption for WTO members. Since then, the Chinese manufacturing industry has attracted a substantial amount of FDI and grown at a remarkable rate.

**(3)** About 2009: The key event explaining this turning point was the 2008 global financial crisis that triggered a prolonged global economic stagnation and the restructuring of global manufacturing. To tackle this challenge, the Chinese government forcefully implemented the 4 trillion RMB investment plan to stimulate local demand. Chinese manufacturers therefore have been encouraged to return and compete in their domestic market from the export market since then—the reverse internationalization phenomenon (Chin et al., 2016).

Overall, the three turning points explicitly highlight the major driving forces for Chinese manufacturing over the past three decades, namely the rapid rise of the GVC and the tremendous inflow of FDI during the 1990s—which to a large extent underscores the pivotal role of the government intervention in China's development trajectory. However, implicit in Fig. 2.1 is the evidence of the employment dilemma—that the ratio of manufacturing employment to total employment kept increasing—despite the contribution of the manufacturing industry to total GDP declining sharply after 2011.

## 2.2.2 Development History of the Chinese Auto Industry

Since China's economic reforms and the opening up of the economy, auto manufacturing has been designated as a pillar industry—a crucial engine fuelling China's economic growth. Referring to Tian (2007) and Yang, Chin, Liu, and Yao (2017), we also divide the development of China's auto industry into three phases: (1) 1953–78, (2) 1979–94, and (3) 1995–present.

In Phase 1, the entire auto industry was totally controlled and subsidized by the central planning economic system. This consisted of 53 small-sized car producers and 166 car parts manufacturers. According to national statistics, there were only 149,000 vans and 2640 sedans produced in 1978 since consumer demand was not a concern at that time (Tian, 2007).

In Phase 2, the auto industry was formally proclaimed by the Chinese government as a 'pillar industry' that could propel the national economy and people's livelihoods. Owing to the deepening of China's open-door policy and market reform, there was a rising demand for cars. Nevertheless, the automotive industry necessitated the implementation of complex production processes (Lockstrom, Schadel, Harrison, Moser, & Malhotra, 2010), but—it was impossible for Chinese firms without sufficient experience to quickly and independently develop all the technical expertise and capabilities required to produce vehicles. To protect and strengthen the competitiveness of local carmakers, since the late 1980s the Chinese government, instead of waiting passively for the 'natural' transfer of advanced technology from FDIs, had enacted a series of 'market for technology' policies to encourage state-owned enterprises (SOEs) to proactively learn know-how from world-renowned automakers by forming joint ventures (JVs) with them (Redding & Drew, 2016). Thus, a few foreign auto brands have been granted privileged access to the Chinese domestic market. The primary goal of these policies was to diversify and reinforce the technology spillover channels between the local firms and the MNCs for accelerating the pace of indigenous innovation (Chou, Chang, & Li, 2014; Yang & Tang, 2014). However, in the 1980s, the above-mentioned 'market for technology' policy permitted only six large SOEs to set up JVs with selected MNCs and to build joint manufacturing bases, which included three large bases as follows: First Automobile Works (FAW), Second (Dongfeng) Automobile Works and Shanghai Automotive Industry Corporation (SAIC), and three small bases: Beijing Jeep, Tianjin Xiali, and Guangzhou Peugeot.

The auto industry benefited greatly from the 1986 to 1991 national 5-year plans. In 1994, the Chinese central government reiterated the significance of vitalizing the auto industry. One of the most influential policies was announced—which pointed out several future development directions enabling Chinese SOEs to cooperate more closely with international auto brands (Motohashia & Yuan, 2010). The three directions were as follows: (1) consolidating small and fragmented local auto producers by raising the entry threshold; (2) further protecting and fostering domestic auto-related industries (i.e. the auto parts and components industry); and (3) better clarifying FDI regulations. As a result, most Chinese automakers formed strategic alliances with well-known foreign car brands during this period.

In Phase 3, the Chinese government continued to position the auto industry as a vital growth engine for the whole country; though the State Council had halted the 'market-for-technology' policy in 2006 in the auto industry, it implemented more preferential treatment policies to support domestic car brands. Since 1995, the demand for vehicles further boomed at a record-setting pace, as the fast-growing economy enabled more families to afford a car. With this trend, vehicle production reached 2 million in 2000, 8.8 million in 2007, and over 20 million in 2013.

To grasp this opportunity, policymakers launched stronger policies in which SOEs and Sino-foreign JVs were given higher priority to expand their production and market shares for achieving economies of scale in China (Gallagher, 2006; Lockstrom et al., 2010). Since 2000, the whole Chinese car market has been dominated by Sino-foreign JVs equipped with superior innovative capabilities over pure SOEs and domestic private firms. It is worth noting that the entry barriers, such as strict FDI constraints preventing foreign carmakers from investing directly in China, remain even today, though the total purchase taxes, such as import tariff and other levies, were reduced from a very high rate of >100% to about 50% in recent years.

### 2.2.2.1 Brief Summary

The above detail confirms that Chinese SOEs have been accustomed to relying on favourable policies to form strategic alliances with foreign auto brands for better profits and rapid product upgrade. Viewed from this angle, the state-controlled Sino-foreign JV, as a unique type of state-owned MNC in China (Curevo-Cazurra, Inkpen, Musacchio, & Ramaswamy, 2014), has evolved to become a kind of interest group with substantial monopoly power. The JVs with their foreign-brand vehicles are the national champions in China's auto market. This kind of JV is very likely to keep occupying the predominant position and more JVs are expected to emerge in the future if the degree of policy support stays the same or increases.

In short, this development history of China's auto market highlights the vital role of governmental intervention/policy agenda in shaping the competition patterns in Chinese manufacturing. However, despite a series of preferential policies issued to encourage domestic companies producing own-brand cars, creating proprietary brands seems to remain difficult for both

SOEs and local private carmakers. For a better understanding of this critical issue, our recent study on relevant topics is presented in the next section.

## 2.3 POLICY SUPPORT FOR OWN-BRAND CAR PRODUCTION: PANACEA OR PLACEBO?

### 2.3.1 Introduction

China surpassed the United States to become the world's largest car market in 2009 and has evolved into a new competitor in the global auto market with fast-growing domestic brands such as Chery, BYD, and Geely (Drauz, 2013; Wang & Kimble, 2013). Consequently, increasing attention has been paid to analysing the determinants for growth of this industry as well as its significant upgrading trajectory from OEM to own-brand manufacturing (OBM) (Chin et al., 2016; Wang & Tanaka, 2011). Among the key success factors, the industry supporting policy is widely recognized as the most crucial one because of its prominent contributions to boosting vehicle sales, knowledge transfer between MNCs and local firms, and the privatization of SOEs via the establishment of international JVs (Curevo-Cazurra et al., 2014; Motohashia & Yuan, 2010; Townsend & Calantone, 2014). The prosperity of the Chinese auto industry occurs within a unique institutional framework comprising various legal constraints, political connections, and bureaucratic rules, where the government intervenes in the market by means of industrial policy. However, although China's strong growth momentum in the past decades has stimulated demand for cars, its automobile industry is confronting unprecedented challenges due to the global economic slowdown and restructuring. It requires more empirical and timely studies to examine the effectiveness and actual influence of policy support on this industry to predict whether policy support can continuously help carmakers achieve sustainable development under China's economic situation. Therefore, we investigate relevant issues in depth from a more pragmatic perspective.

In the 1990s, the Chinese central government explicitly promulgated the view that the automobile industry was an important 'national pillar' industry that should be fully controlled and even monopolized by the central government in consideration of its strong association with the usage of tremendous strategic resources of a nation. As such, the auto industry inherently carries a duty to act as a major driving engine nudging the entire Chinese economy in a certain direction (Tian, 2007). Consistent with this, a variety of industrial policies were stipulated to enhance the innovativeness and protect the competitiveness of local firms, particularly SOEs. Among these, the most influential policies often reinforced the entry regulations for FDI so as to prevent foreign auto firms from investing in China independently. More specifically, though the Chinese government carried out the 'trade market for technology' strategy to facilitate indigenous firms to pursue innovation by collaborating with developed-country partners (Zheng, 2014), the wholly foreign-owned vehicle manufacturers have only been allowed to enter China by partnering with Chinese SOEs via the establishment of JVs. Despite having certain constraints, this national strategy still provided a valuable opportunity for all the world's big automakers to gain legitimate access to the fast-growing Chinese market. As a result, a rising number of Sino-foreign JVs emerged and have been holding a monopolistic position in this context.

However, although SOEs received vigorous policy incentives to form Sino-foreign JVs with world-famous carmakers, their performance was not very satisfactory in terms of developing and marketing their own brands. In 2004, to fuel the desire for cooperative innovation, the Chinese government further put forward a variety of tempting financial initiatives for Sino-foreign JVs to create new car brands, but these initiatives seem to have been ineffective so far. For example, the total sales volume was around 12 million vehicles in 2013 in China, of which only 3.3 million were local-brand vehicles while >8 million were produced by the Sino-foreign JVs under foreign and co-brand names, such as Dongfeng Honda and Bejing Benz. Even worse, some of the JVs that took advantage of the policy support were found to have frequently engaged in rent-seeking behaviour to lobby the government for privileges, rather than being dedicated to public welfare (Ngo, 2008). It is questionable whether policy support fosters independent brand development in the Chinese auto industry, despite the fact that upgrading to OBM status as a national priority constitutes the basis for moving China up the GVC (*China's 12th 5-Year Economic Plan 2011–15*; *China's 13th 5-Year Economic Plan 2016–21*).

Scholars in general acknowledge that industrial policies may exert a positive impact on a firm's innovation activities in emerging economies (Chin et al., 2016; Du & Luo, 2016), but the above-mentioned phenomenon seems to suggest an opposite story. While prior research concerning the nature and influence of policy intervention in China's auto industry has drawn conflicting conclusions (Chen, Firth, & Xu, 2009; Jia, 2016), the existing literature and academic theories remain unable to explain comprehensively the interplay and cause-and-effect relationships among governmental policy, Sino-foreign JVs, and own-brand innovation in the Chinese context. To fill this gap, we demonstrate their relationships from a more context-specific and practical point of view. In this research, we first propose a novel and indigenous approach to measure the degree of policy support and then capitalize on the 2014 data set from China's National Bureau of Statistics to investigate how the degree of policy support affects own-brand innovation in this context.

A main contribution is to identify the mediating effect of Sino-foreign JVs on the relationship between policy support and foreign brand preference, demonstrating that policy support may not always be beneficial but sometimes detrimental to indigenous innovation. Moreover, a novel, context-specific method was employed to evaluate the degree to which policy support in China embodies the distinctive institutional complexity and intricate social network embedded in the local car market. As far as practical implications are concerned, our findings provide valuable information for policymakers to formulate more feasible, or further rectify, existing policies during the critical period of China's socio-economic transformation.

### 2.3.2 Sino-Foreign JVs, Governmental Support, and Own-Brand Innovation

A review of the literature shows that Sino-foreign JVs, as an effective means of attracting FDI into China, have been widely identified as a crucial source of both direct capital input and research and development (R&D) knowledge spillovers from developed-country MNCs to local enterprises (Ma, Yu, Gao, Zhou, & Yang, 2015; Wei & Liu, 2006). FDI usually represents a conglomeration of different types of capital, for example, modern production know-how (i.e. organizational capital), good managerial skills and talent (i.e. human capital), and the trust and relationships with the host country institutions (i.e. social capital). The FDI spillover effects are proven to facilitate cross-border knowledge creation, transfer, and diffusion. All of these factors have a dramatic impact on improvements in the livelihood of local people and the prosperity of host countries, as shown in the East Asian model of economic development (Eapen, 2012; Redding & Drew, 2016). Hence, since China had lagged far behind advanced nations in many aspects of high-tech auto manufacturing, the government implemented the 'market for technology' policy to spur learning from FDIs/developed economy partners within JVs with expedition of technology transfer in mind (Chou et al., 2014; Yang & Tang, 2014). According to the arguments above, we hypothesize as follows:

**Hypothesis 1:** The degree of policy support positively relates to the establishment of Sino-foreign JVs in China's auto industry.

Quite a few studies have elucidated the positive effects of Sino-foreign strategic alliances on technological innovation and independent brand creation in the Chinese manufacturing sector (Chin et al., 2016). Within the electronics industry, Lenovo, TCL, and Huawei are examples of the above. In the early stages, Chinese OEMs, as latecomers, might have drawn on their forging of strategic alliances with global brands (e.g. IBM, Cisco, and Motorola) as a means of being embedded into their GVCs, whereby OEMs make it easier to access state-of-the-art technology and accurate market information owned by the forerunners (Chin, 2014, 2015; Chin & Liu, 2015). As soon as Chinese OEM suppliers acquire core knowledge, technology, and skills from their foreign counterparts, they in turn become eager to embark on OBM for higher economic returns (Horng & Chen, 2008). While transition from the OEM to the OBM mode represents a national initiative, it is a desired goal for many Chinese contract manufacturers to echo the own-brand strategy and, in so doing, catch up with the GVC first movers (e.g. world-class brands and MNCs) (Chin et al., 2016; Horng & Chen, 2008).

However, in terms of the automobile industry, the evidence is indeterminate as to whether Sino-foreign JVs may adversely affect the upgrading of industrial technology, especially concerning own-brand innovation (Tian, 2007). The bulk, just over two-thirds (about 67%), of auto sales in China were contributed by the state-controlled Sino-foreign JVs in 2013, while local-brand cars only accounted for 28% of total sales, in which only one-third (32.6%) were produced by the Sino-foreign JVs (China Automotive Industry Yearbook, 2014). In other words, notwithstanding the fact that government explicitly underscores the imperative of upgrading China's manufacturing industries to a more value-added OBM mode in GVCs, the auto Sino-foreign JVs seem to be more in favour of producing foreign-brand vehicles (e.g. Beijing Benz; Changan Mazda) over own-brand vehicles.

The fact that the Sino-foreign JVs failed to adhere to the national policy of fostering self-developed, indigenous brands may be mainly attributed to the following two reasons. First, according to China's strict restrictions on the mixed ownership of such JVs, foreign investors are not allowed to hold a stake of >50%, resulting in an inherent complexity in terms of share control. From this viewpoint, foreign partners, with less decision-making power, may merely view such JVs as a shortcut to entering China's booming car market (Ma et al., 2015). They are not willing to transfer cutting-edge technologies and knowledge from their foreign parent companies to JVs because of concerns over the protection of their own intellectual property rights (Gallagher, 2006). Noticeably, FDI inflows from developed nations seem reluctant to spawn future Chinese competitors in the world's auto market, while foreign board members often tend to steer Sino-foreign JVs towards producing and selling foreign-brand vehicles in China. Second, the characteristics of the top management teams are a critical contextual factor as they largely affect the strategic choices and performance of international JVs (Ma et al., 2015; Song, Wang, & Cavusgil, 2015). Given the state-owned nature of such JVs, the government, rather than a board of directors or the stock market, has the authority to designate the top managers. For a better understanding, we elaborate next on this unique semiofficial governance system.

In China, the form of public ownership is undertaken and dictated by different types of agencies. Five major types of such agencies can be identified in China's auto industry as per their respective political and economic interests (Chen et al., 2009), These are—from the highest to the lowest class—SAMB/SASAC (the State Asset Management Bureau/the State Assets Supervision and Administration Commission), SOECG (SOEs affiliated to the central government), SOELGP (SOEs affiliated to the local government at the provincial/ministerial level), SOELGM (SOEs affiliated to the local government at the municipal level, and SOELGC (SOEs affiliated to the local government at the county level). The SOEs per se and the governmental committees assigned to supervise specific state-invested companies (i.e. the SASAC SAMB/SASAC) are granted respective political privileges in light of their administrative hierarchy. The key members of the top management team appointed by the government are also given corresponding administrative/political titles like bureaucrats, that is, the bureau-, section-, and office-level cadres, as well as the delegates of the National People's Congress (NPC) and the delegates of the Chinese People's Political Consultative Conference (CPPCC) at the national, provincial, municipal, and county levels.

The above-mentioned agency types largely determine the degree of political support from the Chinese government to the companies (Augier, Guo, & Rowen, 2016). In China, firms with state-owned shares enjoy corresponding benefits and policy supports in conformity with the political powers of the organization and the management committees specified by their administrative hierarchy (Li & Brødsgaard, 2013). Certain state-controlling directors therefore act more like politicians rather than professional managers or entrepreneurs—their focus and energy are mostly placed on maintaining harmonious relationships with government bureaucrats instead of on R&D investment and innovative talent cultivation. It is worth noting that, given the importance of political influence and connections, entrepreneurs of private companies also crave to be awarded political positions in China's auto industry, for example the CEO of BYD auto, Mr. Wang, is an NPC delegate at the municipal level.

Considering the arguments above, it is plausible to assume that policy support is significantly associated with the preference of Sino-foreign JVs for foreign-brand car production and that the establishment of Sino-foreign JVs may attenuate the motivation of the Chinese partners to develop domestic-brand cars while raising the proportion of foreign-brand vehicle production. Hence, we hypothesize the following:

> **Hypothesis 2a:** The degree of policy support is significantly associated with the preference of Sino-foreign JVs for foreign-brand auto production.

> **Hypothesis 2b:** The establishment of Sino-foreign JVs is positively related to the preference for foreign-brand auto production in China's auto industry.

The analysis so far also highlights a peculiar characteristic of the Chinese auto market, namely that the Sino-foreign JVs, as a unique type of SOEs, possess critical comparative advantages relative to private firms, owing to the favourable policy support to this kind of cross-border alliance. With less pressure to survive in the Chinese market, the top management of the JVs are more inclined to set up nonprofit-maximizing goals to avoid high-risk investment and practices and thus safeguard their executive positions. Indeed, producing well-known foreign-brand cars seems to be a relatively easy way for such firms to earn faster returns, compared with investing in the development of domestic car brands that involve the long-term input of substantial R&D.

Based on Institutional Theory (North, 1990), it can be asserted that industrial policies and governmental regulations are key institutional factors that can directly shape innovative activities, such as R&D input and new product launches for firms in emerging economies, where law enforcement may be capricious and the market and financial systems remain opaque (Chen et al., 2009; Jia, 2016; Song et al., 2015). While the government has ambitiously laid out a variety of policies nudging domestic OEMs to upgrade from low- to high-value-added production along GVCs (Chin et al., 2016), the policy support should have also exerted an obvious impact on own-brand creation and technological innovation in the auto industry, as it did in electronic industries (e.g. Haier, Midea, and Gree). Nevertheless, conversely, evidence demonstrates that foreign- rather than domestic-brand cars have dominated the Chinese market since the late 1990s, accompanied by an increasing number of Sino-foreign JVs (Drauz, 2013; Gan, 2003). As a result, we argue that under the premise that policy support in China's auto industry has been mostly focused on international JVs, efforts via governmental intervention to promote domestic-brand cars may be diluted by the establishment of such JVs in favour of producing foreign-brand vehicles.

In the previous section, we postulated that policy support may have a positive association with the establishment of Sino-foreign JVs and that these may have a positive impact on the proportion of foreign-brand car production. Following this logic, we further anticipate that the mediating effect of Sino-foreign JVs between the policy support and the preference for foreign-brand car production may exist. Therefore, we hypothesize the following:

> **Hypothesis 3:** The establishment of Sino-foreign JVs mediates the relationship between the degree of policy support and the preference for foreign-brand car production in China's auto industry.

## 2.3.3 Methodology

### 2.3.3.1 Sample Selection

As indicated at the outset, we used a data set taken from the China Automotive Industry Yearbook (2014), which includes statistical data on all kinds of auto vehicles in 2013, including passenger cars, light buses, minibuses, and trucks. Considering our research focus, all the 39 firms engaged in passenger car production were selected first (e.g. Zhejiang Geely and Great Wall Motors). Next, we further consolidated data from different selected firms that are virtually affiliated to the same parent company into one data set to ensure comparability and accuracy. For instance, Shanghai Volkswagen Co., Ltd. and Shanghai General Motors Co., Ltd. are, as a matter of fact, the subsidiaries of the Shanghai Automotive Industry Corp. (SAIC). The former is a Sino-foreign JV established by SAIC with Volkswagen AG, while the latter was formed by SAIC and General Motors Corporation. Following the same consolidation procedure produced 20 firms for further analysis (GAIG, BAIC,

Jiangnan, Guihang, Changhe, DFM, SAIC, FAW, Changan, FAIG, Brilliance, Hafei, Chery, NAC, BYD, Geely, GWM, HMC, JAC, and Lifan). Taking a close look at our sample, we discovered that 80% of the firms are invested in by the State and 65% of the firms are Sino-foreign JVs formed with world-class automakers and the majority were established in the mid- to late-1990s.

### 2.3.3.2 Measures
#### Policy Support
As illustrated in the previous section, there are five types of agencies whose administrative hierarchies can project the intensity of policy support from the government to a specific enterprise in China's auto industry. Considering the aggregate effects composed of the five agencies in reality, we employed the analytic hierarchy process (AHP) method to create a unique, context-specific equation with five variables to evaluate the sum of the policy support for an auto firm. The details of the rating procedure are described below.

The SOEs per se $(X_1)$, the SASAC$(X_2)$, and the top management of each firm $(X_3)$ are given three values individually according to their respective administrative hierarchies (i.e. SOECG/state/national level$=5$, SOELGP/provincial/ministerial level$=4$, SOELGM/municipal level$=3$, SOELGC/county level$=2$, and NONE/no administrative level$=1$). Referring to China's actual conditions, only two kinds of top executives are seen here as the top management (i.e. Chair of the Board and General Manager) and we merely took into account their political positions outside the organization to avoid doubt counting (i.e. whether they are the delegates of the NPC or PPC). This is because their administrative ratings are equivalent to those granted to their companies.

We calculated the aggregate intensity of policy support to each firm with the AHP method. To ensure the validity of our analysis, we first discussed the judgement matrix with several university scholars and government officers and then based on that we employed AHP software to determine the weight of the above-mentioned three indicators. Finally, the equation $(X=0.577X_1+0.303X_2+0.120X_3)$ for assessing the extent of policy support to each firm was generated.

#### Sino-Foreign JVs
This is represented by dummy variables. A firm that has established a Sino-foreign JV is assigned value 1; otherwise, value 0.

## Proportion of Foreign-Brand Cars

*Proportion of foreign-brand cars of each firm = Annual output of foreign-brand cars /*
*annual output of all cars of each firm.* If a foreign brand has been acquired by a
Chinese company, it is defined as a local brand. For example, China's Geely
group purchased Swedish-brand Volvo from Ford in 2010. Thus, Volvo is
considered to be a local brand in our research.

## Control Variables

Given that firm size (represented by the Napierian logarithm of annual sales)
and firm age (year) may have an impact on the innovation activities of
the firms (Chin, Liu, & Yang, 2015; Chin et al., 2016), we controlled for
these two variables. In addition, since the auto industry has been designated
as a pillar industry for driving economic development, the carmakers located
in less developed regions will thus in general earn more governmental support due to the policy priority. As such, we also controlled for firm location
(represented by dummy variables, the relatively developed regions, including the Pan-Bohai Area, the Yangtze River Delta, and the Pearl River
Delta = 1; others = 0).

## 2.3.4 Results

As noted by MacKinnon, Lockwood, Hoffman, West, and Sheets (2002),
the most commonly cited approach for testing mediation is the hierarchical
multiple regression (HMR) procedure proposed by Baron and Kenny
(1986). Despite its extensive usage, some scholars argue that in terms of nonexperimental research designs, conducting HMR may provide a relatively
weak foundation for inferences about causal connections between variables,
including those in hypothesized mediation models (Stone-Romero &
Rosopa, 2008). However, considering that our sample size was small and
thus not suitable for building a structural equation model, we still adopted
the HMR procedure to test our assumed mediation model but used
the Sobel test as a remedy to examine it for methodological rigour
(MacKinnon et al., 2002; Sobel, 1988).

Table 2.1 shows the descriptive statistics, including means, standard deviations, and correlations for all the variables. Policy support was positively
associated with Sino-foreign JVs ($P < .01$) as well as with the proportion
of foreign-brand cars ($P < .01$). The correlation coefficient between Sino-
foreign JVs and the proportion of foreign-brand cars was also significant
($P < .01$).

**Table 2.1** Means, SD, and Correlations

| | Mean | SD | 1 | 2 | 3 | 4 | 5 | 6 |
|---|---|---|---|---|---|---|---|---|
| 1. Firm scale | 12.1440 | 1.61831 | 1 | | | | | |
| 2. Firm age | 28.5500 | 15.19167 | 0.315 | 1 | | | | |
| 3. Firm location | 0.3500 | 0.48936 | 0.327 | 0.320 | 1 | | | |
| 4. Policy support | 3.0302 | 1.16146 | 0.448* | 0.553* | −0.102 | 1 | | |
| 5. Sino-foreign joint venture | 0.6000 | 0.5026 | 0.256 | 0.044 | −0.257 | 0.638** | 1 | |
| 6. Proportion of foreign-brand cars | 0.4604 | 0.4612 | 0.369 | 0.167 | −0.064 | 0.691** | 0.836** | 1 |

Notes: $n=20$. **,*Correlation is significant at the 0.01 and 0.05 levels (two-tailed), respectively.

**Table 2.2** Results of Regression Analysis

| | Model 1 Sino-Foreign Joint Venture | Model 2 Proportion of Foreign-Brand Cars | Model 3 Proportion of Foreign-Brand Cars | Model 4 Proportion of Foreign-Brand Cars |
|---|---|---|---|---|
| *Independent variables* | | | | |
| Policy support | 0.863** (0.004) | | 0.902** (0.003) | 0.326 (0.215) |
| Sino-foreign joint venture | | 0.831*** (0.000) | | 0.667** (0.004) |
| *Control variables* | | | | |
| Firm scale | 0.016 (0.941) | 0.104 (0.510) | 0.042 (0.845) | 0.031 (0.849) |
| Firm age | −0.427 (0.091) | 0.067 (0.648) | −0.390 (0.112) | −0.106 (0.593) |
| Firm location | −0.037 (0.865) | 0.094 (0.553) | 0.140 (0.521) | 0.165 (0.325) |
| $R^2$ | 0.546 | 0.738 | 0.565 | 0.766 |
| $F$-value | 4.514* | 10.566*** | 4.862** | 9.176*** |

Notes: $n=20$. Significance levels based on two-tailed tests. Standardized regression coefficients are reported; robust SEs are given in parentheses. * $P<.05$; ** $P<.01$; *** $P<.001$.

Table 2.2 lists all the regression results. First, we regressed policy support on Sino-foreign JVs in Model 1 and the proportion of foreign-brand cars on Sino-foreign JVs in Model 2. Second, we entered the proportion of foreign-brand cars that was entered as the dependent variable and policy support as the independent variable in Model 3. Third, we entered policy support and proportion of foreign-brand cars together to test the mediating effect of Sino-foreign JV in Model 4. In all analyses, we controlled for firm size, age, and location.

As per Model 1, policy support is a positive predictor of Sino-foreign JVs ($\beta = 0.863$, $P < .01$), supporting Hypothesis 1. Model 2 indicates that Sino-foreign JVs are positively related to the proportion of foreign-brand cars ($\beta = 0.831$, $P < .001$), supporting Hypothesis 2b. The relationship between policy support and proportion of foreign-brand cars is significant ($\beta = 0.902$, $P < .01$) in Model 3, supporting Hypothesis 2a, while the regression coefficient of policy support on the proportion of foreign-brand cars is insignificant ($\beta = 0.326$, $P > .1$) in Model 4. A comparison of Models 3 and 4 makes it clear that, after adding *Sino-foreign JVs* to Model 3, the standardized coefficient between policy support and proportion of foreign-brand cars changes from significant to insignificant. This result demonstrates the existence of a full mediating mechanism in our variables. To further examine the full mediation effect, we performed the Sobel test (MacKinnon et al., 2002; Sobel, 1988) ($Z = 2.9053$, $P < .01$). The results confirm that Sino-foreign JVs fully mediate the relationship between policy support and the proportion of foreign-brand cars, supporting Hypothesis 3.

## 2.3.5 Discussion

This study investigated whether policy support facilitates own-brand innovation in China's auto industry. Drawing on HMR analysis, our findings show that policy support promotes the establishment of Sino-foreign JVs as well as the propensity of such JVs to produce foreign-brand cars. Moreover, we discovered the full mediating effect of Sino-foreign JVs on the relationship between policy support and foreign-brand preference. As a result, all four of our hypotheses are fully examined, which offers an answer to our research question that policy support may not be able to facilitate the conduct of branding strategy, but rather hinders own-brand development along with the establishment of more Sino-foreign JVs in China's auto industry.

In accordance with prior research (Du & Luo, 2016; Jia, 2016), our findings also indicate that industrial policy as a typical means of governmental intervention plays a crucial role in attracting and leveraging FDI to accelerate the internationalization and development of domestic firms in China's auto industry, especially for SOEs and enterprises with state-owned shares, which make up a large portion of organizations. On the one hand, policy support is particularly conducive to the competitiveness of Chinese enterprises because it can bring about unique, inconceivable resources that compensate for the imperfections and immaturity of China's market structure and legal frameworks (Augier et al., 2016; Chin, 2015). On the other hand, excessive governmental intervention into the market mechanism may also elicit side effects such as low efficiency, institutional inertia, rent-seeking, and corruption, all of which may impede innovation (Chin et al., 2015; Ngo, 2008).

Inconsistent with previous studies addressing the positive technology spillover arising from international strategic alliances (Eapen, 2012; Opper & Nee, 2015), our results implicitly highlight the negative association between Sino-foreign JVs and own-brand innovation. Owing to the potent policy support, the Sino-foreign JVs might have bypassed all institutional constraints and dominated the Chinese auto market. Interestingly, however, such Sino-foreign JVs, as the biggest beneficiaries of government support on subsidies and access to loans and tax breaks, performed relatively poorly in building and promoting domestic brands compared to the privately owned carmakers, such as GWN, Geely and BYD, that have been endeavouring to widen their brand visibility for many years (Drauz, 2013; Wang & Kimble, 2013). As noted earlier, the well-known case of Chinese Geely's acquisition of Volvo from Ford in 2010 elucidates how a Chinese private carmaker gained core technologies, proprietary intellectual property, international marketing channels, and global-brand recognition almost 'overnight'. The Sino-foreign JV model, in this sense, seems to have become an impediment rather than a catalyst for promoting own-brand innovation because the lack of an entrepreneurial culture and a related fear of failure may discourage top leaders of such ventures from making risky decisions. As a result, forming international strategic alliances may lead to excessive reliance on political resources and thus increase the risk-averse behaviour of firms. In contrast, private firms, with a more entrepreneurial spirit and higher risk tolerance, are gradually entering China's economy, fighting for more market share *vis-a-vis* giant national corporations (Opper & Nee, 2015).

Considering the foregoing arguments, the main theoretical contribution of this research is to bring deeper and greater insights into the interplay among policy support, own-brand innovation, and international JVs in China's auto industry. While Japanese and Korean auto industries demonstrate successful examples of industrial upgrading and brand establishment (e.g. Toyota, Honda, Nissan, and Mazda in Japan; and Daewoo, Hyundai, and Kia in Korea) (Kim, 1999; Yang & Tang, 2014), our research illustrates an unsuccessful Chinese story regarding own-brand development. This is not surprising considering that the ratio of expenditure of Chinese companies on technology imports to their technology assimilation is relatively low compared to that in Japan and South Korea. The novel context-specific approach we proposed to measure the degree of policy support is also considered as a valuable contribution to the literature because it embodies the unique institutional complexity and intricate social network embedded in China's SOEs. In addition, implicit in our findings is the possibility that the Sino-foreign JV model as an FDI-led growth strategy may create too heavy a dependence on borrowed technology and marketing skills from the developed-country partners and thus become unable to fulfil the strategic goal of indigenous innovation. Viewed from this angle, we also enrich existing knowledge concerning the impact of FDI on innovation in the Chinese context.

As far as the practical implications are concerned, this research provides valuable information for policymakers to further rectify auto-related policies. As mentioned above, the failure of developing own-brand products by Sino-foreign JVs in China has explicitly drawn our attention to the fact that, from a market perspective, corporate-political ties can not only be an advantage, but can also be problematic. In addition, it seems especially vital to emphasize the strategic importance of top managers in SOEs—firm-level value-creation and innovation rely on the contributions of all employees and this is motivated largely by effective leaders (Foss & Lindenberg, 2013). Whereas the Sino-foreign JV as a symbol of state monopoly still dominates the Chinese car market, it is imperative for the government to formulate more specific policies and strategies for raising the brand awareness of top management so as to motivate these organizations to engage more in own-brand innovation.

## 2.3.6 Conclusion

This case provides strong empirical evidence proposing that policy support may not be a panacea but a placebo for own-brand innovation in the Chinese auto industry. Despite its exploratory nature, this case can be seen as an exciting step that adds to a better understanding of the role of political support in shaping the strategic choices of firms in brand innovation and the building of international JVs in China. According to news reports, China's auto sales continue to increase, with 19 million vehicles sold in the first

10 months of 2015 exceeding the total sales of 2013. However, vehicle usage is often framed in terms of the impact on the environment. Emissions and auto production all carry adverse environmental consequences (Gallagher, 2006). In fact, VW was plunged into a notorious scandal because certain cars contained a device designed to cheat on emission tests (Seow, 2014). Related to this point, the continuous rise in auto use and the corresponding deterioration of air quality across China may be seen as an inevitable challenge as well as an ongoing story worthy of further research—by no means unique to China's experience—about visions of economic development and the ecological costs of industrial modernity (Seow, 2014).

## 2.4 CONCLUSION

Despite being the world' second largest economy and the biggest manufacturing hub, China's industrial success and reputation has mainly relied on the mastery of the role of being the 'world's workshop'. The nature of China's manufacturing is largely low-to-mid tech in form, whose industrial design often derives from foreign sources, international product, and quality specifications, as well as imported high-end machine tools. As noted above, the emergence of GVCs has been the main catalyst to the growth and evolution of China's manufacturing—which to a large extent aroused the official interest and support to attract more FDIs into this sector.

Overall, this chapter has highlighted why the official encouragement/ policy agenda can be seen as the key to the development of Chinese manufacturing. In Chapter 3, we will further illustrate the importance of FDI in terms of the upgrading of China's manufacturing industry and then address how local manufacturers benefit from their partnership with MNCs in Chapter 4.

## APPENDIX

To familiarize readers with some key concepts on industrial upgrading, we elaborate on the concept of GVC and corresponding upgrading terms (i.e. OEM, ODM, and OBM) as follows:

### Global Value Chain (GVC)

The value chain shows the full speculum of value creation processes that firms and their workers engage in to bring a product (i.e. goods or services) from its conception and raw material stage to its end use and beyond.

A product's value chain includes a variety of activities such as design, production, marketing, distribution, and support to the final customer. All activities can be contained within a single organization or divided among different organizations and can take place within a single geographical location or spread over several countries. In fact, today's competitive environment suggests that firms should examine their value chains in a global rather than a domestic-only context, namely from a GVC perspective. This GVC perspective refers to understanding value chains that are divided among multiple firms and spread across wide swaths of geographic space, reflecting the important role of international linkages for firms in global competition (Gereffi, Humphrey, & Sturgeon, 2005; Morrison, Pietrobelli, & Rabellotti, 2008).

## Original Equipment Manufacturer (OEM)

In GVCs, OEM refers to low-cost suppliers of manufacturing parts, components, or even finished products to large international manufacturers, branded companies, or retailers and the name of the OEM is anonymous in the final product market (Ivarsson & Alvstam, 2011). Given that the OEM performs the function of low-cost manufacturing in GVCs, its profit margin is relatively low.

## Original-Brand Manufacturer (OBM)

In GVCs, OBM represents a break from contract manufacturing and to management that requires sophisticated technology, management know-how, and, most importantly, innovation. OBM profit margins are relatively high in GVCs because OBM involves more value-added functions and activities such as design, R&D, and marketing.

## Upgrading Along the GVC From OEM to OBM

Some aggressive OEMs, after entering GVCs as first-tier suppliers of large international buyers, have become full-package suppliers, thereby gradually forging an innovative entrepreneurial capability that involves the coordination of complex production, R&D, and financial networks. As a result, the transition from OEM to OBM, namely, from competing simply on low-cost production to competing on innovation pertaining to design and marketing activities, is made possible for these OEM firms (Gereffi et al., 2005; Ivarsson & Alvstam, 2011; Morrison et al., 2008).

# CHAPTER THREE

# FDI Manufacturers and Their Upgrading Strategies

## 3.1 INTRODUCTION

### 3.1.1 Manufacturing FDI and China's Economic Growth

According to A.T. Kearney's Confidence Index,[1] China maintained its position as the most attractive destination of FDI every year between 2004 and 2012 and ranked as the second popular destination of FDI since 2013 (behind the United States). As mentioned in the previous chapter, owing to the supportive policy environment, export-oriented FDI as an important source of private capital has been, to a great extent, contributing to the growth of Chinese manufacturing. A large number of FDI projects built production hubs for export, helping increase employment of migrant workers and poverty reduction in coastal cities in China.

However, evidence indicates that FDI into China has started to shift preference from manufacturing to service sectors after the exchange rate of US dollar to RMB became lower than seven, as this implies squeezed profit margins in manufacturing and the booming growth of consumption in service industries in local markets. As shown in Fig. 3.1, the 2008 global financial crisis further accelerated this trend. As addressed in Chapter 1, while manufacturers in China have been facing unfavourable conditions, some FIEs conducted upgrading strategies to transform themselves from traditional 'sweatshops' to modern innovation-oriented production bases for higher economic returns.

Nevertheless, given a variety of inherent risks hiding in global value chain (GVC) upgrading, DE firms may not be able to ensure the success of implementing upgrading strategies despite generally being equipped with more sophisticated technology than local firms. This chapter therefore introduces two diverse cases of studies depicting how foreign-invested

---

[1] https://www.atkearney.com/foreign-direct-investment-confidence-index/article?/a/glass-half-full-2017-foreign-direct-investment-confidence-index-article

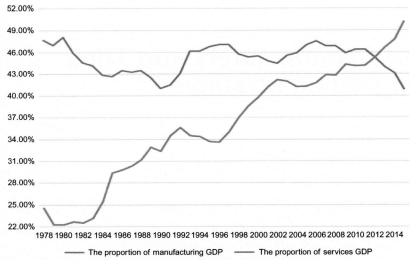

**Fig. 3.1** The proportions of manufacturing and service industry GDP.

manufacturers carried out upgrading strategies in China. The first case incorporates the 'Dynamic Capabilities' perspective (Teece, Pisano, & Shuen, 1997) into the GVC framework, demonstrating how two Singapore-invested OEMs successfully upgraded along the GVC. The second case delineates how a British entrepreneurial OEM suffered a great failure in the Chinese context.

## 3.2 UPGRADING STRATEGIES BY SINGAPORE/FDI OEMs IN CHINA

### 3.2.1 Introduction

Exports are commonly viewed as the main driver of China's economic growth over the past three decades (Gao, Murray, Kotabe, & Lu, 2010). The real engine enabling China to be the global export powerhouse is attributed to a wide range of FDI into this country (Lau & Bruton, 2008). The increasing inflow of FDI is responsible for the majority of China's exports (Wielemaker & Gedajlovic, 2011), promoting its annual GDP and enabling it to become the world's second largest economy in 2010. In terms of the industrial distribution of FDI, about 50% of FDI went into manufacturing sectors since the 1990s, particularly into OEM (National Bureau of Statistics of China, 2012). Following the emergence of GVCs (Gereffi et al., 2005), these foreign-invested OEMs

capitalized on China's abundant supply of low-wage labour to manufacture products for developed-country buyers.

However, China has seen annual wage increases and a 23% appreciation
of the currency over the past 5 years and the trend looks set to continue for
the next 5 years. The low-cost advantages of FDI OEMs are disappearing
and exports may not be sufficient for these firms to remain financially
successful in the future. The literature shows that the most feasible strategy
to enhance economic returns for OEMs is the conduct of functional
upgrading: a process to move upwards along the GVCs from OEM to original design manufacture (ODM) and eventually to OBM (Gereffi et al.,
2005; Morrison, Pietrobelli, & Rabellotti, 2008). If well-implemented,
functional upgrading enables OEM firms to overcome the unequal distribution of profits by engaging in more value-added activities (Humphrey &
Schmitz, 2004).

Since China became the largest consumer market for autos, television
sets, and cell phones and the second largest for luxury goods during the
worldwide recession, its growing domestic market thus symbolizes one
bright point on the horizon for OEMs to implement this upgrading strategy
for value creation. However, the Chinese mass market demonstrates
remarkable heterogeneity and is expected to morph into differentiated
and multitiered segments over the next 10 years. China's domestic market
is actually a conglomeration of separate regional markets protected by provincial barriers and segmented by a variety of economic and industrial factors
(Tse, 2010). Therefore, this multimarket conception inevitably raises
problems for foreign investors to compete in China's huge but disordered
domestic market. As far as the FDI OEMs go, the prominent question is:
what are the specific capabilities these OEMs require for changing to adapt
to the dynamic Chinese market and uncertainties?

Considering the foregoing arguments, this chapter incorporates the
dynamic capabilities perspective (Teece et al., 1997) into the GVC framework and centres its analysis on the premise that manufacturers must invest
to build necessary organizational capabilities to ensure success of functional
upgrade along the GVC. Despite numerous studies investigating the value
creation of FDI firms in emerging economies (EEs) (Horng & Chen, 2008;
Li, Wei, & Liu, 2010; Lin & Hou, 2010; Liu, Wang, & Wei, 2009), there is a
dearth of reliable and timely studies focusing on the key value creation processes of functional upgrading by foreign-invested OEMs in China. To fill
this research gap, we use a multiple-case study to address the functional
upgrading trajectory by FDI OEMs in the Chinese context.

Additionally, since functional upgrading involves high risks associated with system-wide changes and there is no guarantee of success, the vision and persistency of top leadership is vital for pursuing functional upgrading. Hence, we first identify the specific dynamic capabilities and leadership style involved in the upgrading trajectory by FDI OEMs to build a conceptual framework. Then we employ a multiple-case study with a pattern-matching analysis investigating two Singapore-invested OEMs to examine the assumed model. This study makes three unique contributions. First, it presents the evolutionary upgrading strategies of FDI OEMs in China in the face of the new global economy. Further, conducting in-depth interviews with top management in both parent companies in Singapore and their subsidiaries in China, this research responds to a recent call for collecting first-hand timely data to investigate FDI issues in EEs (Lau & Bruton, 2008). Finally, the results offer fresh and critical insights into the practical implications for FDI OEMs to grow and prosper in the Chinese market.

## 3.2.2 Theoretical Foundations

### 3.2.2.1 Functional Upgrading

Globalization has given many OEM firms in developing countries opportunities to participate in international markets by targeting external markets to gain economies of scale and scope, as well as further technological expertise (Kaplinsky, Readman, & Memedovic, 2009). This phenomenon is characterized by the concept of the GVC (Gereffi et al., 2005; Humphrey & Schmitz, 2004; Morrison et al., 2008). Drawing on the GVC system to coordinate global production and distribution, DE exporters are able to manufacture products based on designs supplied by international buyers or just produce small parts of final products. This GVC approach has provided a primary path for Chinese manufacturers to initiate international businesses via offering OEM services to large MNCs and foreign buyers since the reform and opening-up policy over 30 years ago (Li, Wei, et al., 2010; Lin & Hou, 2010). The GVC view reveals not only a holistic map of the global production network and market, but also a comprehensive and integrated approach explaining industrial development and innovation in emerging countries (Morrison et al., 2008). To exploit the opportunities presented by GVCs and meanwhile tackle competitive global markets, firms need to innovate or upgrade their capacities for performance (Kaplinsky et al., 2009).

However, Schmitz (2006) has questioned why in practice, the developing country producers merely specialize on manufacturing activities but delegate higher return activities such as product design and marketing to their international partners? Echoing this, an increasing number of OEM manufacturers have augmented per-unit value of products by carrying out functional upgrading to shift their business functions from competing on low cost production to competing on innovation pertaining to design and marketing activities in GVCs. It is because functional upgrading changes the mix of activities within and between links in the GVC that can be used as an effective means to transform production organizations to design, marketing, and branding corporations. More specifically, research highlights the hierarchy mechanism of functional upgrading in which developing country firms transform from original equipment assembling under contract to global buyers to OEM (producing goods under a buyer's name), to ODM (involving design activities), to OBM (producing own brand products and participating in marketing activities) (Gereffi et al., 2005; Humphrey & Schmitz, 2004).

As far as China is concerned, evidence shows that many OEMs, including both local and FIEs, have followed the path of functional upgrading, successfully upgrading to OBM status, such as Taiwan's Acer and China's TCL and Lenovo (Lin & Hou, 2010). In general, these firms began with OEM, gradually adding postconceptual design services to the manufacturing function, or ODM. After being armed with design capabilities, they then started to manufacture finished products and marketed them under their own brands—this is OBM. As indicated by Matthews (2006), a few Chinese OEMs may start from behind in terms of international arenas, but then overcome deficiencies to become global giants, namely the 'Dragon Multinationals'. Despite the successful precedents, some large manufacturers in China may still choose to continuously provide OEM services to overseas clients after upgrading to OBM as mature market buyers are usually profitable and reliable clients. However, meanwhile these firms may also produce own brand products specifically for their local markets (i.e. the Chinese market).

It is worth noting that OEMs in general attribute the development of upgrading competence to their partnership with DE clients or buyers. Through strategic cooperation, OEMs could rapidly learn about international technology, practices, and standards from advanced economy MNCs (Horng & Chen, 2008; Liu et al., 2009). In this sense, knowledge and technology transfers between OEMs and their developed country clients are of great importance to facilitating their functional upgrading.

### 3.2.2.2 Dynamic Capabilities and Functional Upgrading

In terms of competitive advantage, the resource-based view (RBV) states that a firm's competitive advantage is based on ability to leverage its valuable resources (Barney, 1991). Linking resources to capabilities, Makadok (2001) defines a capability as an organizationally embedded, nontransferable firm-specific resource whose purpose is to improve the productivity of the other resources possessed by the firm. Capabilities are scarce, appropriable, and specialized and are strategic assets that bestow the firm's competitive advantage. Capabilities cannot be bought; rather, they must be built and may only be developed over a long period of time (Malik & Kotabe, 2009). In terms of an organization, the internal capabilities, combined with external partnerships, are seen as a flexible innovation system (Su, Peng, Shen, & Xiao, 2012).

Originating from RBV, dynamic capabilities are the 'abilities to integrate, build, and reconfigure internal and external competences to develop new resources and capabilities' (Teece et al., 1997: p. 516). Dynamic capabilities thus reflect a firm's ability to achieve new and innovative forms of competitive advantage, reconfiguring its capabilities according to its environmental changes (Malik & Kotabe, 2009; Su et al., 2012; Teece et al., 1997). However, how is one to distinguish a dynamic capability from a mere capability? An organizational capability refers to the set of activities performed by the firm which produces outputs that determine its survival and prosperity within its current strategic setting; such outputs will not change the strategic direction of the firm (Sun & Anderson, 2010). In contrast, an organization's dynamic capability should reflect its ability to build new and unique capabilities that help identify new opportunities under turbulent conditions and make strategic responses to situational changes more quickly (Weerawardena, Sullivan Mort, Liesch, & Knight, 2007). In other words, a strategic set of dynamic capabilities does not accrue from the firm, but is built consciously and systematically by the leader's wilful decision-making and actions. Following this logic, scholars argue that corporate profitability may not be sustained by the control over the market (e.g. by using quasimonopolistic practices), but rather by the development of dynamic capabilities to adapt to changing external networks and global situations (Kaplinsky et al., 2009). Viewed from this angle, the dynamic capabilities theory is indeed closely related to the concept of the GVC analytical framework.

Considering the foregoing discussion, our research focuses on discussing the mechanisms between the dynamic capabilities possessed by OEMs and the implementation of functional upgrading. Functional upgrading is the sequence of acquisitions of internal functional capabilities, while the two critical success factors for upgrading within the GVCs are: (1) the acquisition of key functional capabilities, and (2) better exploiting the acquired capabilities to access not only general markets but also particular market channels (Humphrey & Schmitz, 2004). Both acquisitions and access are dynamic in nature because a shift towards an upper specification/function represents a shift in strategic direction. Following this logic, functional upgrading can be seen as a competitive and innovative strategy that requires OEMs to develop bundles of capabilities that help them to overcome the barriers and difficulties in crossing different functions and ultimately increasing economic performance. Taken together, we assume that to ensure successful functional upgrading, firms must possess certain dynamic capabilities that help them react agilely to the uncertainties and complexities in today's world.

### 3.2.3 Conceptual Framework for Pattern Analysis

According to the arguments above, this case thus centres on the three dynamic capabilities that have been identified to be particularly relevant to upgrading under the OEM framework (Lu, Zhou, Bruton, & Li, 2010; Malik & Kotabe, 2009; Su et al., 2012). These are: manufacturing, technological, and absorptive capabilities.

#### 3.2.3.1 Manufacturing Capabilities

These are a significant facilitator for functional upgrading (Chin et al., 2016; Chin, Tsai, et al., 2016). The degree to which they evolve helps determine how an OEM firm performs in increasingly competitive environments. In the beginning, when collaborating with large MNCs in a developed country, OEMs typically manufacture simple products and are weak in high-end production processes. However, in order to survive, OEMs must have a broader range of manufacturing functions at their disposal to meet the dynamic requirements of the outsourcers from mature markets (Chin et al., 2016; Chin, Tsai, et al., 2016; Lin & Hou, 2010). For instance, lean manufacturing methods have been widely implemented to increase operation efficiency and manufacturing flexibility (Malik & Kotabe, 2009). Hence, the evolution of manufacturing capabilities by OEMs, ranging from varying product mixes and production volumes to reducing manufacturing process inventories, is expected.

### 3.2.3.2 Technological Capabilities

These pertain to the intensity of R&D and innovation and are widely viewed as critical strategic assets, whereby firms can create the competitive advantages that determine the success of upgrading by OEMs (Morrison et al., 2008; Su et al., 2012). Technological capabilities are not easy to develop or even to imitate because they are embedded in a firm's operation and, to a certain extent, influence its internal mechanisms (Barney, 1991). Extensive empirical results show that firms with higher levels of technological capability are more likely to compete in hyper-competitive international markets (Zou, Chen, & Ghauri, 2010). By providing manufacturing and assembly services to advanced economy MNCs, OEMs get abundant learning opportunities for acquiring advanced technical and R&D skills to build technological capabilities, including up-to-date technology and the unique capacity to appropriate, adapt, and transform secondary technology (Liu et al., 2009). This reflects the prominent dynamic characteristic in terms of building technological capabilities as the development of such capacity has to cater to the latest need of fast-changing global markets. It is true that, owing to the technology spillover effects within GVCs, some aspirant OEM firms have gradually become proficient in the use of high-tech knowledge after collaborating with global brands for a certain period of time—by which they could further evolve from the bottom of GVCs to be the competitors against their developed-country outsourcers (Humphrey & Schmitz, 2004; Mudambi, 2007).

### 3.2.3.3 Absorptive Capabilities

It is recognized that OEM arrangements promote knowledge transfer associated with sophisticated technology, advanced manufacturing know-how, or new product development skills between buyers and suppliers along the GVC (Liu et al., 2009). As noted above, through providing OEM services to world-class brands, OEMs can acquire a wide range of advanced knowledge that benefits their capabilities development for success in international markets (Weerawardena et al., 2007). 'Learning from outsourcers' can be regarded as a vital catalyst that facilitates OEMs to upgrade from low-end to more value-added status along the GVC. Accordingly, absorptive capabilities that represent a firm's ability to utilize external knowledge through the sequential processes of exploratory, transformative, and exploitative learning (Sun & Anderson, 2010) are is of great importance in functional upgrading.

### 3.2.3.4 Leadership in Functional Upgrading

Leadership is a strategic construct that reflects the extent to which managers are innovative, proactive, and risk-taking in their behaviour and management philosophies (Miller, 1983). It refers to the process, practices, and decision-making activities that top managers use to lead a new entry, including such processes as experimenting with promising new technologies or being willing to seize new product opportunities (Kouzes & Posner, 2007). Leadership is especially important for functional upgrading because upgrading is a high-risk endeavour and there is no guarantee of success. Top managers must have foresight to see the benefits, courage to take the risk, and forbearance and determination to carry through the process. In addition, as described earlier, the achievement of functional upgrading requires OEMs to intensify cross-organizational learning from their international partners for establishing necessary dynamic capabilities. However, owing to the asymmetry of power between buyers and vendors, buyers may not always be willing to provide support for their suppliers' upgrading (Humphrey & Schmitz, 2004; Mudambi, 2007). In this vein, effective leadership (see Rowley & Ulrich, 2014 for an overview) activities that influence a group of individuals to move towards a common goal play a critical role in driving and propelling the whole organization to accomplish functional upgrading.

By incorporating the arguments above, we develop the logic linking the dynamic capability mechanism to the strategy of functional upgrading and a conceptual framework. This is set out in Fig. 3.2.

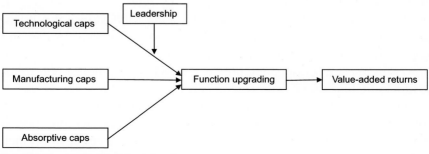

**Fig. 3.2** The conceptual framework.

## 3.2.4 Methodology

Owing to the qualitative nature of this research topic, a case-study methodology is appropriate to explore the evolution and interdependencies of firm capabilities in functional upgrading. Our study thus follows case research design using in-depth archival and field data. According to qualitative methodologists (Rialp, Rialp, Urbano, & Valiant, 2005; Yin, 2003), a multiple-case-based study may serve as a basis for either empirically examining existing theories or establishing new theoretical explanations of the new phenomena being researched. Multiple cases could help to produce replication logic—both literal and theoretical—in which cases are treated as experiments, with each serving to confirm or disconfirm inferences drawn from the others (Yin, 2003). Eisenhardt and Graebner (2007) also argue that multiple-case research typically yields more robust, generalizable theory than single cases. In view of these arguments, our study employs a two-case study to enhance explanatory power.

The pattern-matching analysis that enables researchers to capture subtle similarities and differences within cases and associate them with a specific pattern is believed to further reinforce the systematic application of a multiple-case study (Rialp et al., 2005). Therefore, our study also capitalizes on the pattern-matching approach to analyse findings and examine the assumed conceptual framework.

### 3.2.4.1 Sample Selection

In case study research, sample selection is one of the most difficult procedures (Yin, 2003) because the research samples have to be specific and representative of all cases. We carefully selected two case firms that are Singapore-invested OEMs located in China's Guangdong province chosen for the following reasons. This Southern province of nine large cities with proximity to Hong Kong has attracted many foreign firms engaging in assembling and manufacturing for world leading MNCs since the 1980s, producing large economic growth rates for more than two decades and importance nationally. For example, in 2008 the export volume of processing trade in Guangdong province accounted for nearly two-thirds (64.6%) of China's total exports.

The choice of Singapore-invested OEMs was due to the following reasons. Singapore is widely regarded as an important manufacturing hub in Asia with a strong electronics manufacturing sector and emphasis on high technology (Wielemaker & Gedajlovic, 2011). Manufacturing contributes significantly to Singapore's economic growth, accounting for about one-third of the country's annual GDP. Moreover, since the early 1990s, many Singapore manufacturers decided to invest substantial amounts in China, including establishing subsidiary plants or even relocating main production operations to obtain cost advantages (Lau & Bruton, 2008). Taken together, these points make Singapore-invested OEMs suitable samples for this research.

The criteria for selecting the case OEMs in our study were: (1) the firms located in China are Singapore direct investment companies/subsidiaries; (2) they are subcontracted by large developed country MNCs to manufacture components or parts of final products for them; (3) their names are anonymous in the final products market as there are only brand labels on packaging; (4) they went through functional upgrading processes; (5) they are leading manufacturers in their respective industries. This selection procedure resulted in identification of the following two cases: Company A (listed on the SGX[2]), headquartered in Singapore, a leading MNC providing a full spectrum of high value-added, integrated turnkey manufacturing services in the electronics industry (Case #1) and Company B (listed on the SGX), headquartered in Singapore, a famous global company producing and assembling precision-machined components used in auto and machinery industries (Case #2).

### 3.2.4.2 Data Sources and Informants
Data were collected from three sources: (1) face-to-face and phone interviews with their president/CEO; (2) interviews with managers of different departments in the same company; (3) secondary sources: internal documents provided by the companies, information on company websites, product and firm brochures, as well as newspaper articles, journal articles, research papers, and informal observations. The interviews were semistructured and open-ended. Respondents were the president/CEO/COO, manufacturing managers, R&D manager/senior engineers, CFO/financial manager, and marketing managers.

### 3.2.4.3 Data Collection Methods
To obtain robust data, a triangulation approach was utilized at the collection stage to ensure that different sources were used when gathering data from each firm. The triangulation of data collection, including interview records,

[2] SGX refers to Singapore Exchange Limited.

internal reports, archival data, and literature, can reveal the conditions of enterprises to a maximum extent. To avoid subjectivity, multiple data collection methods were used (Eisenhardt & Graebner, 2007; Yin, 2003). For instance, participants were requested to try their best to provide evidence objectively. The semistructured interviews with open-ended questions in both Chinese and English versions were conducted by at least a three-person team, with one researcher handling the interview questions with the other two recording notes and observations. For the information items that required exploring at length and in depth, the interviewer would ask more follow-up questions. Interviews were tape-recorded at the same time to avoid omitting information and enhance corroborating evidence. To verify the reliability and validity of interviews, the recorded data were processed on the same day they were taped. Also, to resolve inconsistency, researchers listened to the records and returned to the interviewees repeatedly until consensus was reached. If needed, further follow-up telephone interviews would be conducted. Since both firms are listed companies, a wide range of archival records, such as their annual reports and other public statements, were used as supplements. Finally, information and data collected from diverse sources were cross-checked to ensure accuracy and reliability.

## 3.2.5 Empirical Findings

The findings of our case-based empirical analysis are presented as follows. First, the business profiles of the two firms are shown in Table 3.1. Next, each firm's implementation and outcomes of functional upgrading are demonstrated. Finally, the pattern-matching approach is applied to further examine the hypothetical conceptual framework, as displayed in Table 3.1.

## Case #1

Company A, founded in 1984, is a well-known contract manufacturer producing a wide range of high-mix, high-value, and complex electronic products for global leading MNCs, such as IBM and HP. In 1990, Company A first established two plants in Shanghai bonded areas (i.e. the government-appointed tariff-free areas) following the trend of FDI inflow into China in the 1990s and merely offered OEM services for electronic products to global leading companies. This company advanced to the next level of the GVC later, namely providing ODM for foreign buyers. Exploiting a broad range of low-cost advantages, including labour, operations, and land rent, the group augmented its revenue very quickly and thus went

**Table 3.1** Basic Business Profiles of the Two-Case Companies

|  | Company A | Company B |
|---|---|---|
| Constitution year | 1984 | 1981 |
| Listed year | 2002 listed on Singapore Exchange (SGX) | 2001 listed on SGX |
| Parent Co./ subsidiaries | The group is headquartered in Singapore, comprising about 40 companies with global clusters of excellence in South-east Asia, North Asia, America, and Europe | The group is headquartered in Singapore, with other strategic manufacturing locations in Malaysia, China, and Vietnam |
| Current core business and main products | Providing a fully integrated range of electronics manufacturing services (EMS), OEM, ODM, and e-fulfilment services (EFS) for global leading MNEs in electronics industry | Providing highly integrated OEM services on precision-machined components used in automotive and machinery industry, and precision turned parts in imaging and printing industry |
| Main clients | IBM, HP, AVAGO, NCR | TOYOTA, SONY, HP |
| Revenue in 2011 | 12 billion RMB ($1.9 billion) with annual earnings of 786 million RMB ($124 million) | 409 million RMB ($64 million) with annual earnings of 19 million RMB ($3 million) |
| Employees | 14,000 worldwide | 3000 worldwide |

public on the SGX in 2002. Since then, the firm has put more emphasis on developing technological capabilities, such as engaging in a variety of R&D activities and building a world-class R&D team. The technological capabilities development enabled it to provide ODM services that can bring better economic returns.

Several design centres strategically located in Asia, Europe, and the United States were set up to acquire 'state of the art' technological knowledge. In the pursuit of incorporating design and technology, the firm obtained critical know-how and intellectual property with domain expertise in printing, imaging, instrumentation, radio frequency communication, networking, and data storage used in the electronics industry. It has continued to exert effort to deepen and diversify technological capabilities. Through leveraging and reconfiguring existing and new technologies, the firm generated dynamic technological capabilities and made significant strides in providing ODM solutions. In 2010, it made outstanding progress on an ODM project with one key storage client, by augmenting this client's tape library system with Company A-designed and developed precision motion control mechanisms, robotic arms, and system electronics. Moreover, the firm continued to improve its customers' point-of-sale (POS) products, ranging from updating designs to delivering an exceptional combination of reliability and energy efficiency. This enables it to be a primary turnkey supplier, as well as strategic partner to manufacture cash registers for IBM. In addition, Company A's technological capabilities are also supported by its effective enterprise resource planning (ERP) system that facilitates information flow and provides an IT infrastructure linking it with its business partners all over the world in a real-time basis.

As far as manufacturing capabilities are concerned, this firm continually strengthens its manufacturing capabilities to meet global leading MNCs' latest requirements. The constant evolution and improvement of manufacturing capabilities allows Company A to adapt rapidly to sharp fluctuations and declines in demand in advanced economies after the 2008 global financial crisis. More specifically, Company A is highly proficient and cost-effective in manufacturing both high-volume and low-volume yet high-mix, more complex products. To make sure that it had the necessary manufacturing capabilities for the upgrade, the firm established a comprehensive quality control system to meet the requirements of international standards such as ISO 9001:2008, ISO 13485: 2003, ISO 14001:2004, the ODS (Ozone-Depleting Substances), and RoHS (restriction of hazardous substance).

In terms of absorptive capabilities, Company A always looks at commercial relationships as mutually beneficial partnerships and encourages a corporate culture of learning from their strategic partners, particularly from global leading electronic firms. Company A considers the process of transferring knowledge among workers within the supply chain as an important course to brand the group itself. Hence, this company invests a lot of effort into promoting activities that could enhance the organization's absorptive capabilities. For example, top management supports job rotation and enrichment and provides professional training, as well as a wide range of opportunities for employees to acquire, assimilate, and acquire knowledge from their colleagues and business partners. As a result, Company A uses its great absorptive capabilities to maintain long-term, positive relationships with customers and business partners worldwide.

The board committee of Company A is always managed by top-notch professionals from various fields, including MBAs, engineers, and financiers.

The top management team places great premium on talent and innovation, such as attracting experts with special skills to the company's board, hiring outside professional managers with expertise and experience, and adjusting the salary structure of core personnel. They frequently host 'brainstorming sessions' with colleagues to motivate a risk-taking spirit and 'thinking outside the box'. These activities encourage employees to realize and expand their full potential, build strong cohesion, and, most importantly, foster creativity. In the transformation process of upgrading from OEM to ODM status, the top management team withstood uncertainties and showed high flexibility and adaptability to external changes, which enabled the company to survive the 2008 global financial crisis and seize emerging market opportunities. They also displayed potent strategic desires to upgrade to OBM status in the future. In fact, Company A has tried to sell its own-label printers in some shops in the Chinese market since 2009.

## Case #2

Company B, established in 1981, is now a famous contract manufacturer of precision-machined components and assemblies used in the automotive and machinery industry and a well-known OEM of precision turned parts in the imaging and printing industry. The company serves diverse market sectors consisting of many global leading MNCs in imaging and printing, consumer electronics, machinery, automotive systems, and telecommunications. In 1997, it commenced operations in Shanghai to engage in the OEM business and in 2001 went public on the SGX main board after being listed on the SEADAQ[3] board for 3 years. In 2004, to further exploit low-cost advantages and deepen the relationships with its strategic partners, the company set up a factory in Suzhou, China where their major customers of auto components were located. By doing so, the company was able to initiate ODM projects through close collaboration and communication with global leading firms at that time.

To acquire first-tier status as a turnkey supplier of leading MNCs in the GVC, Company B put in a lot of effort in developing technological capabilities for providing total solutions to all customers' machining needs. Emphasizing customer-oriented technical development, the company established an online SPC system that identifies and tracks critical process parameters in production on a real-time basis. This breakthrough in technological capabilities continuously improved Company B's cross-functional

[3] SEADAQ is the second board stock market in Singapore, just like NASDAQ in the United States.

process arrangements in manufacturing, which allowed the company to address the needs of individual customers on service, delivery, and quality, respectively. In addition, with a sophisticated ERP system, Company B has integrated all the activities of its supply chain, whereby it can cater to the various needs of customers in an ever-changing global marketplace.

In terms of upgrading manufacturing capabilities, Company B focused on prioritizing processes in production and thus established multidisciplinary manufacturing processes, such as multiaxis CNC turning centres and multispindle automatic lathes. The company always ensures that the improvement of manufacturing capabilities is matched with relevant global quality standards, and is certified by ISO/TS 16949, ISO 9002, ISO 14001, and OHSAS 18001.

To upgrade to ODM status and meet the ever-changing needs of the marketplace, Company B has built a potent knowledge base that could constantly encourage organizational members to engage in active learning, system thinking, and information sharing with each other and with cooperative partners throughout the GVC activities. The company has operated a comprehensive Institute of Technical Education (ITE), Singapore in-house training programme for foreign worker training and certification, which is an officially approved programme by the ITE in auto maintenance. Through continuous and cross-functional learning in the GVC, this company has developed strong absorptive capabilities that can be employed to recognize external knowledge sources, then assimilate the knowledge acquired and ultimately integrate it into existing knowledge bases.

The board committee of Company B has been led by Mr. Tan, a main controlling shareholder since July 1989. Considering that he also covers the duties of managing director, he is actually the highest/sole leader of Company B with full authority to set overall strategy. With 25 years of experience as a chairman/managing director in the die-casting, electroplating, precision turning, precision machining, and various assembly businesses, Mr. Tan led Company B to build and sustain a strong business foundation, which enabled it to cope with economic uncertainties and business volatility, such as the 2008 global financial crisis and 2010 European debt crisis.

Mr. Tan attached great importance to R&D, innovation, and, most importantly, continuous improvement in operations. He is aggressive, energetic, and resolute with a strong strategic vision and has successfully attracted many talented professionals and experts to work for him. As noted earlier, he was willing to take the risk to initiate the upgrading strategy despite many uncertainties happening in the market. During the global economic slowdown when their business was not thriving, he steered Company B to review and refine many of their work processes for improving production and operation efficiency.

He has extraordinary foresight to seize opportunities during market turbulence. In addition to investing more in advanced technology at a bad time, Mr. Tan also set a customer-centric policy to enhance higher-value business with existing customers rather than looking for new customers. These daring actions raised Company B to a higher level of position as a one-stop solution provider/turnkey supplier for many customers.

## 3.2.5.1 Pattern-Matching Analysis

We conducted the pattern-matching analysis to match our survey findings with the proposed conceptual framework. The results are shown in Table 3.2.

**Table 3.2** Pattern-Matching Analysis

| | Company A | Company B |
|---|---|---|
| Technological capabilities | • Several R&D centres strategically located in Asia, Europe, and America<br>• A high-tech and unique 'Point of Sales' system covering 'point of conception' and 'point of consumption', providing a stand-alone service or as part of the value chain management services to clients<br>• A supportive and effective ERP system<br>• Obtaining critical patents and intellectual property used in electronics industry | • Total solutions to all customers' machining needs (customer-oriented technological development)<br>• An on-line SPC system identifies and tracks critical process parameters in productions on a real-time basis<br>• A supportive ERP system integrating all activities of the supply chain and providing total solutions on customer relationship management |
| Manufacturing capabilities | • A high level of manufacturing flexibility: highly proficient and cost-effective in both high-volume and high-mix, low-volume products<br>• ISO 9001: 2008, ISO 13485: 2003 ISO 14001:2004, RoHS and the ODS | • Optimizing production: building capabilities to deal with multiple manufacturing process simultaneously<br>• ISO 9001:2002; ISO/TS 16949 and ISO 14001:2004 and OHSAS 18001 |

*Continued*

**Table 3.2** Pattern-Matching Analysis—cont'd

|  | Company A | Company B |
|---|---|---|
| Absorptive capabilities | • Encouraging employees to disseminate tacit knowledge acquired within the GVCs through a wide range of activities, for example, staff training, job rotation, cross-department communication, and the company's routine/regular meeting | • Encouraging active learning between cooperative partners in GVC activities<br>• A comprehensive, certificated in-house training programme for foreign workers, an officially approved programme by the ITE in autonomous maintenance |
| Leadership | The top leaders of both firms are quite innovative, visionary, pragmatic, adaptable, and persistent, with particular concerns for attracting and retaining talents, maintaining good relationships with customers, as well as achieving eco-friendly sustainable development | |

## 3.2.5.2 Discussion

In accordance with the assumed conceptual framework, we find that technological, manufacturing, and absorptive capabilities are the key dynamic capabilities for FDI OEMs in China to carry out functional upgrading. Our results show that Singapore-invested OEMs in China have been successfully transformed from OEM to ODM/OBM modes and thus are able to obtain more economic returns. Furthermore, strong leadership plays a pivotal role in driving OEM firms to climb the ladder of the GVC, to engage in more value-added activities, such as ODM and OBM, and eventually earn higher economic returns. Overall, this study illustrates the significance of critical dynamic capabilities in executing the strategy of functional upgrading and highlights the significance of leadership in guiding the upgrading process. Given that the capabilities are dynamic, management should not wait until they are in place before initiating the upgrade. Instead, they can adopt the approach of building the necessary capabilities from the inception or during the process of upgrading.

Our study makes three unique contributions. First, it reveals a holistic picture delineating the upgrading strategies by FDI OEMs in the Chinese context from a dynamic capabilities perspective. More specifically, our study explores how Singapore-invested OEMs exploit the dynamic capabilities developed via collaboration with global leading MNCs to implement functional upgrading, whereby they further cultivate China's huge domestic market. Second, since in-depth interviews with top management were conducted in both parent companies in Singapore and their subsidiaries in China, our study echoes the appeal for collecting more timely, first-hand data, including raw and informal forms, by which we can better capture reality (Lau & Bruton, 2008). Third, on the basis of documenting functional upgrading, our study presents a context-specific dynamic capability mechanism by foreign-invested OEM firms in China, responding to calls for the investigation of dynamic capabilities in specific contexts (Weerawardena et al., 2007).

Our findings also provide insightful managerial implications for FDI OEMs operating in China, perhaps helping them to grow further and prosper. Evidence reveals that creating own brands is likely to cause animosity from main buyers and GVC leaders towards their OEM suppliers (Morrison et al., 2008) because OEMs may leapfrog them to compete against their initial outsourcers in international arenas after developing sufficient capabilities (Matthews, 2006). Despite this, a large number of Chinese manufacturers still view OEM partnerships with global brands as a springboard to learn about creating own brands (Chin et al., 2016; Chin, Tsai, et al., 2016). In contrast, Singapore-invested firms seem inclined to regard OEM collaboration as a long-term stable strategy to secure growth and profits by establishing trust relationships with world-class brands. As such, Singapore OEMs usually endeavour to upgrade to ODM status, but hesitate to proceed to upgrade to OBM status. In this vein, Singapore-invested OEMs in China reflect an idiosyncrasy to establish thicker linkages and dense interactions with GVC partners rather than to build own brands. Following this logic, it is plausible to claim that both foreign-invested and domestic OEMs in China may view the outsourcing trends concerning functional upgrading along the GVC differently.

### 3.2.5.3 Limitations and Recommendations

This exploratory study offers some avenues for future research. However, we acknowledge that it has several limitations. First, in terms of research methodology, a two-case study may not be able to offer sufficient evidence to examine our assumed model. Second, in addition to the three organizational capabilities identified, there may be others; future research could try to identify more vital and relevant capabilities that affect functional upgrading. Third, scholars should pay attention to discussing the mechanisms and interactions among different organizational capabilities, as well as the importance weights and synergy of individual capabilities. By doing so, the path of functional upgrading can be articulated in a more systematic and extensive manner. On the basis of the foregoing arguments, it is also recommended that future research could conduct a comparative study including firms that did not engage in functional upgrading—which may reveal a more comprehensive picture of FDIs and their upgrading strategies in China.

## 3.3 UPGRADING TO OBM BY AN ENTREPRENEURIAL BRITISH OEM IN CHINA

### 3.3.1 Introduction

Global start-up firms that exploit the opportunities of globalization to achieve superior performance in international markets from their inception, or shortly thereafter, have generated significant research in the field of entrepreneurship (Jones, Coviello, & Tang, 2011; Kiss, Danis, & Tamer Cavusgil, 2012; Oviatt & McDougall, 2005). Owing to poor intellectual rights protection and weak legal enforcement coupled with the very complex bureaucratic systems in EEs, global start-up firms with less resources deciding to venture into EEs may face more intricate problems than those internationalizing their business in other developed economies (DEs) with more sound market infrastructures. However, in recent years, there have been an increasing number of entrepreneurial firms from DEs that prefer to enter large EEs such as China at an early stage given the large populations and attractive consumer markets (Jones et al., 2011; Kiss et al., 2012). While the literature still tends to explain how large enterprises from DEs compete in EEs (Lyles & Park, 2013; Yamakawa, Khavul, & Peng, 2013), there has been a scarcity of literature demonstrating why some DE global start-up firms choose to venture into EEs with higher uncertainty instead of into other mature markets with more familiarity.

To fill this research gap, our study uses the Chinese manufacturing sector as a research background because China is the world's largest EE and manufacturing FDI plays a crucial role in its economic growth. Notwithstanding a large body of research that has addressed the upgrading strategies conducted by world class manufacturers from DEs in China (Chin et al., 2015; Herrigel, Wittke, & Voskamp, 2013), the development trajectories of small, entrepreneurial foreign OEMs in this context have been much less covered in the literature. As such, our study employs a case-study approach, investigating how a British OEM accelerated its internationalization process by setting up a plant in China. This study elucidates how a small foreign OEM was willing and daring to bear the high risks of upgrading to OBM status in China by collaborating with Chinese SOEs.

Given that global start-up OEMs as a unique form of international new ventures derive from GVC theory (Chin et al., 2016; Chin, Tsai, et al., 2016), our study takes the GVC framework as the departure point to illustrate how global start-up OEMs from DEs enhanced China's economic development (Gereffi, 2009; Ivarsson & Alvstam, 2011). Seeing that the entrepreneur or SME in general has full authority to make big decisions (Oviatt & McDougall, 2005), we also incorporate the international entrepreneurship view to characterize the unique internationalization and corresponding entrepreneurial behaviours of the case—namely how a British entrepreneur observed, evaluated, and exploited the cross-border opportunities in an unfamiliar Chinese context.

The outline of this study is as follows. First, we integrate international entrepreneurship and GVC perspectives to identify the key external factors that triggered the decision of a British global start-up OEM to enter a psychically distant country, China. Second, a description of the sample case is provided. Finally, we demonstrate how our empirical findings contribute to the literature.

## 3.3.2 Theoretical Foundation

### 3.3.2.1 International Entrepreneurship and GVCs

The label of 'born global firms' or 'global start-ups' refers to early internationalizing firms that span international borders almost at birth (Chin et al., 2016; Chin, Tsai, et al., 2016; Jones et al., 2011; Oviatt & McDougall's, 2005, 1994). The traditional Uppsala model of internationalization (Johanson & Vahlne, 1977) argues that firms' internationalization should be a gradual process that needs sufficient experience and knowledge to reduce the 'liability of foreignness' (Zahra, 2005) and risks. However, Oviatt and McDougall's (1994) theory of international new ventures draws attention to the fact that some small and young ventures may not actually own such experiences and resources, but use their remarkable resourcefulness to compete internationally from their inception. This rapid internationalization framework explains the emergence of the rising power of young, small firms in the global marketplace.

The major difference between these models resides in the choices of entry and operation modes firms adopt for internationalization.

Oviatt and McDougall (1994) claim that global start-ups with inherent entrepreneurial spirit and 'learning advantages of newness' (Autio, George, & Alexy, 2011; Zahra, 2005) transmit and assimilate information very quickly. Such firms may adopt higher and more aggressive modes of foreign market entry, such as building wholly-owned subsidiaries at their inception. In contrast, Johanson and Vahlne (1977) emphasize 'bounded rationality', which suggests that firms learn experientially and measure risks cautiously in internationalization. Firms should, in general, accumulate knowledge to increase their commitments in foreign markets step by step. In other words, the learning trajectories for internationalization by global start-ups and established firms may be varied—which highlights the pivotal role of international entrepreneurship in determining the timing, scope, and scale of internationalizing firms. This raises various issues for researchers to explore. After all, while the background, experience, and personal characteristics of entrepreneurs are of great importance to firms' international entrepreneurial behaviour (Chin, Tsai, et al., 2016; Kiss et al., 2012), it is imperative to investigate the links between global start-ups' learning and their entrepreneurial activities and how the links contribute to firms' competitive advantages. It is also worth further study whether the learning form and content of global start-ups will change as they reach the mature stage of development in host countries.

In sum, as noted earlier, it requires further elaboration as to why some DE global start-ups choose to confront an environment (i.e. EE) that is more volatile, uncertain, and complex and structurally different from their original countries (i.e. DE). Owing to the multidisciplinary nature of the global start-up phenomenon (Oviatt & McDougall, 2005), our research incorporates the international entrepreneurship view into the GVC framework to delve into relevant issues.

### 3.3.2.2 Global Start-Up OEMs

Global start-ups have been classified as one of the four typical types of international new ventures (Oviatt & McDougall, 1994): export/import start-up; multinational trader; geographically focused; and global, according to the differences in the possessions of unique knowledge. However, owing to increasing global complexities, it is highly possible that the internationalizing patterns of global start-ups may vary under different combinations of industry, market, corporation, and entrepreneur-related conditions. There might be more kinds of international new ventures than that presented in the existing literature. For instance, one predominant but previously ignored type is the 'global start-up OEM' that focuses on low cost production and assembly functions within GVCs (Chin et al., 2016; Chin, Tsai, et al., 2016)—yet this is actually a typical and representative type of global start-up firm in the manufacturing industry of DE and EE with large amounts of cheap labour, such as China.

Since the 1990s, in order to reduce costs, quite a few DE MNCs have started to position their core business primarily in brand management and outsourced low value-added production to OEM suppliers in China (Herrigel et al., 2013). This cross-border outsourcing trend has encouraged not only big but also small and medium-sized OEMs from DEs to follow their key buyers' strategic options venturing into China (Chin, Tsai, et al., 2016). As illustrated in the previous section, China had been attracting the world's largest amount of FDI into its OEM industry. Such DE global start-up OEMs, unlike the mainstream model of DE global start-ups emerging from high-tech industries, are mostly labour-intensive rather than technology-intensive because these firms used to exploit the abundant supply of cheap labour in China to compete. Compared with domestic OEMs in China, DE global start-up OEMs often have a relatively broader knowledge base in international marketing and modern technology, despite the weakness of local market knowledge and social networks (Chin & Liu, 2017; Chin et al., 2015). Following this logic, the DE global start-up OEMs in China still possess certain comparative advantages against domestic OEMs when competing in the export and international arenas.

Following the discussion above, it is conspicuous that internationalization by DE global start-up OEMs in China seems to be resource—rather than market-seeking as they position China as a production hub or sourcing platform to acquire low-cost advantages. Yet continuously rising labour costs and sharp currency fluctuations have been squeezing OEM's profit margins in China. Meanwhile, China has grown to be the biggest consumer market for automobiles, televisions, cell phones, and luxury goods (Chin & Liu, 2017). As such, China, in the eyes of many countries and MNCs, has become a very promising market rather than just a low-cost production base. Its fast-growing local demand symbolizes one silver cloud on the horizon— which motivates DE global start-up OEMs, especially those with years of experience in China, to upgrade from OEM to OBM status or to diversify their business activities apart from manufacturing for better returns.

Nevertheless, it remains unknown how and why DE global start-up OEMs conduct their upgrading strategies and increase their commitments in China, as China's FDI policy is often more in favour of supporting large

MNCs. In response, our study integrates the international entrepreneurship and GVC perspectives to demonstrate the 10-year internationalization trajectory of a small British OEM venturing into China, articulating how contextual variables of EE shape DE global start-ups' entrepreneurial behaviours in the process of adapting to the changing competitive context of emerging markets.

### 3.3.3 Methodology

The case study method is particularly appropriate when research covers a real-time environment or when there is little empirical substantiation of relevant issues (Eisenhardt & Graebner, 2007). Considering the salient real-time characteristic and dynamic essence of our research, we conducted an 18-month longitudinal field study (from August 2012 to February 2014) using a single-case research approach to investigate the early internationalization trajectory and subsequent development strategies of a British OEM we called TECHSAVVY[4] in China. To enhance our explanatory power we facilitated continuous mutual learning and understanding between involved researchers and the local firm.

#### *3.3.3.1 Data Collection*

The main form of data collection was regular in-depth interviews (monthly) with the managers of several key departments. We also reviewed the internal reports and archival documents for 10 years (2003 – 13). Therefore, data could be triangulated between real-time observations and retrospective investigations of firm records—which enables the establishment of a chain of evidence (Eisenhardt & Graebner, 2007). Moreover, we conducted semistructured and open-ended interviews at least once every 3 months with the top management team, namely the chief executive officer (CEO), the deputy managing director, and the engineering director. Each of these interviews was conducted in either Chinese or English according to the interviewees' request and lasted about 2 h. To ensure the robustness of data, all interviews were tape-recorded and undertaken with a three-person team, where one researcher handled the interview questions and two researchers were responsible for noting down all the responses.

To verify the reliability and validity of data, the recorded data were transcribed within 24 h of the interviews. Given a participatory action research, we requested the firm to allow us to participate in some decision-making

---

[4] All names of companies and persons were pseudonyms for reasons of confidentiality.

meetings regarding the enactment and implementation of their new internationalization strategies in China. Hence, we attended quite a few meetings discussing their most important strategic move on upgrading to OBM in China—namely building a strategic alliance with an SOE to produce own-brand products—over a period of 16 months (September 2012 to December 2013). Although top management asked us to provide suggestions at the meeting, we strictly adhered to the role of observation and did not voice any opinions during the course of discussion until critical decisions were made.

In the following section, we detail the firm's 10-year internationalization journey. This case chronicles how Chris, the entrepreneur behind TECHSAVVY, spent 10 years leading his firm to upgrade from a low commitment mode (OEM) to a higher commitment mode (OBM) in China. This journey is categorized into six stages: (1) The beginning; (2) from 2003 to 2004; (3) from 2005 to 2007; (4) from 2008 to 2011; (5) from 2012 to 2013; (6) from 2014.

### 3.3.4 Key Findings

We first briefly introduce the background and the crippled start-up of the case firm.

#### 3.3.4.1 Background and Crippled Start-Up

TECHSAVVY, funded in 2003 by the British entrepreneur, Chris, was originally a UK OEM that in the same year established a wholly foreign-owned subsidiary in Guangzhou (GZ), China. TECHSAVVY, producing metal and plastic components for the auto and plumbing industries, had focused on providing OEM services for global leading MNCs that outsourced production of part or finished goods to China for the first 7 years. Until 2013, the firm had another four shareholders. Andrew was an old friend of Chris, dealing with orders related to engineering and based in the United States. Philip who resided in Australia assisted Chris with his expertise in plastics and metal engineering to win orders that required professional technical knowledge. Lili, living in the United Kingdom, was in charge of all nontechnological orders. Julia was promoted to deputy managing director and a business partner in China in 2010 after 7 years of working with Chris. Having about 40 years of working experience in the OEM industry in Latin America and China, Chris established a trusting relationship with his major clients from developed markets and gained a deep understanding of his local competitors in China.

Though Chris himself is not strictly speaking an engineer, his grandfather and great-grandfather were outstanding chief engineers who helped British companies to build the Indian railway network. Inheriting his family's glory, Chris seems to be a 'born engineer' as well as a technological talent and quickly developed a high-quality engineering team in China. With about 40 years of working experience in more than 70 OEMs across the world, Chris established an incredibly trusting relationship with his major clients from developed markets. In addition, serving as the vice chair of the British Chamber of Commerce in GZ for years, he also built good relationships (*guanxi*) with the local government and a variety of domestic OEM suppliers which enabled him to closely watch and gain a deep understanding of his competitors.

### The Beginning: The SARS Crisis

In January 2003, Chris arrived in GZ. After renting a two-room apartment for use as his residence as well as office, he posted a recruiting advertisement for a business contact manager in China that attracted about 60 candidates. He selected a young Chinese woman who was proficient in English, Spanish, Cantonese, and the Shanghai dialect of Mandarin as his manager and another woman as her assistant. Thus, a three-person company was set to go in February 2003.

However, owing to the sudden outbreak of severe acute respiratory syndrome (SARS) in Southern China, the World Health Organization (WHO) issued a global alert. Chris followed the British Embassy's suggestion to fly back to Britain at the end of May and left the office in the hands of the newly hired manager that he barely knew. The WHO continued to issue advisories against travel to China and, therefore, for the next 3 months Chris was compelled to run his business by remote control using the internet and telephone.

Chris flew back to GZ immediately the WHO lifted the restrictions on travel to China in August 2003. Unfortunately and unexpectedly, he found his home office empty, all the Swedish furniture gone, and the operating funds he had remitted to the office missing. From this dramatic incident, Chris learned a valuable lesson. 'It's impossible to manage your business in China via long distance remote control', he said. Accordingly, he made a tough decision to stay long term in GZ. In late 2003, a new manager, Julia, was recruited. She was smart, responsible, and a very capable manager. With her outstanding performance and dedication, she soon became Chris's right-hand person, deputy managing director as well as business partner. Since then, Chris has been able to concentrate on looking for new clients.

### From 2003 to 2004: Early Success

While most major rivals in China were domestic firms that implemented a low-cost strategy, Chris decided to highlight his particular comparative advantages in engineering technologies, locating the competitive position of TECHSAVVY as 'Western quality, China prices'. Thus, 'Chinese people were saying we should buy cheap and sell it at a lower price than our competitors, but to me quality is more important than price', Chris said. This impressive market positioning enabled TECHSAVVY to successfully obtain purchase orders from two important DE buyers.

Using his strong social networks, Chris quickly approached two big European customers after settling the company problems noted above in late 2003. One was a global leader in the manufacture of kitchen and bath products, while the other was a large MNC famous for producing highly sophisticated engines for commercial vehicles. Both companies were suffering from price pressures at about that time and thus keen to outsource the production of plastic parts and metal components to China to reduce costs. However, both companies had high expectations regarding product quality that required advanced manufacturing technologies and practical engineering skills. Therefore, it was not easy to satisfy the needs of these two large clients. Fortunately, Chris's impressive background and work history enabled him to convince them that his OEM firm would be strongly committed to engineering and state-of-the-art manufacturing techniques. The two firms continued to buy products from TECHSAVVY for more than 9 years. Owing to the increasing orders placed by the two key clients, TECHSAVVY's annual sales exceeded US$1 million for the first time at the end of 2004 (see Fig. 3.3).

### From 2005 to 2007: Fast Growth Via Innovative Keyword Marketing

Given that corporate websites were becoming one of the main sales channels around the world, Chris decided to redesign his website in 2005. Despite a website overhaul, Chris could not see any significant improvement in the number of online inquiries to their firm at the beginning. After much research, he found a very interesting book by an author who seemed to be a great internet marketing specialist living in Philadelphia. Without hesitation, Chris made a telephone call to him. Through a 2-h private consultation over the phone that cost US$2000, Chris obtained brilliant ideas and

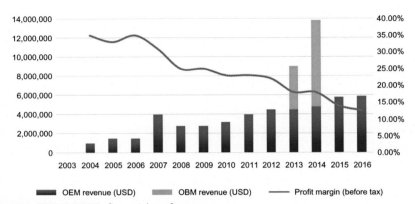

**Fig. 3.3** TECHSAVVY's financial performance.

constructive advice from this American. Despite being exhausted, he felt excited and finally figured out how to use keyword marketing as a pivotal tool to boost online inquiries. 'We had to discover the actual words our clients use when they search for information online about our content topic', he said.

Following the tactics suggested by the American consultant, he rearranged and reorganized the content on his firm's web pages. He hired a professional engineer who updated the keywords daily and optimized the website to achieve the highest possible rankings on search engines. After 3 months' hard work, the number of keywords in TECHSAVVY's website had been added up to about 180 on the first page of Google results without advertising.

Without doubt, the firm's operational effectiveness and efficiency were greatly enhanced by advanced information technology. When a new enquiry came in, Chris was immediately informed by email on his iPhone anywhere in the world. He could respond and give instructions to his staff in minutes. By shortening response times, this internet marketing created a win–win situation for both TECHSAVVY and its buyers. As a result, more and more effective inquiries were received via the website since then. In 2007, TECHSAVVY tripled its revenue to US$4 million (see Fig. 3.3).

### From 2008 to 2011: Global Financial Crisis Hit

Suddenly, the 2008 financial crisis and subsequent global recession swept the world, leading to sharp declines in demand in mature markets. This severely impacted on China's OEM industry (Chin et al., 2015). TECHSAVVY, which relied on exports to DE, therefore suffered a sales drop up to 30%

and its annual revenue fell to about US$2.8 million for the next 2 years. To offset lost high-volume orders from large MNCs, Chris decided to make better use of keyword marketing, striving to get more low-volume orders from SME buyers via the company website. Gradually, TECHSAVVY's sales returned to growth, reaching US$3.2 million in 2010 and US$4 million in 2011 (see Fig. 3.3).

### From 2012 to 2013: Upgrading to OBM

Though Chris started to see sales coming back, the severe pressures of continuous currency appreciation and rising operation costs shrank the profit margin of China's OEM industry. It seemed to become increasingly difficult for TECHSAVVY to manufacture at low prices with superior quality OEM products in this context. Considering how TECHSAVVY's technological and engineering capabilities developed over the past years had equipped the firm with essential technical know-how to create its own-brand products in related industries, Chris decided to make a bold, brave, and aggressive move, upgrading TECHSAVVY from OEM to OBM status for higher profits.

In early 2011, through an old British friend's introduction, Chris encountered an opportunity to collaborate with CMM, a large Chinese mining SOE that had been urgently searching for a strategic partner with sophisticated engineering technologies in plastic and metal moulding, casting, and the like. This SOE wanted the new partner to help technically refurbish its current existing, but obsolete and unreliable, mining safety products and, most importantly, personal protection equipment (PPE). Chris intended to grab this valuable opportunity to achieve the above-mentioned strategic goal of building his own brand in China. He thus persuaded CMM to form a 5-year strategic alliance with TECHSAVVY.

In this contract, CMM allowed TECHSAVVY to refer to CMM's existing but out-of-date and somewhat invalid products and to develop new PPEs under TECHSAVVY's brand name, while TECHSAVVY agreed to use one patented chemical material for generating oxygen supplied by CMM's coal mines in its products. In short, TECHSAVVY would be in charge of the entire design and manufacture and be given an exclusive right to sell the cooperative products in overseas markets (outside China), while CMM would have a monopoly right to sell these products in China. The two companies planned to launch two new products every year during the contract period and CMM could get a 7% commission on the sales made by TECHSAVVY in overseas markets. However, the decisions of selecting, developing, launching, and pricing collaborative products needed to be made through discussion and approved by both sides.

After intensive communication back and forth, TECHSAVVY and CMM finally agreed to overhaul two PPEs of CMM as their strategic objectives for 2012. These were Self-Rescuer (SCSR) and methane gas detector (MGD) products. With CMM's support, the refurbishment process went smoothly. During the co-development period, in addition to regular meetings with CMM, TECHSAVVY's engineering team was working very hard on product innovations, ranging from changing the previous design to adding new features, such as waterproof and quakeproof functions. The samples of the two renewed products had been successively completed in late 2012 and soon after were sent to be thoroughly tested at national and international standards.

The new cooperative products looked good, perfectly refurbished in appearance and technologies. Drawing on this strategic alliance with CMM as a stepping stone, Chris felt that TECHSAVVY had successfully transformed from an OEM to an OBM firm. He was very excited and expected that by selling the two new products TECHSAVVY would increase its annual revenue to US$9 million at the end of 2013 and be able to target a year-on-year growth of 100% for the next 5 years. However, at the end of 2014, the two sides were still unable to reach consensus, and yet there was zero income coming from own-brand products for TECHAVVY (see Fig. 3.3).

### From 2014: Unexpected Difficulties and Challenges Ahead

According to the original plan, the renewed SCSR and MGD products under the brand name TECHSAVVY should have been released in early 2013. However, though TECHSAVVY was all set to globally launch these products at about that time, the release date of the first product (SCSR) had been delayed five times until March 2014 due to some critical disagreements between TECHSAVVY and CMM. This delay incurred unexpected risks and posed a danger to TECHSAVVY's financial stability given that Chris had pumped more than US$500,000 into the R&D process and the certificate application for selling PPEs in different countries. Based on the interviews with Chris, the key problems between TECHSAVVY and CMM are summarized into the following trio.

**1.** Cultural differences between British and Chinese decision-making
Chris, who participated in most of the bilateral meetings with CMM, pointed out that he just could not understand how to get the green light

from CMM top management. More specifically, since Chris was the main decision–maker, the decision–making process on TECHSAVVY's side was quick, smooth, and efficient. In contrast, making decisions seemed to be very time-consuming and complex at CMM. Even worse, conclusions agreed on by both sides at meetings could be overthrown later if a higher level boss of CMM disliked it. Chris felt very confused why the laborious work of preparing the negotiation with CMM always fell through.

**2.** Different opinions on product safety and quality requirements

In terms of product specifications and design, TECHSAVVY suggested that it be in full conformity with the strict international safety regulations since the quality of mining PPEs is significantly related to miners' lives and the thresholds for selling these products are, in general, incredibly high in developed markets. In contrast, CMM thought that strictly conforming to international standards would include redundant and costly functions that might result in excessive pricing beyond the affordable range in the Chinese market. So they suggested following Chinese standards, as China was the major market.

**3.** Disputes on pricing strategies

The different points of view on product specification, as mentioned above, raised further disputes on formulating pricing strategies for the products. CMM, favouring low-price strategies, attempted to position the products as a cost leader in both Chinese and overseas markets, while TECHSAVVY preferred to use 'Western design and quality at a relatively lower price' as the market positioning and thus to differentiate the products in many ways, such as adding hi-tech features and improving display functions. For example, in 2012 TECHSAVVY had followed international standards in designing a MGD model with built-in Wi-Fi, backup battery, and a sensor to measure the densities of methane and carbon dioxide gas in mines. However, CMM used to benefit from cost leading strategy, insisting that the extras of built-in Wi-Fi, backup battery and carbon dioxide gas detector appeared dispensable, as those were not standard equipment for MGD. Hence, CMM suggested to TECHSAVVY to remove them in order to reduce the manufacturing cost as well as selling price. Given that these functions played a critical role in meeting international safety standards, Chris had been trying his best to convince CMM that whereas the specifications of PPE determine the life or death of miners in mining accidents, it is vital to comply with the rigorous international health and safety standards. A similar situation also happened with the SCSR. Nevertheless, despite hard negotiations over relevant topics, no consensus was made for the past 18 months. As a result, the launches of the products had been put off five times. At the end of 2013, TECHSAVVY failed to achieve their initial anticipated annual revenue of US$9 million, only producing US$4.8 million through the OEM business (see Table 3.1).

## 3.3.5 Discussion

Overall, the TECHSAVVY case study presents an inspiring true story about how a British entrepreneur was very courageous in overcoming the 'liabilities of foreignness' by venturing into China at the inception and then exploiting innovative keyword marketing to attenuate the liabilities of smallness, achieving fast growth in export markets within 4 years. The results present an intriguing picture of the 10-year internationalization and entrepreneurial journey of a DE firm in the world's largest EE, China. Although TECHSAVVY's collaboration with a Chinese SOE to upgrade to OBM might be an unsuccessful try, our research still brings insightful and profound implications for other DE global start-ups that have been or will be venturing into an EE context.

As such, the main contribution of our study is to provide valuable first-hand data and empirical evidence at the intersection of the literature of international entrepreneurship and strategic management. First, our findings contribute to the international entrepreneurship literature, as it reveals that knowledge in entrepreneurial firms tend to be individualized to the founder or the top management team and that SMEs are inclined to exhibit speedier entry or higher commitment to internationalization when their entrepreneurs have personal international knowledge or prior living/working experience in foreign markets. Second, consistent with Yamakawa et al. (2013) study on the internationalization choice of EE new ventures, we discovered that DE global start-ups may decide to take the plunge to internationalize into EEs rather than well-established DEs because it seems more advantageous for these firms to exploit their advanced knowledge and technology as competitive advantages in EE than in DE markets. Third, we conducted a comprehensive in-depth case study, ranging from literature retrieval, archival research, a variety of personal interviews to field investigation—which responds to recent calls for collecting more first-hand, timely data to capture what is behind the tremendous FDI inflows into China (Lau & Bruton, 2008).

As far as managerial implications are concerned, our findings show that although upgrading to OBM is recognized as a feasible strategy by foreign

OEMs to benefit from China's huge internal market (Chin et al., 2016; Chin, Tsai, et al., 2016), the approach, path, and industry chosen by individual OEMs, as a matter of fact, influence and restrict the success or failure of such an upgrading strategy in this context. It is not surprising that TECHSAVVY encountered severe difficulties as it chose to work with a Chinese SOE for upgrading in a politically sensitive industry—mining—that the government considers part of its national security interests. As such, we remain quite sceptical about whether TECHSAVVY will finally obtain the returns they deserve from their laborious efforts. This stalemate situation is actually an important lesson for other DE global start-ups in China.

### 3.3.6 Conclusions and Further Suggestions

Considering the foregoing, we conclude that, despite its spectacular growth potential, TECHSAVVY will face more critical challenges in the future, as illustrated next. First, a plethora of studies have discussed the impact of cultural elements such as values, beliefs, and behaviours on the decision-making process (Hofstede, 2015). The differences in decision-making processes between CMM and TECHSAVVY were actually triggered by the cultural differences between the East and the West. As with our findings, it is noticeable that both sides have their own set of core values and basic assumptions on forming strategic alliances. It was imperative for TECHSAVVY to gain a better understanding of CMM's anticipated goal of their strategic alliance; TECHSAVVY will not be able to make a breakthrough until it gets buy-in and approval from key personnel at CMM. In other words, their disputes on product specification and pricing strategies will not be resolved unless TECHSAVVY can enhance its capabilities in cross-cultural negotiation and communication to work with a Chinese SOE. This is an obvious management development need and an interesting opportunity for a quality provider in this area.

Second, previous research indicates that international strategic alliances can be an effective development strategy for entrepreneurial firms to overcome resource deficiencies, especially when venturing into unfamiliar foreign markets (Chin, Tsai, et al., 2016; Drauz, 2013). Given that the administrative and marketing systems in China are very different, TECHSAVVY was supposed to use a strategic alliance with CMM as a stepping stone to gain legitimacy to help foreign firms attach themselves to local business and political networks in the Chinese market. However, despite being a partner with an SOE local partner CMM, TECHSAVVY failed to link itself into an appropriate network that enabled it to become an approved PPE supplier to this company. Viewed from this angle, owing to China's institutional environment, a contractual nonequity governance mode for international strategic alliances may only provide a limited role in the establishment of a trusting partnership.

Third, evidence shows that GVC upgrading from OEM to OBM may not always be a panacea leading to higher profits (Gereffi, 2009). Since upgrading to OBM requires large investment in R&D as well as brand marketing, it faces higher risks of failure (Chin et al., 2016)—which is also very likely to kindle the animosity of GVC leaders in the target domain and, in turn, intensify competition. Hence, it is doubtful that TECHSAVVY will be able to solely rely on OBM business to achieve further growth in today's uncertain and competitive environment. It might be a better option for TECHSAVVY to reconfigure its current production, marketing, and R&D capabilities and conduct a new operational model in parallel that can support OBM activities and improve OEM profits.

### 3.3.7 Limitations and Future Research

In sum, our exploratory longitudinal study offers fruitful avenues for future research. However, it also has limitations. Although our study demonstrates how DE global start-ups venture into China and then deepen their commitments at a more mature phase of development, we may have only scratched the surface of this intriguing entrepreneurial phenomenon. After all, notwithstanding that the longitudinal single-case survey and the use of face-to-face administered investigation are merits of this qualitative research design, self-report data may pose some problems, such as recall bias by respondents. We cannot neglect the possibility that some of our observations could merely reflect a part of the whole story. Findings may have been different had we chosen a different industry or home country. In this vein, scholars are encouraged to carry out more multilevel and multifaceted methods to probe relevant issues in the future.

## 3.4 CONCLUSION

Overall, the foregoing cases discussed in the chapter illuminate valuable implications and new directions for FDI in China's manufacturing, as FDI flowing into this sector still increases and is expected to continuously promote technological innovation and upgrading along the GVCs among

Chinese firms. To better understand the co-evolutionary path of FDI and Chinese institutional environment, we further conducted several informal follow-up interviews with the top leaders of the three case firms in 2016 and 2017. We found that much has happened since our last surveys.

Both the Singapore-invested OEMs (Company A and Company B in Table 3.1) moved their major production bases from China to Malaysia between 2013 and 2016, due to rising labour costs in China coupled with more rigorous antidumping barriers in international markets. In 2013, Company A spent RMB 68 million (US$ = 10.3 million) buying a plot of land in Penang, Malaysia where they built many new, advanced production lines. Company B sharply increased the level of automation and laid off three-quarters of the workers in their China factories by 2016, but meanwhile established a large labour-intensive plant in Xinshan, Malaysia.

In terms of TECHSAVVY, no consensus regarding the product design for the Chinese market had been reached between 2013 and 2016. CMM did not also approve TECHSAVVY's proposal to authorize foreign agents to sell their collaborative products in Latin America. Such an unexpected stalemate allowed Chris to feel that it might be a poor decision to collaborate with a large SOE in China—such kinds of companies are so powerful that small foreign partners do not dare argue against them. As a result TECHSAVVY could not but have returned to concentrate on OEM business since 2015 till now.

Given the latest evidence above, we extrapolate that foreign-invested manufacturers may need to grapple with a greater variety of conundrums during the new round of industrial transformation. Although more and more foreign firms consider contracting an alliance with Chinese SOEs for better cultivating domestic markets and reinforcing their strategic competitiveness, the intricacies of dealing with local officials and partners remain. Hence, despite a lot of manufacturing FDIs that formed IJVs with local partners in the past, many of them have restructured their business into the form of a wholly foreign-owned subsidiary when China announced loosening the ownership restrictions on the entry mode of FDI. We will further discuss in greater detail about the retreat trend of large FDI manufacturers and the emerging trend of local entrepreneurial OEMs in China in the next chapter.

CHAPTER FOUR

# Branding in Reverse Internationalization: Evidence From Local Entrepreneurial OEMs

## 4.1 INTRODUCTION

According to China's national bureau of statistics, SMEs contribute 60% of GDP and 50% of tax revenue; 52% of these SMEs were manufacturers (Child, 2016). As shown in Fig. 4.1, the number of SME manufacturers in China has greatly increased since the early 20th century. Hence, despite the lack of core technologies, brand awareness, and weak product differentiation (Opper & Nee, 2015), SME manufacturers have become an emergent social and economic force in China.

The fast growth of manufacturing SMEs for decades could be attributed to national policies that encouraged FDI into this sector. Numerous local firms grabbed the opportunities to internationalize and grow by providing a variety of OEM services to foreign buyers, especially those MNCs based in China. These OEMs, as typical but context-specific types of global start-up firms emerging from China, indicate a distinctive export-driven internationalization trajectory by SMEs in large EEs or DEs, although business activities of this nature were mainly inclined to be low to mid-tech in form at the beginning. However, evidence reveals that through partnership with world-class MNCs for a certain period, some of these firms with 'entrepreneurial spirit' may gradually evolve their capabilities to innovate and upgrade to OBM status owing to the technology and knowledge spillover effects between lead firms and OEM suppliers within GVCs. It is worth noting that the Chinese government has been playing a leading role in promoting these OEM initiatives to embark on OBM as several favourable policies were promulgated whereby local companies could more easily exploit the massive Chinese market to sell own-brand products.

This branding trend came into more prominence after the 2008 global financial crisis, given that OBM was viewed as a competitive advantage for

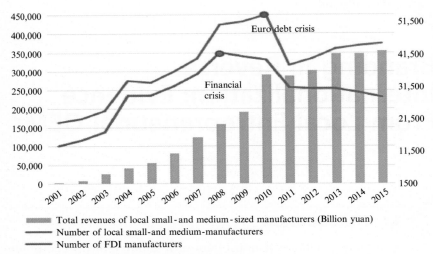

Fig. 4.1 FDI and local entrepreneurial OEMs.

Chinese OEMs to shift their focus from exports to domestic markets. More specifically, while the number of foreign-invested manufacturers started to decline in China after the 2008 financial and 2010 Euro debt crises, the number of local manufacturers, conversely, kept rising during 2008 and 2010 (see Fig. 4.1). This is because the government carried out the 4 trillion RMB (about US$0.6 trillion) economic stimulus plan to boost internal demand and strongly motivated local firms to produce own-brand products catering to local customers. This unique entrepreneurial phenomenon by Chinese OEMs can be characterized as 'reverse internationalization'—which will be clearly addressed in the following two studies.

## 4.2 REVERSE INTERNATIONALIZATION BY CHINESE GLOBAL START-UP OEMS

### 4.2.1 Introduction

While much of the literature suggests that global start-ups from North America and Europe mostly engage in high-tech or knowledge-intensive business (Tolstoy, 2014), scarce attention has been devoted to understanding an unusual, yet typical, type of global start-ups emerging from China— namely the manufacturers who supply labour-intensive OEM services for large MNCs in international markets from the beginning of their export business (Child & Rodrigues, 2005; Chin et al., 2016; Chin, Tsai, et al., 2016). Whereas the prevalence of GVCs promoted MNCs to outsource low-end production to firms in less-developed countries in the 1990s (Gereffi, 2009), numerous Chinese OEMs initiated a distinctive export-driven internationalization route since then, that is, drawing on China's low-cost advantages to produce and export components or finished goods to mature market clients (see Warner, 2014). This OEM path could particularly help OEM firms escape from severe institutional voids, such as governmental interference and weak legal protection, in China. Hence, many such OEMs work with international buyers from their inception, becoming a unique type of global start-up emerging from the Chinese context.

However, as DEs slowed down after the 2008 global financial crisis (Das, 2012), the pressure for sales growth has driven more Chinese OEMs to seek opportunities in their vast, but disordered, domestic markets. Despite being armed with valuable knowledge acquired via internationalization, such firms may meet unexpected difficulties when moving from well-regulated export markets to their home markets where legal institutions supporting market transactions are not well established (Cardoza, Fornes, Li, & Xu, 2015). Unlike typical market diversification—a firm's expansion into more markets—this recent entrepreneurial phenomenon reflects the prominent direction changes regarding the growth and learning trajectories of Chinese global start-up OEMs in response to the launch of a new, fundamental transformation of the global economy. Hence, we define this as reverse internationalization.

The early literature argued that Chinese OEMs seek vital knowledge from their developed country partners and relied on them to compete abroad (Luo & Tung, 2007). In contrast, this reverse internationalization shows a 'reverse' direction of expost knowledge exploitation and flow since these Chinese OEMs further exploit the knowledge gained via internationalization to cultivate their domestic market.

As such, the following research questions arise:
1. Does the critical knowledge gained via internationalization help Chinese global start-up OEMs to compete domestically?
2. What is the main strategy that have often been conducted by Chinese global start-up OEMs in reverse internationalization?

It is argued that the dynamic capability theory embodies a global start-up firm's competence to create, extend, and manipulate its resource base (Monferrer, Blesa, & Ripolles, 2015). Given that the knowledge acquired through internationalization is an essential theme for analysing Chinese

OEMs' reverse internationalization behaviour, we first identify knowledge-acquisition capability as a vital, high-order dynamic capability required for global start-up OEMs to compete domestically and then develop hypotheses based on the dynamic capability perspective.

The main contributions of this research are twofold. First, to identify a novel, context-specific type of 'born global', the global start-up OEMs in China, recognizing knowledge-acquisition capability as a high-order dynamic capability for such firms. Second, to introduce the novel entrepreneurial phenomenon of reverse internationalization to the literature.

## 4.2.2 Literature Review and Hypotheses

### 4.2.2.1 Chinese Global Start-Up OEMs

Although the Uppsala model (Johanson & Vahlne, 1977) viewing internationalization as an incremental process had dominated the field of firm internationalization, Oviatt and McDougall (1994) claim that some SMEs, referred to as 'born globals', generate their revenues mostly in overseas markets from the beginning and bypass the maturing process accompanying domestic development. 'Born globals' highlight an early leap made by entrepreneurial firms to enter international markets without considering 'psychic distance', while the Uppsala model emphasizes a gradual, more risk-averse, and constrained pattern of internationalization (Kuivalainen, Saarenketo, & Puumalainen, 2012).

According to Johanson and Vahlne (2009), the most salient difference between these two models above lies in the choice of internationalization modes. The former claims that companies gradually accumulate knowledge stock for entering into more risky, but also potentially more beneficial and controllable, modes of international operations. The latter indicates that rapid technological change and increasing globalization force entrepreneurial firms to adopt a more flexible mode of foreign operations such as forming strategic alliances with incumbents or joining GVCs in order to leapfrog to developed markets as soon as possible to avoid obsolescence of technology and imitation processes (Gerschewaki, Elizabeth, & Lindsay, 2015; Kuivalainen et al., 2012). This explains why developed country 'born globals' seem to be more inclined to be knowledge-intensive or technology-based firms (Cannone & Ughetto, 2014).

However, 'born globals' from EEs such as China, India, and Brazil may act differently from the above-mentioned technology-driven ones in DEs (Gerschewaki et al., 2015; Uner, Kocak, Cavusgil, & Cavusgil, 2013). The Chinese global start-up OEMs represent a typical example—they are mostly labour-intensive factories rather than hi-tech firms (Chin, 2014, 2015; Chin et al., 2015). From the 1990s, the relentless focus on financial performance has led DE MNCs to position their core business primarily in high value-added activities such as brand management and R&D design, but to outsource low-end production to firms in EEs with cheaper costs, which signals the emergence and prevalence of GVCs (Gereffi, 2009). Following this trend, China, with prominent cost advantages, has become a major recipient of such offshore outsourcing business, attracting FDI into its manufacturing sector (Drauz, 2013).

### 4.2.2.2 The GVC Analytical Framework

Given that a large number of FDIs have been flowing into China to benefit from GVCs, Chinese OEMs may not need to bear higher risks of exploring business overseas, but rather to internationalize themselves rapidly through building strategic partnerships with foreign entrants. More specifically, by participating in GVCs, Chinese OEMs could cooperate with inward FDI easily, which enables them to gain access to export markets at home and avoid high risks of R&D and marketing failure to internationalize almost from inception (Drauz, 2013; Herrigel et al., 2013).

The case of Galanz manifests the successful application of such internationalization. It was founded in 1978 with just seven workers, but has grown to become the world's largest OEM of microwave ovens with 40,000 employees, producing for >200 international brands. In early 2000, it capitalized on the marketing and technological knowledge gained from global brands, initiating the business of OBM, and up until now has built three microwave brands: Galanz, Yamstsu, and Almison. With abundant international experience, Galanz entered the Chinese market in 2005. This case confirms that the OEM partnership can be an effective means for Chinese firms to alleviate domestic institutional constraints via early internationalization, such as lack of law enforcement, poor protection for property rights, underdeveloped factor markets, and various political hazards (Cardoza et al., 2015; Child & Rodrigues, 2005).

Although some notable exceptions may exist, the unique global start-up approach of SME OEMs in China is mainly attributed to the effective insertion into GVCs and often displays the following four characteristics: (1) major focus on labour-intensive, low-end manufacturing; (2) heavy or even sole reliance on exports; (3) high dependence on cost advantages at home; and (4) benefits from FDI at home. Furthermore, these OEMs generally provide services to three main types of foreign outsourcing clients: (1) global brand owners as the lead firms of GVCs, for example, Nike and Gucci; (2) large international manufacturers as the OEM turnkey/ first-tier suppliers for well-established brands, for example, Foxxcon; and (3) other developed country buyers, for example, trading companies or second/third-tier suppliers producing subparts for primary/turnkey OEM suppliers (Gereffi, 2009; Morrison, Pietrobelli, & Rabellotti, 2008). In summary, the accelerated internationalization of Chinese OEMs is propelled by the proliferation of GVCs, coupled with the unique Chinese institutional environment, thus forming a distinctive type of global start-up firms that in general have fewer than 1000 full-time employees with annual sales of no more than Yuan 500 million (about US$7.3 million).

### 4.2.2.3 Impact of the 2008 Global Financial Crisis

However, as noted above, the negative effects of the 2008 financial crisis quickly spread through GVCs to all around the world, including China (Chin, 2014, 2015; Chin et al., 2015). For Chinese OEMs, this crisis resulted in a precipitous decline of orders and synchronized collapse of demand from mature economies for quite some time, thus jeopardizing export growth and financial health (Shen & Netto, 2012). Evidence reveals that the production of the OEM industry in China began falling sharply in 2009, while capability utilization of most factories was reduced to about 50% (Chin et al., 2015). Under such circumstances, as described by Das (2012), the Chinese government adopted a Keynesian policy prescription to combat the recession accompanying the crisis, stimulating aggregate demand in the domestic economy.

As a result, global start-up OEMs in China have, in recent years, felt increasing pressure to look to reverse internationalization, namely returning to expand home markets to compensate for their loss in exports. Viewed from this angle, this reverse internationalization strategy can be seen as a growth strategy by global start-up OEMs to exploit their knowledge acquired in accelerated internationalization as a competitive advantage to competing domestically. This 'reverse' direction of expost knowledge exploitation and flow by the Chinese global start-up OEMs to a certain extent echoes the concept of 'reverse knowledge transfer' from subsidiary to parent companies (Mudambi, Piscitello, & Rabbiosi, 2014) and that of 'reverse technology transfer' from host to home countries (Criscuolo & Narula, 2007) in MNC contexts. Moreover, as shown by the Galanz case, it might be a strategic trend for global start-up OEMs to upgrade from OEM to OBM status and compete in domestic markets ultimately. In other words, the financial crisis may have speeded up this trend.

#### 4.2.2.4 Knowledge-Acquisition Capability Developed Via Internationalization: A Dynamic Capability Perspective

A firm's dynamic capabilities that characterize an organization's capacity to purposely reconfigure, create, or even modify its external and internal resource bases in response to environmental changes (Teece, 2007; Teece et al., 1997) are of particular importance to facilitate the firm's early internationalization and superior performance (Monferrer et al., 2015). Woldesenbet, Ram, and Jones (2012) claim that a dynamic capability is actually a kind of higher-order ability for better leveraging a firm's existing resources and capabilities, with which SMEs could have a greater chance to survive unanticipated market turbulence and a continuously changing environment. Given that the 2008 financial crisis triggered reverse internationalization was a disruptive change, it is imperative for global start-up OEMs to identify key dynamic capabilities required for competing domestically.

The literature illustrates that despite constrained resources and liabilities of foreignness, global start-ups still can succeed in international markets if they possess a strong capability to acquire critical knowledge, whereby they can stimulate awareness of opportunities more easily and respond more rapidly than do incumbent and older firms (Zhou, Barnes, & Lu, 2010). The ability to acquire crucial and even tacit knowledge via internationalization has been recognized as a key determinant for Chinese entrepreneurial firms to overcome latecomer disadvantages in global arenas by leveraging their 'learning advantages of newness'; that is, fewer deeply embedded routines, less structural rigidity, and less cognitive complexity (Kuivalainen et al., 2012; Li, Li, Liu, & Yang, 2010; Li, Wei, et al., 2010; Monferrer et al., 2015). Indeed, in order to upgrade along the GVCs for higher economic returns, aspirant OEMs often strive to internalize the critical knowledge gained from their developed country clients (Morrison et al., 2008). Therefore, the knowledge-acquisition capability that enables Chinese global start-up OEMs to better digest the valuable knowledge acquired via internationalization can be identified as a higher-order dynamic capability to build their own brands and survive the new competitive conditions at home.

However, what knowledge acquired via internationalization would benefit these firms most in domestic competition? Given that OEMs are contracting producers, the mature economy outsourcers as the lead firms of specific GVCs must provide sufficient manufacturing and technology know-how on production-related activities to ensure the quality of their end products (Lin & Ho, 2010; Lin & Hou, 2010). For example, they may frequently introduce better practices of high-tech manufacturing to their OEM suppliers, such as lean manufacturing systems (Malik & Kotabe, 2009). Hence, Chinese OEMs could draw on a variety of sophisticated technological and manufacturing knowledge gained from DE MNCs to outperform their domestic competitors without international experience. Furthermore, the novel marketing knowledge acquired from global brands, such as managing advertisement agencies, market segments, and distribution channels, may allow Chinese OEMs to gain deeper insight into customer needs and product innovation so as to surpass their domestic rivals (Luo & Tung, 2007; Lu et al., 2010). Taken together, the acquisition of manufacturing, technological and marketing knowledge appears to be the most prominent benefits obtained through collaboration with foreign clients by OEMs in China.

Given this, we focus on three elements of the knowledge-acquisition capability (manufacturing, technological, and marketing) here, assuming that the knowledge acquisition capability developed by Chinese global start-up OEMs via internationalization could help them achieve further competitive advantage in reverse internationalization, whereby they also enhance their overall performance. This produces two hypotheses:

**Hypothesis 1:** The reverse internationalization/domestic performance of Chinese global start-up firms is positively related to their overall performance.

**Hypothesis 2:** The knowledge-acquisition capability (in manufacturing, technology, and marketing domains) is positively associated with the domestic/reverse internationalization performance.

As noted earlier, an unexpected long-term economic stagnation in the developed world after the 2008 financial meltdown was the key pressure impelling Chinese global start-up OEMs to shift their focus from export dependency to serving domestic customers (Das, 2012; Shen & Netto, 2012). However, what is the effective strategy commonly used by these firms to compete with incumbents/first movers at home, such as SOEs or MNCs?

Under the GVC framework, a typical successful lead firm from a DE is usually the one with global brand recognition for sophisticated technology or high quality products in the form of proprietary of intellectual property rights (Gereffi, 2009; Morrison et al., 2008). Also, own branded products can create more value and bring greater economic returns to the firms (Eng & Spickett-Jones, 2009). As noted above, the knowledge spillover/transfer between foreign buyers and OEM suppliers has facilitated some ambitious OEMs in China, such as Acer and Galanz, to quickly develop their own technological and marketing competence by which they have evolved into OBM status (Lin & Ho, 2010; Lin & Hou, 2010). Hence, by acting as latecomers, more and more Chinese OEMs are seeking to catch up with the GVC first movers (i.e. the lead firms) and thus expand domestic sales by pursuing their own brands.

However, this upgrading strategy that transforms OEMs into competitive rivals to their clients is prone to create a hostile climate in buyer–supplier relationships. The suppliers upgrading to OBM status may thus lose revenue from their original OEM business. For instance, when Acer and Asus initiated their OBM projects, their main buyers immediately replaced them with other OEMs who did not branch out into OBM (Horng & Chen, 2008; Lin & Ho, 2010; Lin & Hou, 2010). To do branding for OEMs actually implies a structural change of their business model because it requires a longer lead time to acquire capabilities beyond manufacturing technology, as well as a greater amount of investment in R&D and marketing. Evidence indicates that firms often have to carry on their OEM business to finance their long-term investment in OBM-related activities. Hence, although upgrading to OBM seems to be an ideal path in the GVC framework, in reality such an upgrading model may be too risky for some Chinese OEMs to adopt. Several large OEMs, such as Foxconn and Taiwan Semiconductor Manufacturing Company (TSMC), have decided to assure their customers that they will not 'cross the line' and undertake branding.

Despite high risks, engaging in branding activities by Chinese OEMs is spurred by China's local governments. In response to the deteriorating demand of mature markets in recent years, the government carried out a variety of expansionary fiscal policies to encourage firms to venture back to domestic markets. More importantly, it has specifically encouraged local OEMs to build own brand recognition and compete on the world frontier at home (Herrigel et al., 2013; Uner et al., 2013). In China's latest 5-year economic plan, the government explicitly highlights the importance of motivating local OEMs to build own brands through the exploitation of internal markets so as to help move the country up the GVC (China's 12th 5-year Economic Plan 2011–15). With the government's proactive support, domestic markets have become a convenient platform for Chinese OEMs to upgrade to the most value-added OBM stage, especially when there is less room for increasing exports to DEs in future. The conduct of an own brand strategy by Chinese global start-up OEMs to compete domestically is thus becoming a more mainstream phenomenon (Chin, 2015; Herrigel et al., 2013).

Given that the importance of branding may vary by industry, our study only targets global start-up OEMs embedded in buyer-driven commodity GVCs. This kind of GVC refers to the industries in which the lead firms with strong brand names command decentralized production networks in a variety of exporting countries, such as electronics, home decoration, and apparel industries, for example, Sony, IKEA, and Nike (Eng & Spickett-Jones, 2009).

As indicated previously, a switch from OEM to OBM is a high-risk practice. Apart from undermining original buyer–supplier relationships, OEM firms have to engage themselves in R&D and marketing and produce for their own inventories rather than for order when embarking on OBM (Eng & Spickett-Jones, 2009; Horng & Chen, 2008). They need to take an innovative mode, with a certain amount of investment, instead of playing an efficiency game as a contract manufacturer. The critical knowledge acquired via internationalization may thus become even more critical.

Hence, on the premise that the knowledge-acquisition capability may affect Chinese global start-up OEMs' domestic performance (see Hypothesis 2), we further posit that these firms need to use knowledge capability as their core competitive advantage to carry out their own brand strategy in expanding domestic markets. More specifically, we expect a mediating mechanism of utilizing own brand strategy on the relationship between the OEM's knowledge-acquisition capability and reverse internationalization performance. This produces the following hypotheses:

**Hypothesis 3:** Knowledge-acquisition capability is positively associated with the conduct of own brand strategy by Chinese global start-up OEMs.

**Hypothesis 4:** The conduct of own brand strategy is positively related to domestic/reverse internationalization performance.

**Hypothesis 5:** The relationship between knowledge-acquisition capability and reverse internationalization performance is mediated by the conduct of own brand strategy.

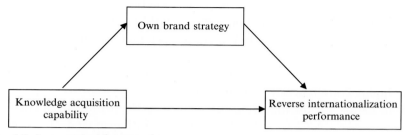

**Fig. 4.2** A conceptual framework.

For a better understanding, we summarize the hypotheses above and put forward our conceptual framework in Fig. 4.2.

## 4.2.3 Methodology

### 4.2.3.1 Sample and Data Collection

Global start-ups are widely defined as entrepreneurial firms with export sales accounting for at least 20% of their total sales within 3 years of inception (Zhou et al., 2010). However, considering the export-oriented characteristic of OEMs, we define 'Chinese global start-up OEMs' as domestic SMEs with export sales accounting for at least 50% of their total sales at inception (OEMs refer to the contract manufacturers who are not responsible for the overall value of R&D technology and the ultimate products and anonymous in the final product market).

To generate a large sample, we identified respondents from the exhibitor list of the 115th Canton Fair published in February 2014. On the basis of this information, we randomly chose 300 firms that matched our definition of Chinese global start-up OEMs. To control for the influence of extraneous variables, we excluded those firms with foreign or state-owned shareholders.

We first contacted the HR division of the firms and then mailed or emailed a Chinese questionnaire to the 165 firms that agreed to participate. Since 32 firms declined to join this survey after receiving questionnaires and 10 firms claimed that they still focused on exports (no domestic sales), we deleted them, leaving 113 firms. To ensure the representativeness of the data, we asked the top executives to complete our questionnaire. Accordingly, the key informants of each firm were selected from senior executives or managers with job titles such as managing director, business director, and/or manager. To assure data validity, we conducted follow-up telephone interviews with all 113 respondents shortly after they returned the completed questionnaires. During this process, we first asked the respondents to indicate their responses to a set of selected questions used in the question-naire to reduce common method variance (CMV) bias (Lu et al., 2010). We then requested each firm to provide a second informant from different divisions to confirm some answers, especially those concerning firm performance, given the lack of credible accounting data. The postsurvey responses were highly consistent with the prior results.

Our sample has the following characteristics: 31.9% came from Guangdong province, 16.8% from Fujian, 30.1% from Zhejian, and 21.2% from other provinces. A total of 65.5% had 500 or fewer employees and 35.5% had >501 employees. Some 22.1% were in household appliances, 31.0% in home decoration or furniture, 20.4% in consumer goods, 18.5% in electronic components, and 8% in textile garments. The average firm age was 13.8 years, indicating that most of were established in the late 1990s. This echoes the argument that unless a certain amount of time elapses, we may not be able to comprehensively understand a 'born global's' knowledge acquisition and strategic actions (Kuivalainen et al., 2012).

About 56.6% claimed that they have had their own-brand products, while 43.4% still focused on OEM business. Also, 62.8% stated that their proportion of domestic sales to total sales was <25%, while 37.2% reported that their proportion of domestic to total sales was between 25% and 50%. The average time of entering the Chinese market was about 5 years; the average time of engaging in OBM activities was about 3 years. Hence, the 2008 financial crisis was clearly a turning point because our firms, as typical Chinese global start-up OEMs, had not intended to compete domestically or create own brands until the financial crisis hit.

### 4.2.3.2 Measures

To evade official tax inspection, many smaller, privately owned organizations in China are often unable and unwilling to provide explicit and objective information. Hence, we referred to previous research using qualitative measures rating firm performance on five-point Likert scales (Lu et al., 2010). These are as follows.

### 4.2.3.3 Overall and Domestic/Reverse Internationalization Performance

We asked respondents to assess the growth of overall and domestic sales as well as profits in the most recent 3 years on a five-point Likert scale (from 1 = a large decrease to 5 = a large increase), respectively ($a = 0.822$ for overall performance; $a = 0.903$ for domestic). Scholars have widely employed similar subjective financial measures in China since entrepreneurs tend to hide or distort their firms' financial performance to avoid unwanted attention from corrupt government officials or criminal circles (Bruton, Ahlstrom, & Li, 2010).

### 4.2.3.4 Knowledge-Acquisition Capability Developed Via Internationalization

Referring to Wu and Chen (2012), we measured knowledge-acquisition capability by asking respondents to evaluate the extent to which they agree or disagree with the following statements on a five-point Likert-type scale: through internationalization, the firm had acquired or gained: (1) advanced technological knowledge from foreign buyers; (2) sophisticated manufacturing knowledge from foreign buyers; and (3) novel marketing knowledge from foreign buyers ($a = 0.921$).

### 4.2.3.5 The Conduct of Own Brand Strategy

We asked whether they engaged in OBM business (yes $= 1$; no $= 0$).

### 4.2.3.6 Control Variables

Given that firm age, firm size, industry type, and domestic experience may impact on performance (Lu et al., 2010), we controlled for these variables. We used a dummy variable to control for firm size (equal to or $<500$ employees $= 0$; between 501 and $1000 = 1$) and another dummy variable to control for industry type (technology and capital-intensive industries $= 0$, labour-intensive industries $= 1$ (referring to the 2002 version of the Chinese Standard Industrial Classification). We measured domestic experience by counting the number of years a firm had engaged in domestic expansion.

Prior research has examined the impact of market uncertainty (Zhou et al., 2010) and relationship strengths between OEM exporters and foreign buyers (Kwon, 2011) on an entrepreneurial firm's performance. We thus controlled for market uncertainty (vulnerability to the change in trade policies across borders) and the relationship strengths between OEMs and their foreign buyers using two indicators—trust and commitment—on a five-point Likert-type scale. Following Kwon (2011), trust was measured by: you and your foreign buyers: (1) treat each other fairly and (2) are always honest with each other ($\alpha = 0.825$); commitment was measured by: you and your foreign buyers: (1) would rather seek long-term than short-term interests and (2) care about the fate of each other ($\alpha = 0.896$).

### 4.2.3.7 Scale Reliability and Validity

The values of Cronbach's a for all constructs were in excess of 0.70, indicating a high degree of reliability. We then employed confirmatory factor analysis (CFA) by AMOS7.0 to test the construct validity following the procedure recommended by Anderson and Gerbing (1988). The CFA results revealed an adequate model fit for the proposed seven-factor structure ($\chi^2_{n=113} = 98.997$, df $= 43$, $\chi^2/\mathrm{df} = 2.302 < 3$, $P < .001$; GFI $= 0.904 > 0.9$; NFI $= 0.913 > 0.09$; IFI $= 0.949 > 0.09$; CFI $= 0.947 > 0.09$; PNFI $= 0.504 > 0.5$). Convergent validity would be ensured if items load significantly on their designated latent variables (Anderson & Gerbing, 1988). As shown in Table 4.1, all factor loadings were larger than 0.50; therefore, the convergent validity for our measures was present.

**Table 4.1** Factor Loadings of Perceptual Scales

| Construct | Measurement | Factor Loadings |
|---|---|---|
| Knowledge-acquisition capability | Through internationalization, the firm had acquired or learned: | |
| | Advanced technological knowledge from our foreign partners | 0.707 |
| | Sophisticated manufacturing knowledge from our foreign partners | 0.691 |
| | Novel marketing knowledge from our foreign partners | 0.678 |
| Overall performance | Overall sales growth | 0.664 |
| | Overall profit growth | 0.665 |
| Domestic performance | Domestic sales growth | 0.755 |
| | Domestic benefit growth | 0.717 |
| Trust | You and your foreign buyers: | |
| | Treat each other fairly | 0.947 |
| | Are always honest with each other | 0.866 |
| Commitment | You and your foreign buyers: | |
| | Would rather seek long-term than short-term interests | 0.707 |
| | Care about the fate of each other | 0.697 |
| Market uncertainty own brand strategy | Vulnerability to the change in trade policies across borders | 1 |
| | Whether your firm has engaged in OBM, creating own brands | 1 |

### 4.2.3.8 CMV

We employed the approach suggested by Podsakoff, MacKenzie, Lee, and Podsakoff (2003) to limit the possible threat of CMV. We entered all items into an exploratory factor analysis. If CMV is an issue, either: (1) a single factor will emerge from the factor analysis or (2) one general factor will account for the majority of the covariance among the variables. Results showed five distinct factors (an eigenvalue >1.0), accounting for 72.343% of the total variance with no single factor accounting for a majority of the variance. Hence, CMV should not be a serious concern in our data.

## 4.2.4 Results and Analysis

The means, standard deviations, and correlations of all variables are reported in Table 4.2. This confirms that there were no outliers or major violations of regression assumptions.

We conducted hierarchical regression analysis using the ENTER regression method to test Hypotheses 1 and 2, as shown in Table 4.3. In all models, we controlled for firm age, firm size, industry type, domestic experience, market uncertainty, OEM supplier–foreign buyer trust and commitment. To assess the explaining power of each set of variables, we included only controls in Models 1a and 2a and added independent variables in Models 2a and 2b. The results show that the proposed positive relationships between the reverse internationalization/domestic performance of Chinese global start-up OEMs and their overall performance (Hypothesis 1) were supported ($\beta = 0.397$, $P < .001$) and that knowledge-acquisition capability developed via internationalization is a positive predictor of domestic performance ($\beta = 0.441$, $P < .001$), confirming Hypothesis 2. We also computed the variance inflation factors (VIFs) for the variables. VIF values were <2 in all regression models, much lower than the critical value of 10, which showed no serious multicollinearity.

To examine Hypotheses 3–5, we adopted the structural equation modelling (SEM) approach suggested by Mackinnon, Lockwood, Hoffman, West, and Sheets (2002) to build a mediation model, given that SEM helps to control for measurement errors and provides clearer and more comprehensive information on the degree of fit of the proposed models. The significance of mediation could be examined by comparing the fit for the direct effect model with that of the predictor–mediator–outcome model (with and without the direct path from the predictor and the outcome constrained to zero). Full mediation would be supported if the model with the direct path

**Table 4.2** Descriptive Statistics and Correlations

| | Mean | SD | 1 | 2 | 3 | 4 | 5 | 6 | 7 | 8 | 9 | 10 | 11 |
|---|---|---|---|---|---|---|---|---|---|---|---|---|---|
| 1. Firm size | 0.3451 | 0.47753 | 1 | | | | | | | | | | |
| 2. Firm age | 13.8761 | 5.54709 | 0.205* | 1 | | | | | | | | | |
| 3. Industry type | 0.8319 | 3.9872 | 20.161 | 0.035 | 1 | | | | | | | | |
| 4. Domestic experience | 5.0531 | 3.04678 | 0.355** | 0.185* | 20.051 | 1 | | | | | | | |
| 5. Market uncertainty | 2.83 | 0.533 | 0.020 | 0.256** | 20.092 | 20.159 | 1 | | | | | | |
| 6. Commitment | 3.2832 | 0.89611 | 0.010 | 20.122 | 0.097 | 0.277** | 20.376** | 1 | | | | | |
| 7. Trust | 3.6770 | 0.71001 | 20.116 | 20.082 | 0.027 | 0.208* | 0.032 | 0.471** | 1 | | | | |
| 8. Knowledge-acquisition capability | 3.5015 | 0.82028 | 20.020 | 20.132 | 0.105 | 0.210* | 20.296** | 0.481** | 0.429** | 1 | | | |
| 9. Domestic performance | 3.1283 | 0.86545 | 20.097 | 20.190* | 0.089 | 0.292** | 20.340** | 0.589** | 0.533** | 0.695** | 1 | | |
| 10. Overall performance | 3.1106 | 0.84709 | 0.026 | 0.172 | 0.095 | 0.299** | 20.384** | 0.664** | 0.561** | 0.675** | 0.726** | 1 | |
| 11. Own brand strategy | 0.5664 | 0.49778 | 0.034 | 20.052 | 0.034 | 0.457** | 20.345** | 0.488** | 0.446** | 0.552** | 0.628** | 0.485** | 1 |

$n = 113$.

* Correlation is significant at the 0.05 level (two tailed); ** Correlation is significant at the 0.01 level (two tailed).

**Table 4.3** Regression Analysis

| Dependent Variable | Model 1a Overall Performance | Model 1b Overall Performance | Model 2a Domestic Performance | Model 2b Domestic Performance |
|---|---|---|---|---|
| *Constant* | 1.241** | 0.677 | 1.453** | 0.424 |
| | (0.474) | (0.444) | (0.532) | (0.498) |
| **Control variables** | | | | |
| Firm age | 20.010 | 20.005 | 20.014 | 20.011 |
| | (0.010) | (0.010) | (0.012) | (0.010) |
| Firm size ($\leqq 500$ employees $=0$, others $=1$) | 0.118 | 0.181 | 20.161 | 20.174 |
| | (0.125) | (0.114) | (0.140) | (0.121) |
| Industry type (labour-intensive $=1$, others $=0$) | 0.096 | 0.071 | 0.066 | 0.005 |
| | (0.137) | (0.124) | (0.154) | (0.133) |
| Domestic experience | 0.020 | 0.003 | 0.045† | 0.038† |
| | (0.020) | (0.019) | (0.023) | (0.020) |
| OEM-buyer commitment | 0.345*** | 0.233** | 0.288** | 0.187* |
| | (0.077) | (0.073) | (0.088) | (0.076) |
| OEM-buyer trust | 0.456*** | 0.291** | 0.423*** | 0.257** |
| | (0.091) | (0.089) | (0.102) | (0.092) |
| Market uncertainty | 20.361** | 20.243* | 20.303* | 20.166 |
| | (0.117) | (0.109) | (0.132) | (0.116) |
| **Independent variable** | | | | |
| Domestic performance Knowledge-acquisition capability | | 0.388*** | | |
| $R^2$ | 0.583 | 0.662 | 0.498 | 0.630 |
| $R^2$ *change* | | 0.079 | | 0.131 |
| *F* value | 20.991*** | 25.488*** | 14.903*** | 22.094*** |

$n=113$.
† $P<.10$; * $P<.05$; ** $P<.01$; *** $P<.001$ (significance levels based on two-tailed tests).
*Note:* Unstandardized regression coefficients are reported; robust standard errors are given in parentheses.

between the predictor and the outcome demonstrated a better fit (Lu et al., 2010).

Similar to other studies (Chin, 2015; Zhou et al., 2010), we posited the full mediation model as our baseline model (see Table 4.4), in which the conduct of own brand strategy completely mediated the relationship between knowledge-acquisition capability and domestic performance, and thus there was no direct path from knowledge-acquisition capability to domestic performance. However, the results showed that this model did not fit our data very well ($\chi^2_{n=113} = 42.762$, df $= 16$, $\chi^2/\text{df} = 2.673 < 3$,

**Table 4.4** Hypothesis Test of Alternative Models

| | $\chi^2$ | df | $\Delta\chi^2$ | $\Delta$df | GFI | IFI | NFI | CFI | RMSEA |
|---|---|---|---|---|---|---|---|---|---|
| Baseline model | 42.762 | 16 | – | – | 0.935 | 0.920 | 0.878 | 0.912 | 0.122 |
| Model A | 16.714 | 14 | 26.048 | 2 | 0.972 | 0.992 | 0.952 | 0.991 | 0.042 |
| Model B | 89.550 | 15 | 46.788 | 1 | 0.909 | 0.777 | 0.744 | 0.755 | 0.211 |
| Model C | 37.881 | 18 | 4.881 | 2 | 0.940 | 0.940 | 0.892 | 0.935 | 0.099 |
| Model D | 89.594 | 16 | 54.738 | 0 | 0.910 | 0.779 | 0.744 | 0.758 | 0.203 |

$n = 113$.

Baseline model, full mediation (no direct paths from the predictor to outcome); Model A, partial mediation model (the path from the predictor to outcome was added; Model B, direct effects model (the path from the predictor to mediator was constrained to zero); Model C, nonmediation models (the path from the mediator to outcome was constrained to zero); Model D, reverse causality models: own brand strategy knowledge capabilities domestic performance.

$P < .001$, GFI $= 0.935 > 0.90$; CFI $= 0.912 > 0.90$; NFI $= 0.878 < 0.90$; IFI $= 0.920 > 0.90$; RMSEA $= 0.122 > 0.08$).

Following Anderson and Gerbing (1988), we tested a series of nested models against our baseline model through sequential chi-square tests with the parameter constraints of interest in our research. First, we compared our baseline model with a partial mediation model (Model A) in which the path from knowledge-acquisition capability to domestic performance was added to the baseline model. As seen in Table 4.4, we found that Model A was much improved and more acceptable than the baseline model ($\chi^2_{n=113} = 16.715$, df $= 14$, $\chi^2/$df $= 1.1943$, $P = .272 > 0.05$; GFI $= 0.972 > 0.09$; CFI $= 0.991 > 0.90$; NFI $= 0.952 > 0.90$; IFI $= 0.992 > 0.90$; RMSEA $= 0.042 < 0.05$) and the chi-square difference ($\Delta\chi^2 = 26.048$) between Model A and the baseline model was significant, as per the critical chi-square of 7.82, $P < .05$.

Next, to rule out alternative explanations, we continued to test other possible alternative models. Model B is a direct effect model assuming that there was no causal relationship between knowledge-acquisition capability and own brand strategy, as own brand strategy may just contribute to domestic performance in the same way that knowledge-acquisition capability did. Model C is a nonmediation model assuming that own brand strategy may only play a trivial role in enhancing domestic performance. Model D is a reverse causality model that treats own brand strategy as an antecedent of knowledge-acquisition capability, namely knowledge-acquisition capability in turn mediates the relationship between own brand strategy and domestic performance. As seen in Table 4.4, the results show that the fit indices for Model A were significantly superior to those for Models B, C, and D. Overall, the partial mediation Model A best fits our data in terms of our hypothesized mediation framework.

## 4.2.5 Assessment of Hypotheses

On the basis of the above conclusions, the best-fit Model A is the final model for illustrating the results of our hypothesis testing. According to Model A, the direct path from knowledge-acquisition capability to domestic performance is still significant ($\beta = 0.387$, $P < .001$), while the indirect path from key acquisition capability via the conduct of own brand strategy to domestic performance is significant (from key acquisition capability to the conduct of own brand strategy: $\beta = 0.926$, $P < .001$; from the conduct of own brand strategy to domestic performance: $\beta = 0.203$, $P < .05$). Hence, Hypothesis 3, that knowledge-acquisition capability is positively associated with the conduct of own brand strategy, and Hypothesis 4, that the conduct of own brand strategy is positively related to domestic performance, are supported. Hypothesis 5 assumes that the conduct of own brand strategy mediates the impact of knowledge-acquisition capability on domestic performance. Given that the conduct of own brand strategy partially mediates the effect of knowledge-acquisition capability on domestic performance as per Model A, Hypothesis 5 is strongly supported as well.

In terms of the control variables, according to Models 1b and 2a in Table 4.3, market uncertainty is negatively related to the overall performance ($\beta = 20.243$, $P < .05$) as well as domestic/reverse internationalization performance ($\beta = 20.303$, $P < .05$). Model 2b indicates that OEM domestic experience influenced reverse internalization performance ($\beta = 0.038$, $P < .1$). Referring to Models 1b and 2b, the relationship strength about OEM-buyer trust had a positive effect on OEM overall performance ($\beta = 0.291$, $P < .01$) and domestic performance ($\beta = 0.257$, $P < .01$); the relationship strength about OEM-buyer commitment had a positive effect on overall performance ($\beta = 0.233$, $P < .01$) and domestic performance ($\beta = 0.187$, $P < .05$). In sum, Hypotheses 1–5 were fully supported.

## 4.2.6 Discussion

Our findings lent support to our five hypotheses. We examined if Chinese global start-up OEMs' domestic performance was positively related to their overall performance (Hypothesis 1) and if knowledge-acquisition capability built via internationalization had positive and significant effects on global start-up OEM domestic/reverse internationalization performance (Hypothesis 2). Moreover, we looked at if knowledge-acquisition capability has a significant impact on the conduct of own brand strategy (Hypothesis 3) and if own brand strategy had a positive association with domestic performance (Hypothesis 4). Consistent with our predicted mediation model, the conduct of own brand strategy by Chinese start-up OEMs mediates the positive relationships between knowledge-acquisition capability developed via internationalization and reverse internationalization performance (Hypothesis 5). In short, our research sheds light on the unique reverse internationalization phenomenon in China showing that being a global start-up could be viewed as a stepping stone for Chinese OEMs to acquire critical manufacturing, marketing, and technological knowledge in export markets by which these firms join brand competition in domestic markets later on.

Our research yields several contributions. First and foremost, this study provides empirical evidence regarding the pursuit of reverse internationalization by Chinese global start-up OEMs representing a challenge to the Uppsala model of internationalization (Johanson & Vahlne, 1977). In alignment with the revised Uppsala model (Johanson & Vahlne, 2009), this reverse internationalization behaviour also underscores the significance of business prospects on increasing resource commitment in promising markets. However, different from that model, this entrepreneurial action demonstrates a distinct pattern of immediate rather than gradual expansion into foreign or domestic markets with tempting opportunities in response to the changes of external environment.

Scholars claim that venturing into diversified markets by Chinese OEMs is often driven by 'pull' factors, such as the desire to gain access to consumers, accumulate financial assets, and develop advanced capabilities abroad (Zhang et al., 2014). Conversely, this reverse internationalization phenomenon by Chinese global start-up OEMs is triggered by 'push' rather than 'pull' factors, namely the unexpected global recession owing to the 2008 financial crisis. In contrast to the concept of de-internationalization elucidating an exit strategy to withdraw from overseas markets (Velazquez-Razo & Vargas-Hernandez, 2011), this reverse internationalization characterizes a growth strategy by OEMs to expand domestically as a result of the uncertainty in DEs coupled with huge profit potential at home.

In view of the above, the main contribution of our research is as follows. First, we identify a specific type of international new venture-Chinese global start-up OEMs—and introduce a novel concept—reverse internationalization—by which such firms enter the entrepreneurial domain. This is in answer to calls for more contextually embedded treatment of entrepreneurship (Bruton et al., 2010). Second, whereas the pivotal role of knowledge-acquisition capability for Chinese OEMs in creating own brand equity and competing domestically has been examined, we corroborate the theoretical logic that the knowledge-acquisition capability developed via internationalization is a vital, high-order dynamic capability for global start-up OEMs to pursue success in new and competitive markets. Third, our findings show that this knowledge-acquisition capability can be transformed into superior performance in the process of reverse internationalization by a crucial intermediate variable, the conduct of own brand strategy. Fourth, in terms of control variables, our findings support prior research that trust and commitment are key social capital components constituting the relationship strengths between buyers and suppliers and thus may help to improve firm performance (Kwon, 2011). In most strategic buyer–supplier relationships, both parties strive to shape their attractiveness to make the other party put more effort into their ties, in order to better leverage their relationships to obtain competitive advantage. Nevertheless, under the GVC framework, OEMs usually make a lot of unilateral investment to keep buyers, whereas buyers hold dominant positions. Hence, it seems even more imperative for OEMs to enhance mutual trust and commitment with their clients.

With regard to managerial implications, our results show that it seems plausible to assume that building own-brand labels can lead Chinese OEMs to become more profitable. However, in reality, the outcomes may be a bit disappointing sometimes. The Chinese market is actually a fragmented internal market, a conglomeration of separate regional markets protected by a variety of provincial barriers and controlled by individual local officials (Chin et al., 2015). This multimarket structure is highly uncertain, complicated, and unregulated relative to well-developed mature markets. Also, there have been well-established local brands and products designed specifically for some regions in China. These local brands possess the advantages of brand familiarity. Hence, will the heterogeneous experience during internationalization render Chinese global start-up OEMs more innovative and competitive than their domestic-focused rivals? We remain sceptical that the conduct of an own brand strategy would ensure the success of Chinese global start-up OEMs in their home country.

## 4.2.7 Limitations

Our research is subject to limitations, most of which represent fertile avenues for future research in relevant fields. First, our measures regarding firms' capability and performance were not exhaustive. Our use of subjective measures resulted from the difficulty associated with acquiring objective and correct archival data in China. Future research could employ more comprehensive scales to better capture the rich meanings embedded in the data. Second, since the majority of our firms are low-tech, labour-intensive OEMs, they may find it easy to acquire advanced knowledge through transactional linkages with developed country partners and thus count on knowledge-acquisition capability most. Nevertheless, will other types of global start-up firms present the same results? Future studies should take industry characteristics into consideration as well. Third, previous studies suggest that the performance of global start-ups may be contingent not only on firm-level factors, but also on the characteristics of individual entrepreneurs (Tolstoy, 2014). One key advantage of global start-ups is argued to be their entrepreneurial proclivity to identify and exploit opportunities unseen by most other firms (Zhou et al., 2010). Therefore, future research should further explore how human factors affect the reverse internationalization phenomenon.

## 4.2.8 Conclusions

The growth strategy of Chinese entrepreneurial firms has been a significant topic that deserves more attention (Cardoza et al., 2015; Zhou et al., 2010). Building on the dynamic capability perspective, our work brings new insight into relevant fields, delineating the mechanisms among the knowledge-acquisition capability developed via internationalization, the conduct of own brand strategy, and the reverse internationalization performance by Chinese global start-up OEMs. Given that China is expected to continue to be the engine of global economic growth in the future, the trend towards reverse internationalization by export-oriented firms in China may only flourish. In order to better understand the strategic options associated with such entrepreneurial activities in China, in the next section we will further elaborate on how different entrepreneurial orientations (EOs) of China's global start-up OEMs influence their performance in the process of reverse internationalization through more context-specific angles of social networks and strategic flexibility.

### 4.3 ENTREPRENEURIAL ORIENTATION–PERFORMANCE RELATIONSHIPS IN REVERSE INTERNATIONALIZATION BY CHINESE GLOBAL START-UP OEMs: SOCIAL NETWORKS AND STRATEGIC FLEXIBILITY

### 4.3.1 Introduction

EO, as the strategy making process characterizing a firm's proclivity towards entrepreneurship, is generally recognized as a significant driver of firm performance, especially for enterprises operating in rapidly changing and competitive environments (Kraus, Rigtering, Hughes, & Hosman, 2012; Rauch, Wiklund, Lumpkin, & Frese, 2009). However, the effect of EO on performance is not always positive and linear, but contingency-oriented and context-specific (Kiss et al., 2012; Sciascia, D'Oria, Bruni, & Larraneta, 2014). Specifically, the EO–performance relationship will not remain static; the impact of EO on firm performance may differ in various industrial settings, development stages, or under market turbulence and financial crisis (Fuentes-Fuentes, Bojica, & Ruiz-Arroyo, 2015; Hughes & Morgan, 2007; Jones et al., 2011). Hence, despite increasing attention, greater insights into the EO–performance linkage in China are still largely required. This is especially as China is a large EE and at a critical period of reform in developing a socialistic market system with the coexistence of socialist and market-based capitalist characteristics. While the world economy has remained sluggish since the 2008 global financial crisis, it is useful to investigate in depth how small, domestic entrepreneurial firms in China reacted. To fill this gap, this section elucidates the EO–performance mechanisms in China from a wider and contingency perspective.

Since reform and opening up in the late 1990s, an increasing number of FDIs have been flowing into China to benefit from its low-cost production and labour. Many Chinese domestic firms have thus taken this opportunity to serve as OEMs for foreign entrants and rapidly internationalize themselves from inception by exports at home without needing to bear the higher risks of directly doing business overseas. Along with this trend, more and more export-driven global start-up OEMs have come into existence, becoming a prevalent and typical type of entrepreneurial firm in China (Chin et al., 2016; Chin, Tsai, et al., 2016). Prior literature also suggests that global start-up OEMs that compete abroad at an early age learn a variety of advanced knowledge and technology through collaborating with FDIs, whereby some ambitious ones even further upgrade to engage in OBM (Child & Rodrigues, 2005; Chin et al., 2016; Chin, Tsai, et al., 2016).

However, in recent years, when facing global economic uncertainty, Chinese OEMs could no longer rely on exports to well-regulated DEs as in the past but needed to seek opportunities in their vast, yet disordered, home markets where consumer demand is growing despite unsound legal and economic institutions. This distinctive, ongoing entrepreneurial phenomenon in China's manufacturing sector can be defined as reverse internationalization—the prominent direction of growth and learning trajectories of Chinese entrepreneurial OEMs responding to change in the global economy (Chin et al., 2015). Reverse internationalization by global start-up OEM changes reflects the intricate connections between the world's economic problems and China's industrial transition, thus providing a compelling strategic background for us to probe into the context-specific EO–performance relationship with a much broader perspective. Moreover, with the aim of advancing our understanding of the EO effects, we refer to the claims of previous research (Jones et al., 2011), considering EO as a multidimensional phenomenon, that is, concerning innovativeness, proactiveness, and risk-taking.

Scholars argue that more attention should be paid to identify pivotal context-specific factors that may moderate the EO–performance relationship because in prior research the contingency-oriented nature of the EO–performance linkage has resulted in inconsistent findings under different circumstances, especially when involving contextual moderators (Huang & Wang, 2013). Hence, our study focuses on two critical contingent variables: social networking and strategic flexibility that embody the unique institutional idiosyncrasies in China. Despite the fact that the effects of social networks as a critical social capital on entrepreneurial firms' performance have been widely identified (Acquaah, 2012; Anderson, Dodd, & Jack, 2010; McKeever, Anderson, & Jack, 2014), whether social networking (*guanxi*) moderates the EO–performance relationships under the context of reverse internationalization remains an unexplored area. Kraus et al. (2012) indicate that when facing a complex institutional environment like China, a firm's EO might synthesize a certain level of strategic flexibility that enhances the flexible use of its resources to overcome institutional constraints. Considering the foregoing, we aim to investigate how *guanxi* and strategic flexibility intervene in the EO–performance mechanisms in reverse internationalization.

In sum, our study makes several contributions to the literature. First and foremost, we elucidate the unique EO–performance mechanisms in a particular context, reverse internationalization by Chinese global start-up OEMs, thus characterizing the context-sensitive nature of EO (Fuentes-Fuentes et al., 2015). Second, echoing recent calls (Kreiser, Marino, Kuratko, & Weaver, 2013), we analyse the impact of individual EO dimensions on performance. Third, by identifying the moderator of *guanxi* and the mediator of strategic flexibility on the EO–performance linkages, we highlight the importance of contingent variables in steering paths where the individual dimensions of EO may directly enhance or be indirectly translated into firm performance in China.

## 4.3.2 Theoretical foundation and hypotheses
### 4.3.2.1 The conceptualization and dimensionality of EO
Despite the ongoing debates on whether EO should be defined as a disposition or behaviour constructor measured as a reflective or formative construct (Covin & Wales, 2012), most scholars agree with the definition of Miller (1983). That is that EO is a firm's strategic posture of specific processes, practices, and activities is constituted by three idiosyncratic components—innovativeness, risk-taking and proactiveness. These enable firms to create value by engaging in product-market innovation, undertaking somewhat risky ventures, and acting on future demands (Kollmann & Stockmann, 2012; Zhang et al., 2014). Conceptually, innovativeness represents a firm's strong commitment to embrace creative ideas, novel technology, and products; risk-taking refers to a firm's willingness to make large resource commitments with a reasonable chance of costly failures; proactiveness embodies a firm's opportunity-seeking tendency, such as entering new markets and introducing new products and services ahead of the competition in anticipation of future market trends (Kraus et al., 2012; Wales, Gupta, & Mousa, 2013).

Some scholars suggest that these three characteristics of EO should be viewed as a joint/integral construct consisting of three subdimensions that must positively covary in order for EO to be exhibited (Sciascia et al., 2014; Tang & Tang, 2012). This conceptualization posits that the three attributes of EO, acting as a unidimensional *gestalt*, should be aggregated together when measuring EO. However, a recent view seeks to uncover the unique roles played by each of the EO dimensions, clarifying the differential effects of individual EO factors on firm-level outcomes (Dai, Maksimov, Gilbert, & Fernhaber, 2014; Zhang et al., 2014). This multidimensional standpoint underscores the potentially distinct nature of the three EO dimensions and their corresponding unique contributions to firm performance. Research has indicated the significance of assessing the impact of individual EO dimensions on outcome variables, especially examining the performance of SMEs (Dai et al., 2014; Kreiser et al., 2013). Given the possession of constrained resources, each subdimension of EO may mirror a distinctive strategic posture by an SME in determining the level and distribution of resource commitment with its unique cost–benefit trade-offs. Whereas our focus is on a specific type of SME here, we follow this logic and expect that the individual dimensions of EO may exhibit heterogeneous effects on a global start-up OEM performance under the context of reverse internationalization.

### 4.3.2.2 EO–Performance Relationships in the Context of Reverse Internationalization

The EO–performance relationship has been found to be very discordant, complex and particularly context-sensitive (Fuentes-Fuentes et al., 2015; Jones et al., 2011; Kreiser et al., 2013). By adopting a unidimensional EO construct, many studies suggest a positive, linear effect of EO on performance (Sciascia et al., 2014). However, some research analysing Chinese data shows that EO may not always translate into improved performance above a saturation point, but rather has a curvilinear relationship with performance (Tang & Tang, 2012). While taking the dimensionality of EO into consideration, research presents even more discrepant results. Kraus et al. (2012) demonstrates that during turbulent times, risk-taking is negatively related to performance, innovativeness has no impact, but proactiveness still contributes to performance. Kollmann and Stockmann (2012) discover a negative association between risk-taking and performance despite innovative- and proactiveness-performance relationships remaining positive. In contrast, Rauch et al. (2009) manifest a positive association between risk-taking and performance while some scholars even report the presence of nonlinearity in EO–performance relationships (Kreiser et al., 2013). Given the inconsistent findings, Dai et al. (2014) claim that the EO–performance relationships may differ depending on whether the EO construct is presumed to be uni- or multidimensional. The evidence above corroborates the eminent, contingent, and somewhat emic nature of EO with its diversified impact on firm outcomes. Moreover, it implicitly sheds light on the imperative to further investigate the distinct influences of individual dimensions of EO on performance in a specific, representative entrepreneurial environment.

The reverse internationalization by Chinese global start-up OEMs is characterized as a peculiar, entrepreneurial, and increasingly prevalent phenomenon in China that is very suitable for our research setting (Chin et al., 2015). In the past three decades, numerous FDIs have entered China to capitalize on its low-cost production, which actually facilitates the emergence of Chinese global start-up OEMs that embarked on their business by serving as contracting producers for well-known international brands, for example, Nike, Gucci, and Apple, or MNC manufacturers, for example, Foxconn (Child & Rodrigues, 2005; Chin et al., 2015). The outsourcers who usually came from more DEs might frequently transfer a certain level of technology know-how to OEM suppliers in order to ensure the quality of their end products. Hence, the acquisition of manufacturing, technological, and marketing knowledge has been widely recognized as the most valuable benefit obtained by Chinese OEMs through cooperating with foreign clients/buyers at home (Child & Rodrigues, 2005; Chin et al., 2015).

However, the 2008 financial crisis and 2010 Europe debt crisis resulted in a global recession and China's export stagnation, which has further triggered the strategic trend of reverse internationalization by Chinese global start-up OEMs. This is because many such firms have been continuing to lose low-cost advantages in international competition (Chin, 2015; Zheng, 2014) and thus have targeted China's large market to offset their loss in exports. As a matter of fact, the strategic option of reverse internationalization by Chinese global start-up OEMs is also partly encouraged by the Chinese government according to *China's 12th and 13th 5-Year Economic Plans (2011–15 and 2016–20)* (Chin et al., 2015) This reverse internationalization, in this sense, characterizes a new growth strategy by Chinese OEMs to venture back to cultivate their domestic market as a result of choosing between the escalating uncertainty and profit decline in mature markets and the growing demand at home.

One of the severest challenges China confronts is to incorporate two antagonistic ideologies—the socialist and the capitalist—into a unified institutional system. This could impose a variety of stress and confusion, and even generate unexpected institutional frictions and constraints that may diminish the value of EO for such global start-up OEMs (Chin et al., 2015; Zheng, 2014). In this vein, despite huge potential for growth, the Chinese market appears to be very dynamic and complex (Chin, 2015; Zheng, 2014). The global start-up OEMs will therefore still have to change their learning strategies and patterns from learning from DE partners to learning from the incumbents in domestic markets. Viewed from this angle, this reverse internationalization embodies the unique direction changes on the growth and learning trajectories of Chinese entrepreneurial OEMs in an attempt to survive a fast-changing and competitive situation. Taking the aforementioned discussions together, reverse internationalization is particularly appropriate for assessing the impact of the broader conceptualization of EO on firm performance during China's socioeconomic reform.

### 4.3.2.3 Innovativeness and Performance

Innovativeness is often regarded as a critical factor in facilitating growth by introducing and investing in new products, services, and cutting-edge technologies with high profit potential or market value (Covin & Wales, 2012). This EO dimension generally involves a higher level of R&D investment and a large prior expenditure of organizational resources, which tend to provide long-term rather than short-term returns (Dai et al., 2014; Kreiser et al., 2013).

Chinese global start-up OEMs used to confine their business activities to labour-intensive production, relying on China's huge labour pool and low wage advantages to compete in export markets (Chin, 2015). Compared with large and foreign-invested manufacturers, such entrepreneurial OEMs have confronted more institution-based barriers in the area of innovation in China, such as limited access to financial support and weak abilities to protect their intellectual property rights (Zheng, 2014; Zhu, Wittmann, & Peng, 2012). Research also indicates that it seems to be quite difficult for SME OEMs to benefit from innovations in China (Tang & Tang, 2012; Zhu et al., 2012). Hence, global start-up OEMs, without a legacy of innovation, usually invest very little in R&D.

As noted earlier, the 2008 and 2010 crises triggered the reverse internationalization phenomenon in China. Owing to an appreciating currency, rising wages, tighter environmental protection policy, and more severe competition from other EEs, Chinese global start-up OEMs have been facing sharp drops in export volume and endeavoured to benefit from their domestic markets with more promising opportunities (Chin et al., 2015; Zheng, 2014). At this critical time, the strategic priority for most such OEMs was to meet short-term financial obligations by exerting their strength to pursue short-term or current gains, instead of increasing resource commitment to unleash their innovation potential for long-term returns in the Chinese market. More specifically, the substantial costs and upfront investment accompanying the innovative activities may outweigh the profits gained from innovativeness and thus reduce firm performance.

Hence, although many studies show the positive effect of innovativeness on performance, we hypothesize:

**Hypothesis 1a:** In reverse internationalization, innovativeness is negatively related to firm performance.

### 4.3.2.4 Risk-Taking and Performance

Risk-taking that represents a willingness to commit resources to carry out strategies and business activities with significant chances of costly failure is believed to orient SMEs towards a direction of embracing uncertainty as opposed to a fear of it (Lumpkin & Dess, 1996). Despite a positive relationship between risk-taking and performance being often found in the literature (Rauch et al., 2009), more recent studies have shown a negative effect of risk-taking on performance under fast changing or uncertain circumstances, such as in turbulent times (Kraus et al., 2012) and at the embryonic stage of firm development (Kollmann & Stockmann, 2012). Evidence also indicated a concave (inverted U-shaped) relationship between risk-taking and international expansion (Dai et al., 2014) and a convex (U-shaped) association between risk-taking and SME performance (Kreiser et al., 2013), which reveal that lower or higher levels of risk-taking may both lead to the highest level of performance according to different contexts.

On the basis of the contradictory findings above, risk-taking may not represent a worthwhile endeavour sometimes, particularly for smaller firms operating in turbulent markets, due to the risk-averse nature of such firms and the substantial resource commitment of risk-taking. Following this logic, given that Chinese global start-up OEMs are still striving to neutralize the loss of export revenue in reverse internationalization activities, we argue that these firms may bear a relatively low fault tolerance—high levels of risk-taking are likely to be too hazardous and counterproductive. Hence, we make the following hypothesis:

**Hypothesis 1b:** In reverse internationalization, risk-taking is negatively related to performance.

### 4.3.2.5 Proactiveness and Performance

Proactiveness orients firms towards taking the initiative to position themselves in anticipation of changes, being the first to introduce new offerings in existing markets, or to enter and develop new markets (Lumpkin & Dess, 1996). Firms with a higher level of proactiveness are able to accommodate with and identify valuable opportunities more quickly than their rivals in fast-changing contexts (Zhang et al., 2014).

While carrying out the strategy of reverse internationalization, Chinese global start-up OEMs are required to be more sensitive to market signals and better position themselves to obtain a more solid foundation for organizational legitimacy since they are shifting from competing in well-regulated international arenas to China, an unpredictable, volatile, and underdeveloped market (Chin et al., 2015; Tang & Tang, 2012). As such, proactiveness is of greater importance to firms in reacting to 'the rules of the game' of unprecedented and vigorous market competition situations.

Indeed, proactiveness per se entails certain levels of innovativeness and risk-taking (Hughes & Morgan, 2007; Miller, 1983). However, acting proactively is far less risky because proactiveness primarily enables firms to compete in a more agile manner and in general will not result in as much upfront investment as do innovativeness and risk-taking. Hence, we hypothesize:

> **Hypothesis 1c:** In reverse internationalization, proactiveness is positively associated with firm performance.

### 4.3.2.6 Social Network Relationships/Guanxi: The Moderating Effect

According to the literature (Hughes & Morgan, 2007; Kollmann & Stockmann, 2012), the controversial and conflicting findings highlight the significance of identifying other factors influencing the EO–performance relationship. The EO–performance linkage has been found to be moderated by a variety of internal and external contingency factors, such as a firm's capabilities and resources, internal social context, as well as the technological level of the industry and cultural variables (Kreiser et al., 2013). However, moderators have not yet been sufficiently articulated so far (Wales et al., 2013), while there remains a scarcity of knowledge about how an entrepreneurial firm's social networks are leveraged and applied in specific business circumstances, such as reverse internationalization. Thus, we examine the moderating effect of a key contingent factor—social networks/*guanxi*—on EO–performance relationships in the Chinese context of reverse internationalization.

In China, where legal and financial institutions are still immature, entrepreneurial firms, in order to achieve competitive advantage, may capitalize on establishing informal social networks with main stakeholders as a critical source of social capital to build legitimacy and credibility in economic exchanges (Huang & Wang, 2013; Kiss et al., 2012; Lim & Cu, 2012;

McKeever et al., 2014). Such social network relationships may encompass personal and business relations such as buyer–supplier relationships or strategic alliances. Nevertheless, we chose to concentrate on the social networking/*guanxi* pertaining to informal structures of personal ties as this mirrors one salient cultural propensity in China.

Built on interpersonal trust and goodwill, *guanxi* as an indigenous Chinese concept with Confucian origins is often characterized by informal interpersonal connections bonded with reciprocal expectations (Rowley, 2016) and has been extended from individual to corporate levels (Chin, 2015; Luo, Huang, & Wang, 2011). Evidence indicates that *guanxi* provides abundant information benefits and has significant value in enhancing firm performance and entrepreneurial success in the unique institutional environment of China (Lim & Cu, 2012). In general, on the basis of building linkages involved in a business transaction, firms operating in China have to develop and exploit *guanxi* at the organizational level with two major groups of economic actors that provide crucial advantages. First, local business network ties: *guanxi* with managers of business stakeholders, for example suppliers, buyers, intermediaries, and competitors. Second, local institutional network ties: *guanxi* with government officials, key members in trade or industry associations, bankers, and professionals, for example, professors and scientists (Baron & Tang, 2009; Kiss & Danis, 2008).

*Guanxi* seems to become more critical for Chinese global start-up OEMs to benefit from reverse internationalization activities. While these firms are actually latecomers in the Chinese market, the development of *guanxi* with local business and institutional partners can provide a buffer for their weak legitimacy, enabling them to mobilize limited resources in China's undeveloped, diversified, and fragmented regional markets so as to cope with constraints imposed by highly bureaucratic institutional structures (Luo et al., 2011). We thus hypothesize:

**Hypothesis 2a:** In reverse internationalization, *guanxi* moderates the negative relationship between innovativeness and performance; the negative relationship is less pronounced when *guanxi* is better.

**Hypothesis 2b:** In reverse internationalization, *guanxi* moderates the negative relationship between risk-taking and performance; the negative relationship is less pronounced when *guanxi* is better.

**Hypothesis 2c:** In reverse internationalization, *guanxi* moderates the positive relationship between proactiveness and performance; the positive relationship is more pronounced when *guanxi* is better.

### 4.3.2.7 Strategic Flexibility: The Mediating Effect

Scholars point out the imperative to empirically identify more variables intervening in the causal chain between EO and outcomes (Wales et al., 2013), whereas previous research dealing with the mediation mechanisms of EO–performance relationships mostly focuses on knowledge-based variables, such as organizational learning and knowledge creation process. To fill this gap, we examine the mediating effect of strategic flexibility on EO–performance relationships in China.

Strategic flexibility refers to a firm's intrinsic ability to leverage and flexibly use resources in reaction to substantial and rapidly occurring environmental changes and seems to be a peculiarly effective approach for SMEs to handle institutional constraints embedded in EEs. It can impel the entrepreneurial performance of SMEs in unstable and unpredictable EEs like China by encouraging firms to break down institutional routines, make precipitate commitments, and undertake competitive actions when facing a variety of changes (Nadkarni & Herrmann, 2010; Zhou & Wu, 2010). Strategic flexibility can be seen as an organizational trait as well as one type of complementary organizational capability that enables entrepreneurial firms to alter their business practices and strategic initiatives faster than their competitors in terms of grasping new opportunities and tackling threats. In this sense, proactive firms may be more inclined to exhibit strategic flexibility. Research has implicitly suggested that proactiveness as one of the EO dimensions indeed synthesizes a certain level of such strategic flexibility (Kraus et al., 2012). Hence, we hypothesize:

**Hypothesis 3a:** Proactiveness is positively related to strategic flexibility.

Some findings highlight the positive effect of strategic flexibility on SME performance during economic downturns because stability may provide a comfort zone with minimized uncertainty and scarcity, which usually hinders a firm's tendency towards risky entrepreneurship and thus undermines intentions to achieve full potential and flexible usage of key resources (Kraus et al., 2012; Nadkarni & Herrmann, 2010). In contrast, while entering an EE like China, SMEs may have to perform proactive behaviours to establish business networks, gain access to new niches, and seek out diverse opportunities ahead of their rivals. As a result, strategic flexibility may play a critical role in helping SMEs to continuously depart from the *status quo* and recalibrate their strategies in fast-changing environments. Following this logic, it is plausible to postulate that strategic flexibility has a positive impact on firm performance in the context of reverse internationalization.

Integrating the arguments above, we further propose that strategic flexibility is likely to act as a mediator through which Chinese global start-up OEMs transfer proactiveness into their reverse internationalization performance. This produces the following hypothesis:

> **Hypothesis 3b:** During reverse internationalization, strategic flexibility mediates the positive relationship between EO and performance.

## 4.3.3 Methodology

Our study was reviewed and approved by an Institutional Review Board at the Institute of Innovation and Development, Hangzhou Dianzi University (ethics committee).

### 4.3.3.1 Sample and Data Collection

Referring to Chin et al. (2016) and Chin, Tsai, et al. (2016), considering their prominent export-oriented nature, Chinese global start-up OEMs are defined as SMEs in China with export sales accounting for at least 50% of their total sales within 3 years of inception. OEMs are contract manufacturers who are not responsible for the overall value of R&D technology as well as the trademarks of the ultimate products and anonymous in the final product market. Given that over 50% of FDI into China was pumped into the OEM sector, the number of OEMs has been increasing since the late 1990s. For instance, there were >5000 OEMs specializing in shoe production in just Guangdong province (Chin, 2013). As such, to generate a large and representative sample, we relied on the 113th Canton fair exhibitor list to select our sample firms. As a well-known, comprehensive exhibition held biannually in GZ, this fair has the longest history (55 years) and the largest scale (i.e. the most complete exhibit variety, broadest distribution of foreign buyers, and greatest business turnover) in China. More importantly, the participants of this trade fair must supply the organizers with clear and accurate demographic and business information about the firm. Hence, in February 2013, we randomly chose firms from the list that fit our definition of Chinese global start-up OEMs as shown in Section 4.2.2. To control for extraneous factors, firms with foreign or state-owned shareholders were excluded.

We first made telephone calls to the 300 selected firms and then mailed or emailed a questionnaire to the firms that agreed to join our survey. Some 21 firms stated that they had not undertaken reverse internationalization activities and still focused on exports, while 200 firms returned the completed questionnaires. To ensure the representativeness of the information, we requested each firm's top management to answer our questionnaire. Informants were thus chosen from key decision-makers, for example, managing director, chief executive officer, or general manager. To reduce CMV, we assured respondents that this was an anonymous survey and there were no right or wrong answers (Podsakoff et al., 2003). To validate data, we carried out follow-up telephone interviews shortly after the questionnaires were returned. During this process, we first requested the respondents to indicate their answers to a set of selected questions and then asked them to recommend a second informant to further confirm the answers. The postal survey responses were highly accordant with previous answers.

The final sample included a variety of business domains, for example, gifts, home decorations, textile garments, electronics, and pharmaceutical products as well as locations: 24% from Guangdong province, 14.5% from Fujian, 23.5% from Zhejian, 8.5% from Guangxi, and 29.5% from other provinces. According to the 2002 version of China's Standard Industrial Classification, 23.5% of firms were from technology/capital-intensive industries while 76.5% were from labour-intensive industries. The average number of employees per firm was 159 and the average age was 12.1 years. We also conducted a nonresponse bias test using a within-sample extrapolation method (Chin et al., 2015). We compared the early response group (the first 129 responses) and the late response group on key firm characteristics such as firm age, firm size, and industry type. The results of mean comparison $t$-tests did not return any significant differences between the two groups ($P > .1$ in all three characteristics).

### 4.3.3.2 Measures
All items except the firms' information were anchored on a five-point Likert scale (from 1=strongly disagree to 5=strongly agree; from 1=a large decrease to 5=a large increase).

### 4.3.3.3 Domestic Performance
Given that entrepreneurs in China experience strong incentives to hide or distort their firms' financial performance to avoid unwanted attention from corrupt government officials or criminal circles, performance in reverse

internationalization was measured by three self-reported indicators (sales, market share, and profitability) following previous studies (Chin et al., 2015; Hughes & Morgan, 2007) (Cronbach $\alpha = 0.942$).

### 4.3.3.4 Entrepreneurial Orientation

Using Covin and Wales (2012), innovativeness was measured by asking respondents about their firm's tendency to invest heavily in cutting-edge R&D activities, to be a technological leader, and to introduce innovative products and services during reverse internationalization (3 items, $\alpha = 0.906$). Proactiveness was measured by the propensity to be proactive to change competitive approaches, reorganize operations processes, and to initiate new programmes (3 items, $\alpha = 0.800$). Risk-taking was measured by preference for taking bold actions and engaging in high-risk projects such as diversifying into new products or service lines, acquiring companies in very different industries, and initiating unknown new business (3 items, $\alpha = 0.740$).

### 4.3.3.5 Social Network Relationships/Guanxi

Considering the inherent complexity of the definition of *guanxi* and our commercial-oriented backdrop, we merely focused on studying the moderating effect of instrumental and utilitarian *guanxi* (i.e. business and institutional network ties) rather than that of affective, obligatory, or reciprocal *guanxi*, for example, family, friend, and acquaintance's relations (Chen, Chen, & Huang, 2013). Hence, referring to Kiss and Danis (2008), we measured social networking relationships by asking respondents to describe how close the links were between their firms and the six parties (three on business network ties; three on institutional network ties): (1) key clients; (2) key suppliers; (3) key competitors; (4) governmental officials; (5) key members in trade associations or industry policy committees; (6) professionals (e.g. professors, scientists, and bankers) (Cronbach $\alpha = 0.875$).

### 4.3.3.6 Strategic Flexibility

Consistent with Nadkarni and Herrmann (2010), we measured strategic flexibility by asking respondents to assess the extent to which their firms responded to environmental variations or market turbulence, such as the 2008 financial crisis, This was by: (1) regularly sharing information with all stakeholders; (2) frequently changing strategies to derive benefits from external changes; our strategy: (3) emphasizes exploiting new opportunities arising from environmental variability; (4) reflects a high level of flexibility in managing financial and political risks; (5) emphasizes versatility and empowerment in HR allocation (Cronbach $\alpha = 0.878$).

### 4.3.3.7 Control Variables

Whereas firm size, firm age, and industry type may influence SME success (Sciascia et al., 2014), we controlled for these variables. Firm size was measured as the number of full-time employees and firm age as the number of years since it was established. We used a dummy variable to classify industry type into technology and capital-intensive industries (0) or labour-intensive industries (1). In addition, environmental dynamism has been found to significantly influence the EO–performance relationship, particularly in highly dynamic environments riddled with dramatic and rapid changes (Huang & Wang, 2013; Wiklund & Shepherd, 2005, 2011). Therefore, given the dynamic nature of reverse internationalization as noted above, we controlled for environmental dynamism using three indicators according to Wiklund and Shepherd (2005): (1) products have a short life; (2) customers' demands are highly unpredictable; (3) competitors' actions are highly unpredictable (Cronbach $\alpha = 0.777$).

### 4.3.3.8 Reliability and Validity of the Measurement Model

Cronbach $\alpha$ for all constructs was above 0.70, indicating adequate reliability. We then evaluated the construct validity of the proposed five-factor model by CFA. CFA results provided a good model fit ($\chi^2_{n=200} = 233.613$, df=119, $\chi^2$/df=1.963<2, $P<.001$, CFI=0.952> 0.90, IFI=0.954>0.90, RMSEA=0.070<0.08). The assumed five-factor model displayed a good fit to the data, confirming its nomological validity. We further assessed the convergent and discriminant validities by checking for the values of construct reliability (CR) and average variance extracted (AVE). As shown in Table 4.5, except for the second item of the risk-taking scale, all the values of factor loadings are higher than 0.5; except risk-taking, all the CR and AVE values are above the acceptable levels of 0.6 and 0.5, respectively (Chin et al., 2015). One plausible explanation for this is that during reverse internationalization global start-up OEMs may be unable to bear excessive financial risks like company acquisition (i.e. the second item of the risk-taking scale). Overall, our key measures captured distinct constructs.

**Table 4.5** CFA Results

| Constructs | Factor Loadings | T Value | CR | AVE |
|---|---|---|---|---|
| Innovativeness | | | 0.9406 | 0.8409 |
| Investing heavily in cutting-edge R&D | 0.909 | 68.361*** | | |
| Tending to be a technological leader | 0.950 | 72.689*** | | |
| Introducing innovative products and services | 0.891 | 65.665*** | | |
| Risk-taking | | | 0.6531 | 0.3933 |
| Preferring to undertaking bold actions/ high-risk projects | 0.631 | 50.162*** | | |
| Acquiring companies in different industries | 0.473 | 49.551*** | | |
| Initiating unknown new business | 0.747 | 61.418*** | | |
| Proactiveness | | | 0.7443 | 0.5020 |
| Changing the competitive approaches | 0.822 | 63.310*** | | |
| Reorganizing the operations processes | 0.691 | 66.684*** | | |
| Initiating specific programmes for competing domestically | 0.594 | 57.561*** | | |
| Strategic flexibility | | | 0.8946 | 0.6335 |
| Regularly sharing information with stakeholders | 0.828 | 64.450*** | | |
| Frequently changing strategies | 0.938 | 61.538*** | | |
| Emphasizing on the exploitation of new opportunities | 0.823 | 67.339*** | | |
| Flexibility in managing financial and political risks | 0.627 | 48.007*** | | |
| Emphasizing versatility and empowerment in HRM | 0.729 | 59.684*** | | |
| Social networking relationship (guanxi) | | | 0.8574 | 0.5041 |
| Guanxi with key clients | 0.607 | 52.499*** | | |
| Guanxi with key suppliers | 0.658 | 56.049*** | | |
| Guanxi with key competitors | 0.822 | 67.525*** | | |
| Guanxi with governmental officials | 0.790 | 73.608*** | | |
| Guanxi with key members in trade associations | 0.612 | 63.944*** | | |
| Guanxi with professionals | 0.741 | 58.985*** | | |

*** Correlation is significant at the 0.001 level.

## 4.3.3.9 CMV

Since information about the dependent and independent variables is given by the same respondent, we recognize the potential for CMV. Given that we had built a five-factor CFA model to examine the construct validity as shown above, we further created a first-order latent marker with all of the measures as indicators to the original CFA model to address CMV issues. This latent variable approach used in a large body of research allows us to control for the effects of a single unmeasured latent method factor (Podsakoff et al., 2003). In comparison with the original five-factor model ($\chi^2_{n=200} = 233.613$, df $= 119$, $\chi^2/\text{df} = 1.963$, $P < .001$, CFI $= 0.952$, IFI $= 0.954$, RMSEA $= 0.070$), the new model with the latent CMV factor still fits the data well ($\chi^2_{n=200} = 225.494$, df $= 108$, $\chi^2/\text{df} = 2.088$, $P < .001$, CFI $= 0.951$, IFI $= 0.953$, RMSEA $= 0.074$) and did not make any significant differences ($\Delta\chi^2 = 8.119$, $P > .05$). We believe that CMV is unlikely to be a major threat here.

## 4.3.4  Results and Analysis

### 4.3.4.1  Multiple Regression Analyses

Scholars have pointed out that examining moderation effects using SEM (i.e. a multigroup model) continues to be extremely difficult (Little, Bovaird, & Widaman, 2006) and comes with the obvious disadvantage of lower statistical power (Semrau & Sigmund, 2012). As a result, many scholars still choose to use the HLM to test moderation effects (Lian et al., 2014; Semrau & Sigmund, 2012). In view of this, we also chose to use HLM rather than SEM to test moderation effects in our study.

Table 4.6 presents the means, standard deviations, and correlations of the variables included in our analysis, which confirms that there were no outliers or major violations of regression assumptions. We referred to Cohen, Cohen, and Stephen's (2003) recommendation to mean-centre all independent and moderator variables for minimizing the probability of multicollinearity. The calculated VIFs were all lower than the cut-off point of 5 (Cohen et al., 2003; Mackinnon et al., 2002), indicating no apparent multicollinearity.

To assess the explanatory power of each set of variables, we followed prior research (Kraus et al., 2012; Tang & Tang, 2012) using an HLM with SPSS 21.0 to test the direct influence of each EO dimension on performance and the moderating effect of *guanxi* on the EO–performance relationship. Following the sequential steps of HLM practices, we included all control variables in Model 1A, added independent variables in Model 1B, and added the assumed interaction terms in Model 1C. Table 4.7 presents the summarized results.

Of the control variables, environmental dynamism and firm age had a negative impact on firm performance, as shown in Model 1A

**Table 4.6** Mean, SD, Correlations

| | M | SD | 1 | 2 | 3 | 4 | 5 | 6 | 7 | 8 | 9 |
|---|---|---|---|---|---|---|---|---|---|---|---|
| 1. Firm size | 170.63 | 146.341 | 1 | | | | | | | | |
| 2. Industry type | 0.765 | 0.42506 | -0.902 | 1 | | | | | | | |
| 3. Firm age | 12.065 | 6.08737 | 0.315** | 0.099 | 1 | | | | | | |
| 4. Environmental dynamism | -3.547 | 0.72336 | -0.06 | -0.044 | 0.049 | 1 | | | | | |
| 5. Innovativeness | 3.5735 | 0.9949 | 0.056 | -0.092 | -0.114 | -0.415** | 1 | | | | |
| 6. Risk-taking | 3.4821 | 0.73448 | -0.103 | -0.053 | -0.112 | -0.483** | 0.394** | 1 | | | |
| 7. Proactiveness | 3.732 | 0.70784 | 0.005 | -0.043 | -0.197** | -0.422** | 0.555** | 0.482** | 1 | | |
| 8. Guanxi | 3.6012 | 0.67682 | 0.042 | -0.034 | -0.091 | -0.422** | 0.555** | 0.482** | 0.472** | 1 | |
| 9. Strategic flexibility | 3.6802 | 0.65895 | 0.068 | -0.02 | -0.211** | -0.499** | 0.549** | 0.414** | 0.614** | 0.413** | 1 |
| 10. Domestic performance | 3.5131 | 0.67913 | -0.039 | -0.046 | -0.333** | -0.267** | 0.156* | 0.244** | 0.398** | 0.401** | 0.377** |

$N = 200$.
** Correlation is significant at the 0.01 level (2-tailed); * Correlation is significant at the 0.05 level (2-tailed).

**Table 4.7** Hierarchical Regression Analyses

| Variables | Model 1A | | Model 1B | | Model 1C | |
|---|---|---|---|---|---|---|
| **Domestic Performance** | $\beta$ | S.E | $\beta$ | S.E | $\beta$ | S.E |
| **Control variables** | | | | | | |
| 1. Firm size | 0.000 | 0.000 | 0.000 | 0.000 | 0.000 | 0.000 |
| 2. Industry type | 0.006 | 0.112 | 0.010 | 0.002 | −0.039 | 0.097 |
| 3. Firm age | −0.042*** | 0.008 | −0.037*** | 0.008 | −0.033*** | 0.008 |
| 4. Environmental dynamism | −0.240*** | 0.067 | −0.086 | 0.076 | −0.039 | 0.006 |
| **EO dimensions** | | | | | | |
| 5. Innovativeness | | | −0.137* | 0.060 | −0.167** | 0.059 |
| 6. Risk-taking | | | −0.007 | 0.075 | 0.053 | 0.072 |
| 7. Proactiveness | | | 0.356*** | 0.092 | 0.363*** | 0.092 |
| **Moderators** | | | | | | |
| Social networking relationships/guanxi | | | 0.227** | 0.081 | 0.218** | 0.077 |
| **Interactions** | | | | | | |
| Guanxi*Innovativeness | | | | | 0.061 | 0.093 |
| Guanxi*Risk taking | | | | | −0.012 | 0.081 |
| Guanxi*Proactiveness | | | | | 0.343** | 0.131 |
| $R^2$ | | | 0.341 | | 0.423 | |
| Adjusted $R^2$ | | | 0.311 | | 0.386 | |
| $F$-value | 10.229** | | 11.145*** | | 11.272*** | |
| $\Delta R^2$ | | | 0.153*** | | 0.082*** | |

$N=200$.
* $P<.05$; ** $P<.01$; *** $P<.001$ significance levels based on two-tailed tests. Unstandardized regression coefficients are reported; robust standard errors are given in parentheses.

(environmental dynamism: $\beta = -0.240$, $P < .001$; firm age: $\beta = -0.042$, $P < .001$). According to Model 1B and Model 1C, proactiveness made a significant direct positive contribution to firm performance ($P < .001$), while innovativeness showed a significant negative impact on performance, supporting Hypothesis 1a and 1c. Risk-taking did not have a direct effect on performance, leading to the rejection of Hypothesis 1b.

In Model 1C, the interaction of social networking relationships with proactiveness was significantly and positively related to firm performance ($\beta = 2.185$, $P < .01$), supporting Hypothesis 2c. The estimated coefficients of the interactions between *guanxi* and innovativeness and between *guanxi* and risk-taking were not statistically significant, leading to the rejection of Hypotheses 2a and 2b.

Additionally, Model 1A showed that the control variables explained only 18.9% of the variance in domestic performance. After including three EO variables and *guanxi*, Model 1B explained 34.1% of the variance in performance ($\Delta R^2 = 15.3\%$, $P < .001$). In Model 1C, the inclusion of interaction terms explained 42.3% of the variance in performance, further adding another 8.2% ($P < .001$) in terms of the explanatory power.

In sum, full support was found for Hypotheses 1a, 1c, and 2c, while Hypotheses 1b, 2a, and 2b were rejected.

### 4.3.4.2 Mediation Tests

To test the mediating role of strategic flexibility between proactiveness and reverse internationalization performance, we used the SEM approach suggested by Mackinnon et al. (2002) to build mediation models. Testing a series of nested models against the presumed baseline model with sequential chi-square tests enables researchers to better rule out alternative explanations so as to discern the model that best illustrates the results of the hypotheses (Anderson & Gerbing, 1988; Chin et al., 2015). This approach, advocated by Anderson and Gerbing (1988), has been widely applied to examine the intervening effects in previous studies (Chin, 2015; Jones, Willness, & Madey, 2014; Lu et al., 2010; Semrau & Sigmund, 2012). The significance of mediation can be examined by comparing the fit for the direct effect model with that of the predictor–mediator–outcome model (with and without the direct path from the predictor and the outcome constrained to zero) (Jones et al., 2014; Lu et al., 2010). A full mediation would be identified if the model with the direct path between predictor and outcome displays a better fit.

**Table 4.8** Hypothesis Test of Alternative Models

|  | $\chi^2$ | Df | $\chi^{2*}$ | Df* | IFI | NFI | CFI | RMSEA |
|---|---|---|---|---|---|---|---|---|
| Baseline Model 2A | 25.690 | 11 | – | – | 0.939 | 0.897 | 0.934 | 0.082 |
| Model 2B | 9.345 | 9 | 9.027 | 2 | 0.999 | 0.963 | 0.998 | 0.014 |
| Model 2C | 68.218 | 10 | 42.528 | 1 | 0.757 | 0.727 | 0.738 | 0.177 |
| Model 2D | 37.791 | 10 | 12.101 | 1 | 0.884 | 0.849 | 0.875 | 0.118 |
| Model 2E | 28.998 | 10 | 3.308 | 1 | 0.921 | 0.884 | 0.914 | 0.098 |

$n = 113$.
* The differences between the model and the basic model 2A. Baseline model, full mediation (no direct paths from the predictor to outcome); Model 2B, partial mediation model (the path from the predictor to outcome was added; Model 2C, direct effects model (the path from the predictor to mediator was constrained to zero); Model 2D, nonmediation models (the path from the mediator to outcome was constrained to zero); Model 2E, reverse causality models: strategic flexibility to proactiveness to domestic performance.

Table 4.8 shows the results of the mediation tests. Consistent with prior studies (Chin, 2015), we estimated a baseline model as the full mediation, which has no direct path from proactiveness to domestic performance. The results of this full mediation model (Model 2A) showed an unsatisfactory model fit $(\chi^2_{n=200} = 25.690$, df$= 11$, $\chi^2$/df$= 2.335 > 2$, $P < .01$; CFI$= 0.934 > 0.90$; NFI$= 0.897 < 0.90$; IFI$= 0.939 > 0.90$; RMSEA$= 0.082 > 0.08$). Then we tested a series of nested models against our baseline model via sequential chi-square tests with the parameter constraints of interest in our research. We compared Model 2A with a partial mediation model (Model 2B) in which the path from proactiveness to performance was added. As seen in Table 4.8, the fit indices of Model 2B look more acceptable than those of the baseline model $(\chi^2_{n=200} = 9.345$, df$= 9$, $\chi^2$/df$= 1.038 < 2$, $P = .406 > 0.05$; CFI$= 0.998 > 0.90$; NFI$= 0.963 > 0.90$; IFI$= 0.999 > 0.90$; RMSEA$= 0.014 < 0.05$), considering the significant chi-square difference between Models 2A and 2B ($\Delta\chi^2 = 16.345$, df$= 2$, $P < .05$).

Model 2C is a direct effect model, where there is no causal relationship between the proactiveness and strategic flexibility, as proactiveness, and strategic flexibility were set to directly link performance. Model 2D is a nonmediation model assuming that the path from strategic flexibility to performance was constrained to zero. Model 2E represents a reverse causality model that treats strategic flexibility as an antecedent of proactiveness, whereby proactiveness conversely mediated the relationship between strategic flexibility and performance. Table 4.8 shows that the fit indices of Model 2B are significantly superior to those of Models 2A, 2C, 2D, and 2E. Overall, the results suggest that the partial mediation Model 2B best fits our data.

### 4.3.4.3 Assessment of Hypotheses

Fig. 4.3 delineates the parameter estimates of the final best fit Model 2B for examining our Hypotheses 3a and 3b. Hypothesis 3a states that proactiveness is positively related to strategic flexibility. As shown in Fig. 4.3, the direct path from proactiveness to domestic strategic flexibility is significant ($\beta = 1.280$, $P < .001$), supporting Hypothesis 3a. Hypothesis 3b assumes that strategic flexibility mediates the effect of proactiveness on domestic performance. Fig. 4.3 shows that the direct path from proactiveness to performance is still significant ($\beta = 0.014$, $P < .001$), while the indirect path from proactiveness via strategic flexibility to performance is significant (from proactiveness to strategic flexibility: $\beta = 0.1280$, $P < .001$; from strategic flexibility to performance: $\beta = 0.1231$, $P < .001$). So Hypothesis 3b is strongly supported as well.

## 4.3.5 Discussion

Our research illustrates that during China's economic transition period the link between EO and firm performance presents more complicated interrelationships than a simple direct relationship and the individual dimensions of EO may have different influences on firm performance. As per our findings, in the context where global start-up OEMs return to compete domestically, proactiveness is positively related to firm performance; risk–taking is not statistically associated with performance; innovativeness is negatively related to performance. In alignment with recent findings (Dai et al., 2014; Kreiser et al., 2013), our results confirm that three dimensions of EO demonstrate differential associations with SME performance. More specifically, in the

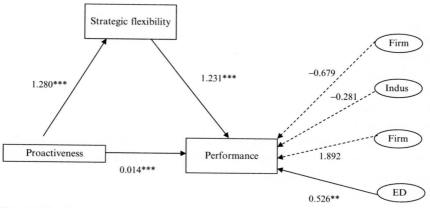

**Fig. 4.3** The mediation model.

context of reverse internationalization by Chinese global start-up OEMs, proactiveness is generally considered a cornerstone of the role EO plays in driving firm performance (Hughes & Morgan, 2007; Kraus et al., 2012) and exhibits exclusively positive effects.

In contrast, during reverse internationalization, innovativeness that entails lots of R&D cost may impede performance, whereas risk-taking that deals with large possibilities of failure has no significant impact on performance. SMEs with higher levels of innovativeness are believed to be beneficial in dynamic EEs (Chin et al., 2015). However, on the basis of our findings, entrepreneurial OEMs operating on thin profit margins may not be able to rely on undertaking innovative projects to increase revenue in China owing to the fact that a variety of institutional barriers and less intellectual property protection can diminish the value of innovativeness (Zheng, 2014). Kraus et al. (2012) also suggest that in the face of an economic slowdown SMEs with severe financial pressure will need to have a legacy of innovativeness to draw upon when entering new markets as opposed to building it directly from new markets. As such, it seems plausible that Chinese global start-up OEMs may typically not capitalize on innovativeness to generate competitive advantage in the context of reverse internationalization since they used to prefer imitation and low-cost manufacturing rather than innovation and R&D input, thus remaining weak in the initiation of new technologies (Chin et al., 2015).

The contradictory findings about the impact of risk-taking on performance have led to an increasing level of scrutiny in recent entrepreneurial literature (Kreiser et al., 2013). A large body of studies has found that risk-taking behaviours often do not represent a worthwhile entrepreneurial endeavour for SMEs, but display a predominantly direct or U-shaped negative relationship with firm performance (Dai et al., 2014). Consistent with Kraus et al. (2012), risk-taking does not show a direct association with performance in our research. However, this may be caused by the fact that the second indicator of our risk-taking scale, as noted above, seems not suitable for our background setting of reverse internationalization because Chinese global start-up OEMs with heavy financial burdens are unlikely to view the acquisition of new business as their strategic priority.

Our study demonstrates that social networking relationships (*guanxi*) significantly moderate the effect of proactiveness on performance, while the interactions of *guanxi* with risk-taking and innovativeness have no significant impact on performance. Implicitly, our findings corroborate the vital role of social networking with two dominant resource controllers—the key persons of local government agencies and business communities—in facilitating SME awareness and access to valuable market information in China (Luo et al., 2011; Tang & Tang, 2012; Zhang et al., 2014). With *guanxi* as a precious information source, it would be easier for proactive firms to foresee future trends of Chinese markets. This shows why the positive effects of proactiveness on performance become stronger when interacting with *guanxi*.

In terms of the mediating effect, our results find that proactiveness can be translated into firm performance through strategic flexibility. As is well known, China's socialist political structure allows regional governments to be directly involved in the enactment of market policies in their jurisdictions, and thus market structures vary regionally (Chin, 2013; Krug & Hendrischke, 2012). Owing to such complicated political embeddedness in the Chinese market with the corresponding decentralized and segmented market design (Chin, 2014; Kiss et al., 2012; Krug & Hendrischke, 2012), merely engaging in proactive behaviours could be ineffective if entrepreneurial firms are unable to compensate for their resource shortages. Hence, strategic flexibility embodying the firm's ability to coordinate and leverage limited resources appears to be particularly instrumental for SMEs to transform their entrepreneurial efforts, such as adjusting competitive approaches and reallocating resources into actual performance. In other words, without a certain degree of strategic flexibility, Chinese global start-up OEMs, despite possessing high levels of proactiveness, may still not be able to achieve superior performance when undertaking reverse internationalization.

It is worth noting that firm age as a control variable elicits a negative impact on firm performance according to our results. Our findings, to a certain extent, support the learning advantages of newness (LAN) Theory (Zahra, 2005), which assumes that latecomers may not suffer from the same inertial forces that stifle mature incumbents' adaptation to new changes in target markets. In this regard, global start-up OEMs, as newcomers in their domestic competitions, might also derive competitive advantage from accelerated cross-border learning.

Overall, several contributions emerge from our research. First, we explore how the individual dimensions of EO benefit, suppress, or have no significant effect on firm performance in a particular environment, thus responding to recent calls for unravelling the heterogeneous characteristics of each subdimension of EO as well as for more contextually embedded treatment of the EO–performance association (Fuentes-Fuentes et al., 2015; Jones et al., 2011). Second, by testing the moderating role of *guanxi* and the mediating mechanism of strategic flexibility on EO–performance relationships, we advance the understanding of how such contingent factors help entrepreneurial OEMs to break down institutional barriers and reap the most from EO in the EE of China. Third, we contribute to the literature by introducing and elucidating a novel entrepreneurial phenomenon, reverse internationalization, by Chinese global start-up OEMs. Although China's tremendous domestic market and huge consumption demand have become a major source of growth for the world economy, such entrepreneurial activity has had limited examination in the literature (Chin et al., 2015; Zheng, 2014). Our study therefore delivers a clearer, holistic picture of this intriguing entrepreneurial scene in the Chinese market, providing valuable and practical implications for other OEMs in China to deal with relevant issues in a better manner.

## 4.3.6 Limitations and Future Research

This study, like other research, has its boundaries and limitations, which may open up fertile avenues for future research in relevant fields. First, using cross-sectional data may not be sufficient for establishing proper causality between EO and performance (McKeever et al., 2014). Future research could conduct a longitudinal study to interpret the key issues more comprehensively and precisely. Second, employing a perceived and aggregated performance index may mask the effects of EO on individual financial indicators, nonfinancial performance, and growth potential (Kraus et al., 2012). Future research should take into consideration the utilization of more solid financial performance indices such as archival information and the inclusion of various types of performance measures (e.g. customer satisfaction). Third, there are limits in data collection. So future research is encouraged to enlarge the sample size, incorporate multiple informants, and add more diverse control variables for a deeper understanding of relevant issues. Fourth, though most scales of social networking relationships/*guanxi* assess only the perceived value of *guanxi*, future studies should consider the development of more objective measurements to capture the quality of business and institutional network ties. Additionally, given that the EO–performance relationship is bounded to contextual contingencies (Dai et al., 2014; Lumpkin & Dess, 1996), it is vital to further investigate under what circumstances SMEs with high EO can outperform competitors and how the subdimensions of EO interact with other idiosyncratic factors to affect performance. Doing so will provide valuable reference points for future generations of EO researchers.

In conclusion, the fast-changing and complex Chinese market, coupled with the tough issues of overcapacity and rising labour cost in China's OEM industry, might be able to best elaborate on why our distinctive results occur. Our research—which brings new insights into how Chinese global start-up OEMs benefit from EO in the process of reverse internationalization—unveils a distinctive EO–performance mechanism in a given context that is quite different from that in mature and developed markets.

## 4.4 CONCLUSION

### 4.4.1 Branding in Reverse Internationalization: A Reflection of Chinese Yin–Yang Harmony Thinking

Luo and Child (2015) claim that the major reason why some entrepreneurial OEMs in China could develop a unique composition capability to integrate low cost advantages with new product functions and innovate is because of a unique set of external conditions. Branding in reverse internationalization appears to be a typical example that links China's unique institutional environment and where there still exists tenacious institutional hardship to local SME OEMs' entrepreneurial endeavours. More specifically, these entrepreneurial OEMs perceive fresh opportunities occurring in their domestic market, thus organizing in ways that permit a quick response to such changes—OBM is instrumental to provide increased value or convenience to domestic customers.

Viewed from this angle, this branding in reverse internationalization to a certain extent mirrors the overwhelming propensity of Chinese entrepreneurs to set a kind of 'Yin–Yang' harmony strategic orientation (Chin et al., 2015; Luo & Child, 2015)—they seem to possess a unique integration ability to achieve the arbitrage through continuously balancing firm-specific advantages against economically fragmented and institutionally harsh environments. In other words, this Yin–Yang harmony cognition indicates the prominent cultural idiosyncrasy of identifying complementary components in conflicts. It explains why Chinese entrepreneurial OEMs do not regard low cost and costly innovation (i.e. OBM) as adversaries, but instead are open to unifying them (Luo & Child, 2015) and often keen to advocate a harmonious coevolution and coadaptation with the external changes.

Considering the ubiquitous influence of the Yin–Yang harmony view on the behaviours of China's firms and workers (Chin, 2014, 2015), we will elaborate on this cultural ideology in this chapter and further relate it to the resolution of labour conflict in Chapter 5.

# CHAPTER FIVE

# A Yin–Yang Harmony Cognition to Employer–Employee Relationships

## 5.1 INTRODUCTION

### 5.1.1 'Harmonious Mentality' of Chinese People

'Harmony' is recognized as a predominant cultural idiosyncrasy of Chinese people, a core value of Chinese 'mental software' (Hofstede, Hofstede, & Minkov, 2010; Leung, Brew, Zhang, & Zhang, 2011), as numerous lines of evidence indicate that the Chinese particularly value group harmony and collective spirit, and prefer to trust long-term member affiliations and patriarchal systems (Han & Altman, 2010; Leung, Koch, & Lu, 2002; Ngo, Lau, & Foley, 2008; Redding, 2005; Westwood, 1997). The notion of harmony dominating Chinese culture ascribes primacy to reciprocity, interdependence, and interrelatedness among individuals, not just the individuals themselves, thus involving a broader context—even including the entire universe. With a distinctive mode of holistic and all-encompassing thinking, the Chinese tend to maintain harmony not only at the individual level, but also at interpersonal, group, and corporate levels (Chin, 2014, 2015; Tjosvold, Wu, & Chen, 2010; Xiao & Tsui, 2007).

This Chinese harmonious culture originated from *Yijing* (i.e. *The Book of Changes*) and is comprehensively decoded by the eight-trigram model at its heart (see Fig. 5.1). According to the CCP's claims, an ideal organization/firm should be a harmonious unity in which people of differing talents and professions occupy their proper jobs, perform their proper functions, and are all equally satisfied and not in conflict with one another. We will elaborate on the origin, features, and connotations of this indigenous Chinese concept of Yin–Yang harmony in the next sections.

Compared with Western corporate governance systems where the organizational structure and position design are usually impersonal

**Fig. 5.1** The eight-trigram diagram.

(Westwood, 1997), Chinese managerial systems may see the policies, decisions, and procedures introduced by a leader as his personal orders and allow for interpersonal harmony to take precedence where some jobs can be specifically tailored to persons with *guanxi*. Evidence shows that the ultimate goal for Chinese workers to cope with contradictions at the workplace is not to pursue an ideal noncontradictory solution like the West, but for a balanced yet continuously dynamic status of harmony—a constantly changing process of 'harmonization'. These ambiguous, dynamic, and dualistic psychological qualities constitute a salient feature of Chinese personality, namely the 'harmonious mentality', which significantly affects the working attitude and behaviour of employees as well as management styles in China.

As far as China's manufacturing sector is concerned, understanding the unique, indigenous harmonious mentality seems to be particularly critical, as nearly half of the employed population working in manufacturing—>100 million workers—represents the world's largest manufacturing workforce (see Fig. 5.1). Hence, in the next section, we introduce two studies that use China's manufacturing as a case to address how this cultural idiosyncrasy shapes employer–employee relationships in labour-intensive organizations.

## 5.2 HARMONY AND OCB IN CHINESE ORGANIZATIONS

### 5.2.1 Introduction

The great impact of OCB on firm success has been recognized by a plethora of studies (e.g. Chang & Smithikrai, 2010; Euwema, Wendt, & van Emmerik, 2007; Kabasakal, Dastmalchian, & Imer, 2011; Organ, Podsakoff, & Mackenzie, 2006; Paille, 2013; Podsakoff, MacKenzie,

Paine, & Bachrach, 2000; Sun, Aryee, & Law, 2007; Teh, Boerhannoeddin, & Ismail, 2012). OCB, defined as positive behaviour that goes beyond the formal requirement of the job but promotes effective functioning of the organization, improves employees' task performance by freeing up resources, helps to coordinate activities between employees, and boosts co-worker productivity (Organ, 1988, 1997; Podsakoff et al., 2000; Van Dyne, Graham, & Dienesch, 1994). Hence, while many firms failed following the 2008 global financial crisis and 2010 European sovereign debt crisis, studies of HRM have paid increasing attention to topics regarding the enhancement of employee OCB for improving firm performance. China, the world's second largest economy employing >243 million workers (China Statistical Yearbook, 2010), has the largest workforce in the world. With its distinctive political and sociocultural environment, it provides a large and novel setting for HRM researchers to investigate OCB-related issues in depth.

However, evidence illustrates that the dimensions and meaning of OCB vary widely across cultures (Euwema et al., 2007; Farh, Zhong, & Organ, 2004; Gelfand, Erez, & Aycan, 2007). This is because different nations, particularly for those from the East and West, are distant in their philosophies, cultural values, and beliefs about people's attitudes and behaviours at work (e.g. Adler, 2008; Bruton et al., 2010; Chen & Miller, 2010; Hofstede et al., 2010; Stone & Stone-Romero, 2007; Tsui, Nifadkar, & Ou, 2007).

It is widely acknowledged that the content domain of OCB in China differs from that developed in the West, mainly due to the impact of Confucian doctrines on Chinese work behaviour (Farh, Hackett, & Jian, 2007; Han & Altman, 2010; Keister & Zhang, 2009; Tsui et al., 2007). Compared to the West, people in China, as collectivists, value harmony much more, which reflects a cultural characteristic and proclivity originating with Confucian ideology at the heart of *Yijing*, the most critical ancient Confucian canon (Chen & Miller, 2010; Han & Altman, 2010; Hofstede et al., 2010; Ngo et al., 2008; Tjosvold et al., 2010; Yu & Zaheer, 2010). Emphasis on harmony is 'the software of Chinese mindset' (Hofstede et al., 2010) and enhancing the degree of harmony appears to be a useful approach to encourage positive employee behaviour within Chinese organizations.

Although research has found some OCB indicators of harmony stemming from Confucian moral roots that are specific to China (Farh et al., 2004; Han & Altman, 2010), the existing models of Chinese OCB are still built on Western theories (Farh et al., 2004; Han & Altman, 2010).

Thus, OCB models are ripe to be 'contextualized theories' (developing theories in context or contexualizing extant theory) rather than 'context-effect theories' (developing the theories of the specific context or using context to formulate new theories) (Rowley, 2016; Tsui, 2007; Whetten, 2009). Despite the contributions made by existing research on Chinese OCB, it is vital to build an indigenous context-specific model that can explain the impact of harmony on OCB in China from a more context-sensitive angle (Whetten, 2009).

To fill this research gap, our study explores the relationships between harmony and OCB within Chinese organizations employing an indigenous model that conceptualizes the abstract notion of Chinese harmony at the workplace (Chin, 2010). Furthermore, since job satisfaction, a fundamental assessment associated with employee well-being and morale, could trigger employee displays of OCB (Gonzalez & Garazo, 2006; Kabasakal et al., 2011), we also investigate the interactions among harmony, job satisfaction, and OCB.

Our research yields three contributions to the literature. First, despite the existence of numerous studies on OCB and job satisfaction, we develop a new indigenous framework examining their relationships with the prominent cultural characteristic—harmony—in the Chinese context. This is a response to calls for introducing context-specific measures and considering the impact of cultural variables on HRM (Stone & Stone-Romero, 2007; Tsui, 2007). Second, whereas the way Confucian codes are reflected within organizations is still poorly understood (Han & Altman, 2010), we empirically investigate the mechanism between the values of harmony derived from Confucianism and the levels of OCB and job satisfaction from Western theories, which provides a useful theoretical foundation for future research. Third, we encourage non-Chinese managers to motivate OCB in China effectively by enriching their understanding of the unique cultural trait of harmony.

## 5.2.2 Theoretical Foundations and Hypotheses

### 5.2.2.1 An Art-Based View

The rising use of an art-based view to investigate organizational development and change has emerged recently (Adler, 2006; Harrison, Leitch, & Chia, 2007; Rhee, 2010; Taylor & Ladkin, 2009; Tung, 2006). Weick (2007) states that traditional business tools of logic and rationality are ill-suited to a complicated and chaotic environment and that the art-based method may provide a different means or new lens from which to approach the world. In short, the art-based method can be defined as the systematic use of the artistic process, namely the actual making of artistic expressions in all of the different forms of the arts, as a primary way of understanding and analysing human experience, entities, or phenomena in the world (McNiff, 1998). The art-based view therefore leads people to make use of a larger spectrum of creative intelligence to generate illustration or information that often feels more accurate, original, and intelligent than does more conventional, verbal, and mathematic descriptions (McNiff, 1998; Taylor & Ladkin, 2009).

Adler (2006) documents the recent increase in the use of arts-based methods as part of broader cross-fertilization between business and the arts. Her research reveals that business leadership potentially learns courage from the arts—the courage to see reality, envision possibility, and to bring reality to possibility. Extending Adler (2006) study, Tung (2006) argues that one principal difference between North American and East Asian management practices is that in the former, management is considered primarily as a science, whereas in the latter, it is typically viewed as an art, even though management education is valued. Western society, through its growing awareness of the potential merits to be derived from cross-fertilization of the arts and leadership, is converging towards the Asian tendency to view management as an art rather than as a science (Tung, 2006).

Taylor and Ladkin (2009) have pointed out that the study of culture is a particularly good example of where an art-based method is useful. Unlike most western cultures that traditionally favour linear and logic thinking modes, Chinese wisdoms, philosophies, and culture that espouse the Yin–Yang dynamics reflect a salient art orientation. As Rhee (2010) claims, classical Chinese literature is written in a fairly poetic and figurative way. Hence, to address the logic of Chinese values and beliefs, scholars need to use imagination to extract theoretical insights from Chinese traditional philosophies and literature.

### 5.2.2.2 Chinese Perception of Harmony Based on Yijing

As indicated at the outset, the Chinese concept of harmony originated from the most influential philosophical scripture *Yijing* written 3000 years ago. This represents the pivotal source and basic mode of Chinese philosophical ideologies, including two major mainstreams of Chinese philosophy, Confucianism and Taoism (Cheng, 2011; Fung, 1948; Huang, 2008; Lai, 2008; Li, 2008). The ancient text of *Yijing* was originally used as an oracle for divination, but later the Confucianists continued to develop and extend its ancient text into a wider spectrum, including cosmological, metaphysical, and ethical interpretations and explanations for thousands of years, as first shown in Yizhuan (易传 in Chinese), the earliest and most well-known Confucian annotations to Yijing (Fung, 1948; Lai, 2008; Zhou, 2004). It explains why in terms of the Confucian values system, maintaining Yin–Yang harmony is the essential tenet to doing things 'the right way', representing 'noble character' in a 'gentleman' (sic) (Cheng, 2006; Fung, 1948; Lai, 2008).

The central thought pattern of Yijing is symbolized by the eight-trigram model—which was believed to be created by the Confucian mythical sage, Fuxi, one of the earliest legendary rulers of China who also created ancient Chinese characters (traditional dates 2800 BCE) (Fung, 1948; Lai, 2008; Zhou, 2004). Fuxi, relying on sustained obser-vations of changes in nature, further used imagination in drawing eight trigrams which were constituted by a combination of three Yin (a bro-ken line) or Yang (an unbroken line) elements as primary substances to delineate eight primordial forces in the universe (i.e. Heaven, Lake, Fire, Thunder, Wind, Water, Mountain, and Earth, respectively) (Fung, 1948; Lai, 2008; Miller, 1991) (See Fig. 5.1). As per ancient Chinese writings, the essence of the Yang element usually characterizes sunshine, light, or an entity/subject's strong, bright, and positive side, while the essence of the Yin element mirrors the absence of sunshine such as shadow, dark-ness, or an entity/subject's supple, dark, and negative side. Following this logic, the eight trigrams are virtually analogous to 'symbols' where the particular semiotic connotation and denotation on Yin and Yang are delivered. By combining any two of the eight trigrams with one another into diagrams of six lines each, the total 64 hexagrams epitomizing the unique paradigm of Yijing were obtained (Zhou, 2004).

It is worth noting that the symbols mentioned above are very similar to what in symbolic logic are called 'variables' in the West (Fung, 1948; Zhou, 2004), but people need to translate the artistic insights concealed in the images of the trigrams into descriptive language by an intuitive, aesthetic knowing, that is, inspiring creativity, to realize the outside realm of rational thought (McNiff, 1998). For example, the trigram 'Qian' consisting of three Yang lines can symbolize 'Heaven' and 'Masculine', while the trigram 'Kun' consisting of three Yin lines can symbolize 'Land' and 'Famine'. Scholars argue that the Yin–Yang interacting philosophy should be seen as a unique frame of thinking for exploring complex phenomena and an open system as a duality to accommodate a balance between all 'either/or' and 'both/and' situations, whereby the changing pattern of relatively abstract things can also be clearly codified (Cheng, 2006; Gu, 2005; Li, 2012).

To conclude, the central theme of *Yijing*, as its English title *The Book of Changes* implies, is the axiom of the continuous and eternal changing paradigm of all tangible and intangible entities in the universe (Lai, 2008; Miller, 1991; Zhou, 2004). The 64-hexagram system can be considered as 64 semiotic terms to account for the unitary transformation law which every single thing ought to obey so as to activate the world; the eight trigrams as the primary components forming 64 hexagrams are essential image symbols that are constantly undergoing transformation standing for different transitional states. In fact, with time passing by, the eight-trigram model with its Yin and Yang components, in addition to the eight natural sources noted above, have been frequently exploited by Eastern scholars as a convenient and easy-to-understand open system to substitute for a variety of objects and dynamic concepts (e.g. animals, directions, numbers, and members of family), or to embody a large scope of abstract transformation processes and intangible presences (e.g. energy, spirit) (Fung, 1948; Li, 2012; Miller, 1991; Zhou, 2004).

Considering the foregoing arguments, it is understood that Chinese culture has been art-oriented since the very beginning (Huang, 2008; Rhee, 2010; Tung, 2006), and the way Chinese define harmony based on *Yijing* is more proximate to art than to science.

### 5.2.2.3 The Art-Based View to the Yin–Yang Dynamics of Chinese Harmony

Taking together the foregoing discussions, it is understood why the Chinese notion of harmony constituted by the Yin–Yang interactions is more like art than science.

Following the above logic, employing an art-based perspective, Chin (2010) conducted an empirical study examining if the harmony realized and cognized by employees in Chinese organizations project the concept of harmony demonstrated in *Yijing*. The results showed an eight-factor construct. The eight dimensions encompass a wide range of cognitive harmony at the workplace by individual employees, ranging from self-cultivation and self-development for harmony to the harmony between external and internal organizations. Chin (2010) further used creative imagination, a typical art-based approach (McNiff, 1998; Taylor & Ladkin, 2009), to match the eight dimensions with the eight trigrams, based on the theoretical implications concerning harmony decoded by the Yin–Yang dynamics of the eight trigrams (see Table 5.1).

As a result, the two models were found to fit each other very well. The symbolic logic (the denotation) combined with the connotation of the eight-trigram model could be applied to characterize the notion of Chinese

**Table 5.1** The Symbolic Meaning of the Eight Trigrams and Their Counterparts in the Eight-Factor Model

| Trigram | Name | Symbolic Meaning of Each Trigram and Its Counterpart of Eight-Factor Model |
|---|---|---|
| ☷ | Kun (Earth) | Factor 1: harmony of employee with himself<br>Kun represents the image of Earth. Its spirit is to yield, serve and bring forth as soft and generous as the Earth. With it, employees will be stable, willing to protect working environment and respect company's disciplines |
| ☴ | Sun (Wind) | Factor 2: harmony of employees<br>Sun represents the image of wind. Its spirit is to be gentle, humble, and penetrate things from below just like the way the wind kisses the grass. With it, employees will maintain smooth and beautiful emotions and avoid irritating colleagues, which therefore bring them into harmony |
| ☲ | Li (Fire) | Factor 3: harmony of employee with his team<br>Li represents the image of fire. Its spirit is to cooperate together with warmth and rely on other people's power to achieve goals just like burning woods to bring brightness. With it, team members will work together towards a shared aim with warmth |
| ☱ | Dui (Lake) | Factor 4: harmony of employee with his supervisor<br>Dui symbolizes the image of lake. Its spirit is to spread joyfulness, profitable transparent exchange and cheerful interaction just like a lake of clear water. With it, supervisors will treat subordinates kindly, and vice versa, which enhances a harmonious subordinate–boss relationship |
| ☶ | Gen (Mountain) | Factor 5: harmony of employee with management system<br>Gen represents the image of mountain. Its spirit is to keep still, stop things or to follow the rules with good discipline as firm and solid as mountain It not only encourages employers to build sound management systems, but also urges employees to comply with them |

**Table 5.1** The Symbolic Meaning of the Eight Trigrams and Their Counterparts in the Eight-Factor Model—cont'd

| Trigram | Name | Symbolic Meaning of Each Trigram and Its Counterpart of Eight-Factor Model |
|---------|------|----------------------------------------------------------------------------|
| ☵ | Kan (Water) | Factor 6: harmony of departments<br>Kan symbolizes the image of water. Its spirit is to dissolve things and overcome obstacles in danger of stagnation as brave as rapidly flowing water (torrent). It helps employees from different departments to control emotions, and reduce misunderstanding and conflicts among them |
| ☳ | Zhen (Thunder) | Factor 7: harmony of grassroots employee with the highest leader<br>Zhen represents the image of thunder. Its spirit is to produce courage to burst forth from the below, raising confidence to take risks, just like surviving a lightning storm. It arouses a leader's dominant energy and vision for prospect, and motivates the whole organization to act decisively in the pursuit of success |
| ☰ | Qian (Heaven) | Factor 8: harmony of internal and external organizations<br>Qian represents the image of heaven. Its spirit is representative of divine power that inspires and strengthens creative inner forces, deep contemplation and positive movement towards a greater interconnection in the world. It symbolizes the highest power in Chinese culture, facilitates an organization to achieve superior harmony, and establishes internal and external rapport |

harmony in all aspects at the workplace. More specifically, Chin (2010) developed an indigenous eight-factor framework measuring the degree of harmony that the employee perceives at the workplace, including with themselves, other employees, their team, supervisors and management systems and the harmony between departments, employees, and the highest leader, internal and external organizations. For a better understanding, the way in which the eight trigrams epitomized the concept of Chinese harmony and were matched with their counterparts of Chin's (2010) eight-factor model is illustrated in Table 5.1 (the symbolic meaning/spirit of each trigram on harmony refers to the book Formal Interpretation of *Yijing* written by Kong Yingda in the Tang dynasty).

While taking a closer look at the items measuring harmony at the workplace in Chin (2010) model, we found that it seemed to be composed of many separate constructs in terms of Western organizational behaviour theories, for example, organizational justice (the firm has a fair wage system), leadership (the leader listens to employees' different opinions), and OCB (colleagues help each other overcome difficulties). This is not surprising because from the art-based view to decode Chinese harmony by the Yin–Yang dynamics, all forms of interaction of polarities of whatever degrees of complexity can be regarded as symbolic of Chinese harmony. In contrast to the Western viewpoint, Chinese harmony rooted in *Yijing* encompasses a broader spectrum of content and elements, including all relevant values, tradition, and practice, such as moral cultivation, authentic leadership, and organizational politics, which are central to arranging the individual, social, world, and even universal orders in the pursuit of harmony (Cheng, 2006; Qian, 2010). Despite being exploratory in nature due to the lack of prior empirical research, Chin (2010) model reflects the prominent characteristic of Chinese harmony noted above as it displayed a holistic and comprehensive description on how Chinese employees define and describe the ideal status of harmony at the workplace. In other words, this model could be used as a distinct construct to measure the level of harmony at workplaces perceived by employees in China. Hence, it is appropriate to employ Chin (2010) model here.

Taken together, the foregoing arguments lead us to focus on exploring the mechanism between the cultural variable 'harmony' and OCB in our study.

### 5.2.2.4 OCB

Employee behaviours are conceptually divided between in-role (task-dependent behaviour) and extra-role (individual behaviour above the standards normally expected by employers) actions (Organ, 1988; Van Dyne et al., 1994). OCB is widely viewed as individual extra-role behaviour that 'goes beyond the call of duty', not directly or explicitly enforced on the basis of formal role obligations, nor elicited by a formal reward system and, in the aggregate, promotes the effective functioning of the organization and supports task performance (Bergeron, 2007; Lam, Chun, & Law, 1999; Organ, 1988, 1997; Organ et al., 2006; Podsakoff et al., 2000). In short, OCB is the critical 'lubricating machinery' of an organization that reduces friction and/or increases efficiency (Podsakoff et al., 2000).

Social Exchange Theory argues that individuals who choose to engage in OCB benefiting organizations may actually expect a successful reciprocity with their employers because they hope that their supervisors take their exhibition of OCB into account when evaluating their performance (Gong, Chang, & Cheung, 2010; Walumbwa, Cropanzano, & Goldman, 2011). Researchers have also examined OCB as a group-level model since OCB develops positive feelings among group members and departments that may result in 'group think' and facilitate effective collaboration among cross-functional teams (Gong et al., 2010). Overall, we could conclude that when employees demonstrate more OCB, their work performance improves (Chang & Smithikrai, 2010; Rotundo & Xie, 2008).

It is worth noting that the boundary between in-role and extra-role behaviours remains ambiguous because contextual factors, such as national culture and institutional environment, affect how in-role and extra-role behaviours are defined, and therefore the content domains of OCB may vary across different countries (Euwema et al., 2007; Farh et al., 2004; Gelfand et al., 2007; Van Dyne et al., 1994). From a divergence perspective, individuals hold onto their national cultural values, and hence HRM practices are deeply rooted in a nation's culture (Rotundo & Xie, 2008; Rowley, 1997a, 1997b; Rowley & Benson, 2002, 2003). For example, Lam et al. (1999) suggest that, compared with employees from Australia and the United States, employees from Hong Kong and Japan are more likely to consider sportsmanship and courtesy as in-role rather than extra-role behaviours (as defined by Organ, 1988). Consequently, a number of OCB models with slight variations in their dimensionality have emerged from different socio-environments (e.g. Lin & Ho, 2010; Yen, Li, & Niehoff, 2008).

In the Chinese context, building on Confucian moral values, Farh et al. (2004) revise the OCB scale proposed by Organ (1988) to give the new Chinese OCB scale two distinctive factors—interpersonal harmony and protecting company resources—that were not identified in prior Western research. Han and Altman (2010) summarized 12 types of OCB, including helping co-workers; individual initiative and/or functional participation; group activity participation; self-development; social welfare participation; promoting company image; voice; protecting and saving company resources; interpersonal harmony and keeping the workplace clean; and maintaining departmental harmony and coexistence during adversity. Taking Confucian culture as the background, their research also highlights that two dimensions—interpersonal and departmental harmony—have not been reported conceptually or empirically as OCB dimensions in Western literature.

On the basis of the above arguments, there is no doubt that harmonious orientation characterizes the salient Chinese cultural characteristic, acting as a critical contextual element determining OCB in China. Thus, it is reasonable to propose that the Chinese display of OCB is strongly related to the level of harmony at the workplace. This produces the following hypothesis:

**Hypothesis 1:** The degree of harmony an employee perceives within an organization is positively related to their display of OCBs.

### 5.2.2.5 Job Satisfaction as a Mediator of Harmonious Spirit on OCB

Job satisfaction refers to an employee's pleasurable or positive emotional state resulting from one's job or job experience (Harrison, Newman, & Roth, 2006; Schmidt, 2007; Zhang & Zheng, 2009). Job satisfaction may arise from different sources, including level of job ambiguity, quality of supervision, and social relationships, for instance level of support in the workplace (Moura, Abrams, Retter, Gunnarsdottir, & Ando, 2009; Schmidt, 2007). Research suggests that job satisfaction is an important indicator not only of employee well-being and psychological health but also of numerous desirable organizational outcomes and employee behaviours (Lam, Baum, & Pine, 2001; Moura et al., 2009; Zhang & Zheng, 2009). Research has shown that for Chinese employees a harmonious working environment is a significant component fostering their job satisfaction (Lam et al., 2001). In this vein, we thus assume that employees may experience a higher level of job satisfaction if they perceive and sense a higher degree of harmony within their company. This produces the following hypothesis:

**Hypothesis 2:** The degree of harmony an employee perceives within an organization is positively related to their job satisfaction.

The social psychological perspective suggests that attitudes influence behaviour (Ajzen & Fishbein, 1980; Yavas & Bodur, 1999). Ajzen and Fishbein (1980) developed the 'compatibility principle', proposing that an attitude drives behaviour only when the two models are compatible in their actions, target, context, and time. The attitude–behaviour connections are strongest when the attitude is matched specifically or generally to the behaviour. In the light of the attitude–behaviour compatibility, job satisfaction should kindle a general force to engage in (positive or negative) behaviours that express or manifest this attitude (Harrison et al., 2006). According to the Social Exchange Theory, when employees feel satisfied with their jobs, they display OCB reciprocally towards the organization that has benefited them (Chiu & Chen, 2005; Kabasakal et al., 2011). In fact, abundant evidence has found that job satisfaction has robust correlations with employee exhibition of OCB (e.g. Gonzalez & Garazo, 2006; Kabasakal et al., 2011; Rich, Lepine, & Crawford, 2010).

In addition, researchers have examined the indirect mediating effect on OCB of job satisfaction. For instance, Chiu and Chen (2005) report the mediating role of job satisfaction in the relationship between job characteristics and OCB. Gonzalez and Garazo (2006) propose that employee job satisfaction mediates the relationship between organizational service orientation and OCB. As noted, we argue that both variables—harmony and job satisfaction—may have positive relationships with OCB and that the degree of harmony at a workplace may be positively related to individual job satisfaction in China. Following this logic, we further expect that individual job satisfaction will mediate the relationship between the degree of harmonious spirit and OCB. Since a higher level of harmony within an organization may satisfy a Chinese employee, it is likely to further motivate them to be good organizational citizens. Thus, we hypothesize:

**Hypothesis 3:** Individual job satisfaction mediates the relationship between an employee's perception of harmonious spirit and their display of OCBs.

Fig. 5.2 presents our hypothesized framework for this study.

### 5.2.3 Methods

#### 5.2.3.1 Population and Sample

From May to December 2013, we collected data randomly by questionnaire surveys (in Chinese) from the membership lists of HR associations in four

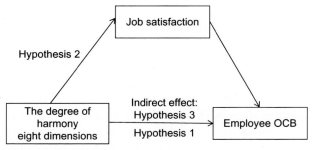

**Fig. 5.2** Hypothesized model of this study.

cities in China: Guangzhou, Shenzhen, Humen, and Dongguang. We first selected 80 private manufacturing companies at random from the lists and telephoned them, of which 50 companies were willing to participate in this study. The sample collection was restricted to full-time employees working in private firms in manufacturing sectors to enhance comparability and to reduce extraneous sources of variation and measurement error (Batt & Colvin, 2011). A total of 1000 questionnaires (20 per firm), accompanied by a note that explained the academic nature of the survey and assured ano-nymity and confidentiality, were distributed to randomly chosen employees by the HR managers. We received 592 usable questionnaires, a response rate of 59.2%. Of these, 40% ($n = 237$) were male and 60% ($n = 355$) were female. A total of 42.4% had less than or equal to 5 years of working expe-rience, 39.3% were 25 or younger, and 19.1% held managerial positions. A total of 60.1% had senior high school or lower diplomas while 39.9% had a bachelor's, a 4-year college, or higher degrees. To assure data validity, we conducted follow-up telephone interviews shortly after about one-third of the completed questionnaires were returned, asking them to indicate their responses to a set of selected questions used in the questionnaire to reconfirm their participation.

### 5.2.3.2 Measures
We integrated three types of measures to examine how the degree of har-mony is related to two employee outcomes: job satisfaction and OCB. The instruments were measured using a six-point Likert-type scale ranging from (1) strongly disagree to (6) strongly agree to the questions to prevent response bias because Chinese people (as do many others, Rowley, 2003) tend to choose the midpoint of the scale regardless of their true feelings or attitudes (Cheng, Jiang, & Riley, 2003). The subsequent analyses used SPSS and LISREL software.

### 5.2.3.3 Degree of Harmony
We referred to Chin (2010) study on harmony in Chinese organizations to measure the degree of harmony that an employee perceives in all aspects. This scale comprised eight factors and 32 items (Cronbach's $a = 0.890$— the reliability value of the aggregated harmony variable): four for harmony of employee with himself or herself (Cronbach's $a = 0.803$); four for har-mony of employees (Cronbach's $a = 0.844$); four for harmony of employee with their team (Cronbach's $a = 924$); four for harmony of employee with their supervisor (Cronbach's $a = 0.896$); four for harmony of employee with

the management system (Cronbach's $a = 0.894$); four for harmony of departments (Cronbach's $a = 0.805$); four for harmony of employee with the highest leader (Cronbach's $a = 0.899$), and four for harmony of internal and external organizations (Cronbach's $a = 0.874$).

### 5.2.3.4 Job Satisfaction
Referring to measures designed by Eisenberger, Cummings, Aremeli, and Lynch (1997), we used a scale consisting of three items to measure an employee's satisfaction with the job ($a = 0.781$). A sample item is: 'I find real enjoyment in my current job'.

### 5.2.3.5 OCB
The boundary between in-role and extra-role behaviours is still the topic of an ongoing debate, particularly on OCB models in different sociocultural environments (e.g. Coyne & Ong, 2007; Gonzalez & Garazo, 2006; Han & Altman, 2010). Thus, referring to the scale developed by Farh et al. (2004), Organ (1988), and Van Dyne et al. (1994), we selected six items of which three pertained to altruism and three to conscientiousness. These were chosen because these two dimensions are less controversial and appear in both Chinese and Western OCB literature. Following Coyne and Ong's (2007) suggestion that the respondent is the only person who knows how much OCB they have actually displayed, we used a self-report measure rather than supervisor or peer ratings. Furthermore, consistent with recent research (e.g. Evans, Davis, & Frink, 2011), OCB was treated as an aggregate-level model (Cronbach's $a = 0.863$). A sample item is: 'I am willing to assist new colleagues to adjust to the work environment'.

### 5.2.3.6 Control Variables
Referring to prior research (Batt & Colvin, 2011; Gong et al., 2010), we included several variables to control for organizational, workforce, and demographic characteristics that may influence employee attitudes towards their organizations. We controlled for workforce size ($>300$ employees $= 1$, $\leq 300$ employees $= 0$) and industrial type (labour-intensive $= 1$, technology and capital-intensive industries $= 0$) using the 2002 version of the Chinese industrial classification. In terms of the demographic variables, we controlled for age (younger than or equal to 25 years old $= 1$, others $= 0$), gender (male $= 0$, female $= 1$), education level (senior high school or lower $= 1$, others $= 0$), work experience (less than or equal to 5 years $= 1$, others $= 0$), and whether they had held a managerial position (management $= 1$, other $= 0$).

### 5.2.3.7 Construct Validity

As noted, Cronbach's $a$ for each construct is above 0.78, indicating adequate reliability. Then we used LISREL 8.7 to test the validity of the constructs following the procedure recommended by Anderson and Gerbing (1988). The CFA (maximum likelihood method) revealed a good model fit for the proposed 10-factor structure (8 factors for the model of harmony, 1 factor for OCB, and 1 for job satisfaction) ($\chi^2_{n=592} = 1756.29$, df $= 701$, $P < .01$; CFI $= 0.98 > 0.90$; NNFI $= 0.98 > 0.90$; SRMR $= 0.04 > 0.08$; RMSEA $= 0.051 > 0.06$). Furthermore, according to Anderson and Gerbing (1988), convergent validity is ensured when items load significantly on their designated latent variables. Table 5.2 lists the CFA results, which presents evidence for convergent validity.

**Table 5.2** CFA Results

| Constructs | Measurement Items | Factor Loadings | t-Value |
|---|---|---|---|
| Satisfaction | I feel satisfied with the accomplishment I get from my job | 0.86*** | 14.51 |
| | I feel satisfied with the praise I get for doing a good job | 0.89*** | 15.65 |
| | I find real enjoyment in my current job | 1.00*** | 17.30 |
| OCB | I cover work assignments for colleagues when needed | 0.59*** | 15.70 |
| | I assist new colleagues to adjust to the work environment | 0.62*** | 17.77 |
| | I help colleagues solve work-related matters | 0.62*** | 16.09 |
| | I keep workplace clean and neat | 0.82*** | 20.32 |
| | I comply with company rules, even when nobody watches | 0.71*** | 17.47 |
| | I take my jobs seriously and rarely make mistakes | 0.68*** | 17.19 |
| Harmony | | | |
| Self-harmony | I maintain good self-discipline | 0.84*** | 11.28 |
| | I cherish work environment | 0.91*** | 20.80 |
| | I strengthen self-cultivation | 0.95*** | 18.88 |
| | I complete assigned jobs | 1.02*** | 21.77 |
| Of employees | Colleagues maintain good relationships outside work | 0.68*** | 14.42 |
| | Colleagues help each other overcome difficulties | 0.74*** | 17.73 |
| | Colleagues maintain a friendly working atmosphere | 1.06*** | 19.48 |
| | Colleagues exercise a fair competition | 0.98*** | 20.91 |

**Table 5.2** CFA Results—cont'd

| Constructs | Measurement Items | Factor Loadings | t-Value |
|---|---|---|---|
| With system | Firm has a fair wage system | 1.09*** | 23.34 |
| | Firm provides good medical insurance | 0.91*** | 18.61 |
| | Firm has a sound welfare system | 1.12*** | 23.34 |
| | Firm has a fair reward system | 1.09*** | 22.70 |
| With direct boss | Direct boss considers performance rather than 'guanxi' in appraisal | 1.06*** | 20.35 |
| | Direct boss allocates rewards impartially | 1.15*** | 24.49 |
| | Direct boss cares subordinates' life outside the office | 1.02*** | 22.09 |
| | Direct boss does not steal contributions from subordinates | 0.99*** | 21.40 |
| Of departments | Firm encourages cross-department cooperation | 0.82*** | 18.17 |
| | Firm encourages employees' job rotation between different departments | 0.88*** | 17.39 |
| | Firm has regular cross-departments meetings for communication | 0.81*** | 15.16 |
| | Firm allocates equal resources to different departments | 1.02*** | 21.39 |
| With firm leader | Leader does not humiliate employees | 1.04*** | 21.03 |
| | Leader understands the capability limits of employees | 1.00*** | 22.48 |
| | Leader listens to employees' different opinions | 1.16*** | 23.75 |
| | Leader empowers employees to work independently | 1.08*** | 23.58 |
| With own team | My team has a cooperative spirit | 1.08*** | 24.82 |
| | My team view our team's common interest as the top priority | 1.05*** | 25.32 |
| | My team does not play politics | 1.00*** | 22.20 |
| | The job roles of all team members are recognized | 1.08*** | 26.43 |
| Of internal and external organizations | My firm competes with rivals following the ethical codes | 0.89*** | 20.92 |
| | My firm shares accurate and timely information with employees | 0.81*** | 18.65 |
| | My firm ensures operations openness to employees | 0.80*** | 18.46 |
| | My firm treats clients and suppliers with honesty and respect | 0.82*** | 20.63 |

Note: *** $P < .001$.

## 5.2.4 Results

The means, standard deviations, and correlations of the variables included in our analysis are reported in Table 5.3. This confirms that there were no outliers or major violations of regression assumptions. Following the aggregation method to reduce the number of parameters to be estimated (Little, Cunningham, & Shahar, 2002), we further averaged the eight sub-dimensions of harmony to form one composite score indicator to test our hypotheses.

To examine our hypotheses, we adopted the SEM approach suggested by Mackinnon et al. (2002) to build a mediation model. SEM, which can be used to control for measurement error, provides information on the overall goodness of fit relating to the hypothesized model and tests multiple mediators (Brown, 1997; Mackinnon et al., 2002). As sketched by Mackinnon et al. (2002), the logic behind testing for mediating effects using SEM resembles that of using regression analysis. More specifically, the significance of mediation could be examined by comparing the fit for the direct effect model with that of the predictor–mediator–outcome model (with and without the direct path from the predictor and the outcome constrained to zero). A full mediation would be supported if the model with the direct path between the predictor and the outcome shows a better fit (Lu et al., 2010; Zhou et al., 2010).

In the light of the procedures above, we tested our hypothesized model. Similar to a large body of precedents (e.g. Lu et al., 2010; Stobbeleir, Ashford, & Buyens, 2011; Zhou et al., 2010), we first estimated a baseline model as the full mediation (see the baseline model in Table 5.4), which did not have direct paths from harmony to OCB. The results show that this model fitted our data adequately ($\chi^2_{n=592} = 82.369$, df$=22$, $P<.001$; CFI$=0.923>0.90$; IFI$=0.919>0.90$; RMSEA$=0.068<0.08$). Next, following the method advocated by Anderson and Gerbing (1988), we tested a series of nested models against our baseline model through sequential chi-square tests with the parameter constraints of interest in our research. In Model A, we examined the partial mediation model in which the path from harmony to OCB was added to the baseline model. As shown in Table 5.4, the chi-square difference between the baseline model and Model A ($\Delta\chi^2=4.322$, $P<.05$) is not significant. Despite this, we also see that Model A may be preferred, since it is still slightly better than the baseline model ($\chi^2_{n=592} = 78.045$, df$=21$, $P<.001$; CFI$=0.927$; IFI$=0.924$; RMSEA$=0.068$).

**Table 5.3** Hypothesis Test of Alternative Models

| | Mean | SD | 1 | 2 | 3 | 4 | 5 | 6 | 7 | 8 | 9 | 10 | 11 | 12 | 13 | 14 | 15 | 16 |
|---|---|---|---|---|---|---|---|---|---|---|---|---|---|---|---|---|---|---|
| 1 Gender | 0.5997 | 0.49038 | 1 | | | | | | | | | | | | | | | |
| 2 Tenure | 0.4240 | 0.49461 | 20.185** | 1 | | | | | | | | | | | | | | |
| 3 Age | 0.3926 | 0.48873 | 0.198** | 20.431** | 1 | | | | | | | | | | | | | |
| 4 Educational level | 0.6010 | 0.49011 | 0.053 | 20.104* | 0.268** | 1 | | | | | | | | | | | | |
| 5 Job position | 0.1909 | 0.39333 | 20.261** | 0.114** | 20.144** | 20.026 | 1 | | | | | | | | | | | |
| 6 Industrial type | 0.0524 | 0.22295 | 0.006 | 20.002 | 0.028 | 20.072 | 0.059 | 1 | | | | | | | | | | |
| 7 Firm size | 0.3678 | 0.48261 | 20.056 | 20.071 | 0.158** | 20.263** | 0.031 | 0.025 | 1 | | | | | | | | | |
| 8 Self-harmony | 4.3799 | 1.06619 | 0.008 | 20.031 | 20.003 | 0.040 | 0.013 | 0.054 | 0.045 | 1 | | | | | | | | |
| 9 Harmony of colleagues | 4.3456 | 0.99190 | 0.019 | 20.052 | 0.086* | 20.011 | 0.009 | 0.056 | 0.029 | 0.554** | 1 | | | | | | | |
| 10 With firm system | 3.8544 | 1.14332 | 20.016 | 20.021 | 0.054 | 0.039 | 0.016 | 0.115** | 0.075 | 0.395** | 0.446** | 1 | | | | | | |
| 11 With supervisor. | 4.1707 | 1.15320 | 0.028 | 20.040 | 0.075 | 0.023 | 20.015 | 0.061 | 0.055 | 0.360** | 0.524** | 0.589** | 1 | | | | | |
| 12 Of departments | 3.9806 | 1.00483 | 0.026 | 20.057 | 0.130** | 0.089* | 0.066 | 0.079 | 0.123** | 0.408** | 0.456** | 0.624** | 0.611** | 1 | | | | |
| 13 With firm leader | 4.0780 | 1.13584 | 20.002 | 0.044 | 0.051 | 20.020 | 0.031 | 0.061 | 0.000 | 0.266** | 0.405** | 0.582** | 0.663** | 0.591** | 1 | | | |
| 14 With team | 4.1852 | 1.11174 | 0.002 | 20.093* | 0.056 | 20.027 | 20.010 | 0.070 | 0.014 | 0.423** | 0.564** | 0.561** | 0.602** | 0.611** | 0.553** | 1 | | |
| 15 Of inside and out-side organizations | 4.3772 | 0.95267 | 0.031 | 20.069 | 0.124** | 0.144** | 20.066 | 0.079 | 0.072 | 0.477** | 0.536** | 0.536** | 0.556** | 0.574** | 0.503** | 0.595** | 1 | |
| 16 OCB | 4.8043 | 0.75427 | 20.035 | 0.006 | 0.027 | 0.072 | 0.063 | 20.048 | 0.001 | 0.278** | 0.407** | 0.361** | 0.385** | 0.432** | 0.379** | 0.462** | 0.521** | 1 |
| 17 Job satisfaction | 3.8481 | 1.08157 | 20.099* | 0.074 | 20.111** | 20.026 | 0.084* | 0.077 | 20.053 | 0.255** | 0.307** | 0.549** | 0.438** | 0.487** | 0.461** | 0.457** | 0.358** | 0.460** |

** Correlation is significant at the 0.01 level (two tailed); * Correlation is significant at the 0.05 level (two tailed).

**Table 5.4** Hypothesis Test of Alternative Models

|                | $\chi^2$ | df | $e\chi^2$ | df | IFI | CFI | RMSEA |
|----------------|----------|-----|-----------|-----|-------|-------|-------|
| Baseline model | 82.369   | 22 | –         | –   | 0.919 | 0.923 | 0.068 |
| Model A        | 78.045   | 21 | 4.322     | 1   | 0.924 | 0.927 | 0.068 |
| Model B        | 373.527  | 22 | 291.158** | 0   | 0.550 | 0.530 | 0.164 |
| Model C        | 118.814  | 22 | 36.445**  | 0   | 0.876 | 0.871 | 0.086 |
| Model D        | 96.117   | 22 | 13.748*   | 0   | 0.901 | 0.905 | 0.076 |

Note: $N = 202$. Baseline model, full mediation (no direct paths from the predictor to outcome); Model A, partial mediation model (the path from the predictor to outcome was added); Model B, direct effects model (the path from the predictor to mediator was constrained to zero); Models C, nonmediation models (the path from the mediator to outcome was constrained to zero); Models D, reverse causality models: OCB! job satisfaction! harmony. Significance levels: * $P < .05$; ** $P < .01$.

Model B is a direct effect model, assuming that there is no causal relationship between the degree of harmony and job satisfaction, as job satisfaction may just contribute to OCB in the same way that the degree of harmony does. Model C is a nonmediation model, assuming that job satisfaction may only play a trivial role in enhancing OCB. Model D treats OCB as an antecedent of the degree of harmony, which in turn becomes the predictor of job satisfaction. As seen in Table 5.4, the findings reveal that the fit indices for Models B, C, and D were not acceptable. Overall, the results suggest that the partial mediation Model A best fits our data in terms of our conceptual framework.

### 5.2.4.1 Assessment of Hypotheses

Hypotheses 1 and 2 state that the degree of harmony is positively related to employee job satisfaction and OCB. As demonstrated in Fig. 5.3, the paths from harmony to OCB ($\beta = 1.136$, $P < .001$) and to job satisfaction ($\beta = 0.882$, $P < .001$) are both significant. Thus, hypotheses 1 and 2 are strongly supported.

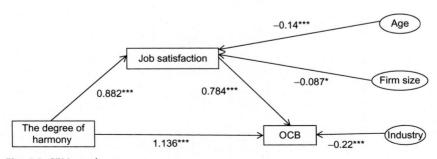

**Fig. 5.3** SEM results.

Hypothesis 3 states that job satisfaction mediates the impact of harmony on OCB. As shown in Fig. 5.3, the direct path from the degree of harmony ($\beta = 1.136$, $P < .001$) to OCB is still significant, while the indirect path from harmony via job satisfaction to OCB is significant (from harmony to job satisfaction: $\beta = 0.882$, $P < .001$; from satisfaction to OCB: $\beta = 0.784$, $P < .001$). Hence, we posited that job satisfaction partially mediates the effect of the degree of harmony on employee OCB. Thus, Hypothesis 3 is strongly supported as well.

In terms of the control variables, industry type is significantly related to OCB while firm size and employee age are significantly related to job satisfaction. In summary, the results of SEM illustrate that Hypotheses 1–3 are fully supported.

## 5.2.5 Discussion

The empirical findings in our study lend support to our hypotheses. First, the results suggest that the degree of harmony an employee perceives within a Chinese organization is significantly related to their job satisfaction and OCB. Second, findings are consistent with the predicted mediation model that job satisfaction positively mediates the relationship between the degree of harmony and OCB. In addition, the positive relationship between job satisfaction and OCB is observable as well. Overall, our main research questions have been answered.

### 5.2.5.1 Contributions

Three unique theoretical contributions emerge from our study. First, we deal with the relationship between a model of Chinese harmony and the measures of OCB and job satisfaction from Western theories, thus responding to calls for developing context-sensitive indigenous models and analysing the country-specific implications (Rowley, 2016; Tsui, 2007; Whetten, 2009). More specifically, we fill a research gap that calls for introducing valid measures on the effect of cultural diversity on HRM in China because existing Western theoretical HRM models do not always consider differences between Eastern and Western cultures and the dynamic nature of the Chinese cultural context was not explored fully (Stone & Stone-Romero, 2007; Zhu, Thomson, & Cieri, 2008). Therefore, we contribute to the HRM literature by offering a useful theoretical foundation for future research that seeks to probe into the effect of China's harmony-oriented culture on HR practices.

Second, our results confirm that the degree of harmony is an important predictor of employees' positive attitude (job satisfaction) and behaviour (OCB). This echoes the divergence perspectives in HRM (Rowley, 1997a, 1997b; Rowley & Benson, 2002, 2003) by showing that cultural contextual factors such as harmony indeed play an important role in swaying people's attitude and behaviour at work.

Third, our findings suggest that the degree of harmony works indirectly through job satisfaction to OCB, which gives an answer to the appeal for examining the mediating effects of cultural values on employee outcomes (e.g. Gelfand et al., 2007; Tsui et al., 2007). By exploring the mechanisms within the variables of harmony—OCB and job satisfaction—we shed some light on testing the intervening effect of job satisfaction in this values–behaviour (harmonious culture–OCB) relationship. The findings also implicitly indicate that if an employee's job satisfaction is low, a higher level of harmony at the workplace may not be effectively translated into exhibition of OCB.

Fourth, the significant correlations reported between the two dependent variables lend support to previous studies (refer to Table 5.3 and Fig. 5.3) on related topics. These include the close associations between OCB and job satisfaction (Chiu & Chen, 2005; Gonzalez & Garazo, 2006; Rich et al., 2010).

Our results have important managerial implications. As employee continue to become less emotionally attached to organizations during the global economic recession, our research, which adds new insights into the linkages between the degree of harmony and OCB, as well as job satisfaction within Chinese organizations. This can guide firms in China to encourage positive employee attitudes and behaviours by promoting the level of harmony in the workplace. China, as a potential model for EEs (Bruton et al., 2010; Ma & Trigo, 2011), has drawn attention for studying how its unique institutional differences and cultural characteristics present a challenge for MNCs operating there. In this case, our findings offer guidelines for MNCs eager to effectively manage Chinese employees and facilitate non-Chinese managers to realize the values of harmony and how to elevate it in the Chinese context.

### 5.2.5.2 Limitation and Future Research

Despite a number of potential research avenues suggested by our study, its limitations and constraints should be noted. First, to reduce extraneous sources of variation, our survey focused on collecting data in Chinese private firms in manufacturing. However, having data from more types of organizations would contribute to the generalizability of the findings. Since numerous MNCs in China also have many Chinese employees, future research could include a broader business context and take MNCs into consideration as well. Second, the subjects of our study were confined to full-time workers from four cities in Guangdong province. Future research could incorporate more diversified samples from different regions in China. Third, self-report measures of OCB may have resulted in an upward bias. Since the OCB rating conducted by supervisors may be even more biased than self-report measures (Kuvaas & Dysvik, 2010), future research could gather both self-report and supervisor or peer measures simultaneously to to rule out the common method variances.

## 5.2.6 Conclusion

While we found positive news concerning boosting the degree of harmony at the workplace, our study also finds negative implications, especially in the practical business context. For instance, our study discovered that Chinese (Asian) employees appear to place a relatively strong emphasis on harmony (Hofstede et al., 2010; Yu & Zaheer, 2010), with a tendency to avoid conflict. However, for organizational success, conflict is not always harmful. There are times when conflict benefits a group's performance.

Researchers express doubts about the existing boundary between in-role and extra-role behaviours because it can be difficult to differentiate these behaviours (Gonzalez & Garazo, 2006; Van Dyne et al., 1994). This has also led to ongoing debates on the definition of OCB dimensions since its components may be inconsistent across time, employees, organizations, and situations (e.g. Farh et al., 2004; Han & Altman, 2010). To a certain extent, our research supported this argument. While the concept of Chinese harmony in the workplace seems to reflect some extra-role behaviours among employees, those may nonetheless be considered as in-role behaviours and not OCBs in China. From a Chinese perspective, an enterprise may be not only a nexus of contracts between the individuals and the firm or a pure economic entity, but also a community with abundant inter- and intrafirm networks of employees beyond the exchange of labour for pay. Thus, organization behaviour issues, especially those concerning broader contextual or cultural factors, need to be explored further in future research.

In short, understanding cultural roots and their dynamic properties in different nations leads to a better understanding of the reasons behind the success and failure of international organizations. Our study, which formulated a new context-effect model of the relationship between employee behaviour and the Chinese cultural orientation, harmony, thus serves as a response to the need for more research on managing global HRs (Adler, 2008; Stone & Stone-Romero, 2007). Many researchers highlight the scarcity of Asia-originated behavioural theory and so encourage Asian scholars to discover the heritage of classical Chinese wisdom, for instance to fill research holes (Tsui, 2007; Whetten, 2009). The underlying goal is to move towards a true sense of the 'melting pot' by integrating Asian ideas into the essential notions of US organizational theories (Rhee, 2010). Our study makes a substantial contribution towards this goal.

## 5.3 HARMONY AS A MEANS TO ENHANCE AFFECTIVE COMMITMENT IN CHINESE ORGANIZATIONS

### 5.3.1 Introduction

Uncertainties and risks in today's postfinancial crisis environment are changing employment landscapes, weakening employees' physical, administrative, and temporal attachments to organizations (Grant, Dutton, & Rosso, 2008). Accordingly, one of the most critical challenges for firms is to seek effective approaches to cultivate employee affective commitment (AC). This is an employee's attitude of emotional dedication and psychological attachment to, and voluntary identification with, organizations (Johnson, Chang, & Yang, 2010; Meyer et al., 2012).

AC entails an acceptance and internalization of the other party's goals and values, a willingness to exert effort on that party's behalf, and a strong emotional attachment to that party (Johnson et al., 2010). AC is widely recognized as a fundamental factor for organizations to enhance employee retention, particularly in industries which struggle to retain employees (Grant et al., 2008; Veitch & Cooper-Thomas, 2009). Owing to the high-speed economic growth coupled with the lack of skills training and vocational education in the past three decades, China has had unfulfilled rising demand for skilled workers in spite of its population exceeding 1.3 billion people. Insufficient skilled workers were found to be one of the biggest barriers to expansion for numerous MNCs as well as domestic firms in China (Davies & Liang, 2011). Moreover, the one-child policy since the 1980s to curb population further exacerbated skilled labour shortages

(Xiao & Cooke, 2012). These crucial facts show an imperative need for firms in China to seek out feasible ways to strengthen employees' AC to their organizations.

A plethora of studies have demonstrated the great impact of cultural differences on employee AC (e.g. Adler, 2008; Meyer et al., 2012; Sidle, 2009; Yu & Egri, 2005). However, as far as Chinese values are concerned, previous research provides ambiguous results. For instance, using the same scales on Chinese traditionality, Zhang and Zheng (2009) examine a positive relationship between Chinese traditionality and employee's AC, while Farh et al. (2007) do not show a direct link between them.

Despite the controversy about Chinese cultural variables, many scholars suggest that the pursuit of harmony, as a unique cultural disposition originating with the Chinese philosophical text, *Yijing* (Fung, 1948; Zhou, 2004), symbolizes the desired means as well as the ultimate goal/end in establishing and maintaining all kinds of relationships in the Chinese context (Chen & Miller, 2010; Chin & Mao, 2010; Han & Altman, 2010). In other words, harmony can be regarded as a prominent representative of cultural variables in China.

However, compelling evidence indicates that the concept of harmony is subject to East–West cultural differences (Leung et al., 2011; Wang & Juslin, 2009). From a philosophical angle, the development of the ideal of harmony in ancient Greek philosophy is based on a linear progressive model with a preset order as a science, whereas the traditional Chinese concept of harmony is best understood as a comprehensive but somewhat abstract expression of the harmonization process, as an art rather than a science (e.g. Leung et al., 2011; Li, 2008; Tung, 2006). The detailed comparison is shown in the next section. Given that harmony is considered as 'the software of Chinese mindset' (Hofstede et al., 2010), we assume that Chinese employee AC to firms may be significantly connected to perceptions of the degree of harmony within workplaces.

To examine the foregoing argument, our study investigates the relationship between the degree of harmony and AC. Furthermore, given that AC is a robust predictor of work behaviour (Grant et al., 2008; Harrison et al., 2006), we explore the mediating mechanism of AC on the relationship between the degree of harmony and compliance behaviour as well. Also, whether the business model fitting traditional scientific logic is ill-suited to a far more complex environment nowadays and an art-based view may provide a new lens from which to approach the world is discussed (Adler, 2006; Weick, 2007). For example, the Chinese notion of harmony seems inclined more to an art than to a science, as mentioned earlier. In response to this, research (Chin, 2012; Chin & Mao, 2010) developed an indigenous model that characterizes the abstract notion of harmony derived from the *Yijing* to assess the level of harmony at workplaces in China. Considering the above, we choose to ground our study in an art-based perspective, employing the foregoing model to measure the degree of organizational harmony.

Our research yields three contributions. First, we build on the Western art-based perspective to probe the links between a predominant cultural variable 'harmony' and employee outcomes which projects a revolutionary way of East–West integrative thinking. Second, we contribute to the literature by providing a useful theoretical foundation for future research to examine the effect of Chinese cultural codes on employee outcomes, thus responding to recent calls for analysing the country-specific implications to further develop context-sensitive theories in the field of HRM (Rowley, 2016). Third, our study particularly helps non-Chinese managers in China to gain a better understanding of how to employ harmony as a means to effectively enhance Chinese employee emotional attachment and loyalty to organizations.

## 5.3.2 Theoretical Foundations and Hypotheses

### 5.3.2.1 East–West Cultural Differences of the Notion of Harmony: Art-Based vs Science-Based Views

While the Sections 5.1 and 5.2.2 have highlighted the importance of Chinese harmonious culture in affecting workplace behaviour and attitude, here we further elucidate the critical East–West cultural differences existing in the concept of harmony (Leung et al., 2011; Li, 2008; McElhatton & Jackson, 2012)—which fortifies the rationale underpinning the use of an art-based perspective to decode how the Yin–Yang dynamic changes characterize Chinese harmony.

According to ancient Greek philosophy, harmony is a kind of rational order established in numbers. A number is sequentially linear in nature and the perfectly rhythmic alternation of odd and even is an unmistakably linear progression (Franklin, 2002). The concept of harmony is often defined as 'a perfect unity of many mixed (elements)', 'a satisfactory agreement between disagreeing (elements)', or 'perfect accordance of the discordant', which is based on the premise of solving conflict of opposing forces in the world (Li, 2008). Hence, the Western ideal of harmony with its strong quantitative tendency from the very beginning is significantly related to the scientific logic of integration, starting with the recognition of contradictions or conflicts and then moving on towards the final goal of seeking a satisfactory reconciliation of contradictions (Franklin, 2002; Leung et al., 2011; Li, 2008).

In contrast, Chinese classical philosophies do not suggest that people pursue a perfect scientific model for 'absolutely' resolving contradictions or conflicts as does Western philosophical thinking. Rather, it tends to embrace paradoxical strategies facing inevitable contradictions in life (McElhatton & Jackson, 2012; Li, 2012). Li (2012), putting forward an integrated framework based on the Yin–Yang balance derived from the eight-trigrams of *Yijing* to illustrate a distinctive cognitive frame of the Chinese paradox. Research compares the differences of reasoning 'contradictions' between the Greek and Chinese philosophies. The Western philosophic logic aims to find an ultimate noncontradictory solution to scientific inquiries of contradictions while the Chinese philosophic thinking encourages people to treat all contradictions as permanent yet relative, thus aiming to maintain a permanently contradictory situation where the two opposites of Yin and Yang in a contradiction entity are acting as a duality to present the relative and tentative forms of contradictions (Fung, 1948; Li, 2012; Zhou, 2004). More specifically, the ultimate goal for the Chinese to cope with contradictions is not an ideal noncontradictory solution, but a 'balanced yet continuously dynamic status of harmony, a constantly changing process of harmonization.' These in-built ambiguous, dynamic, and dualistic qualities embedded in the Chinese notion of harmony characterize the unusual art-oriented nature of Chinese culture (Tung, 2006).

In summary, the development of the ideal of harmony in Western ideology is built upon a science-based linear model with a presupposed, perfect sequence. In contrast, the Chinese concept of harmony is based on an art-based abstract expression with a strong qualitative tendency and multidimensionally dynamic pattern.

### 5.3.2.2 The Eight-Trigram Model and Harmony: An Art-Based Perspective

Following the above discussions, the eight-trigram model of *Yijing* seems to be the most appropriate framework to articulate the development of the Chinese ideal of harmony given that its art-oriented essence is multidimensionally dynamic, analogous to a constantly changing process of harmonization (e.g. Chin, 2012; Chin & Mao, 2010; Huang, 2008; Li, 2008; Zhou, 2004). As noted in Section 5.2.2, scholars (Chin, 2012; Chin & Mao, 2010) followed Taylor and Ladkin (2009) with an art-based approach, utilizing imagination to extract semiotic insights of the eight trigrams and distilled profound implications beyond the ancient text of *Yijing* to characterize the notion of Chinese harmony in the workplace. Their studies proposed an indigenous eight-factor model that displays a similar thought pattern with the eight-trigram model to measure the degree of harmony a Chinese employee perceives at work—which concretizes the rather abstract Chinese concept of harmony. Hence, we also adopted this indigenous model to measure the degree of harmony here. While Table 5.1 has addressed how the eight trigrams decipher the Chinese concept of harmony, we further listed the measurement items of all eight factors in Table 5.5.

**Table 5.5** The Measurement of Chinese Management

| Trigram | Items |
|---|---|
| ☷<br>Kun (Earth) | **Factor 1: harmony of employee with himself**<br>Employees cherish working environment<br>Employees maintain good self-discipline<br>Employees are responsible for job completion<br>Employees are aware of their own duty |
| ☴<br>Sun (Wind) | **Factor 2: harmony of employees**<br>Colleagues keep good relationship outside work<br>Colleagues help each other to overcome difficulties<br>Colleagues maintain a nice working atmosphere<br>Colleagues enhance communication to resolve disagreement |
| ☲<br>Li (Fire) | **Factor 3: harmony of employee with his team**<br>The roles of all team members are well recognized<br>Team members don't play politics<br>Members show cooperative spirit<br>Members view their team's common interest as the top priority |
| ☱<br>Dui (Lake) | **Factor 4: harmony of employee with his supervisor**<br>Direct boss allocates rewards to subordinates impartially<br>Direct boss appraises subordinate performance by competence rather than 'guanxi'<br>Direct boss cares subordinates' life outside the office<br>Direct boss has ethical behaviours |
| ☶<br>Gen (Mountain) | **Factor 5: harmony of employee with management system**<br>Company has a good pay plan<br>Company has a sound welfare system<br>Company has fair appraisal systems<br>Company has clear regulations<br>**Factor 6: harmony of departments** |

**Table 5.5** The Measurement of Chinese Management—cont'd

| Trigram | Items |
|---|---|
| ☵<br>Kan (Water) | Firm has regular cross-dept. meetings to communicate<br>Firm allocates equal resources to all departments<br>Firm emphasizes on cross-dept. cooperative programmes<br>Firm encourages job rotation between different depts |
| ☳<br>Zhen (Thunder) | **Factor 7: harmony of grassroots employee with the highest leader**<br>Leader empowers followers to work independently<br>Leader is willing to listen to different opinions<br>Leader understands the limit of individual capabilities<br>Leader does not humiliate followers |
| ☰<br>Qian (Heaven) | **Factor 8: harmony of internal and external organizations**<br>Firm commits to comply with the codes of ethics in business competition<br>Firm ensures operations openness to employees<br>Firm shares accurate and timely information throughout supply chain<br>Firm embraces transparency in reporting |

### 5.3.2.3 AC

In the wake of organizational downsizing induced by the global recession, the concept of organizational commitment that reflects the special bonds between individuals and organizations remains a compelling and significant topic for scholars in the field of HRM to consider. It is recognized that a healthy and committed workforce is crucial to enhancing organizational performance and competitiveness (Brooks & Wallace, 2006; Xiao & Cooke, 2012). Notwithstanding different conceptualizations of the organizational commitment used in the literature, important for HRM practices is the concept of AC. AC has been found to be the most consistent and strongest predictor of positive organizational outcomes, reflected in a desire to see the organization succeed in its goals and a feeling of pride at being part of the organization (Tornikoski, 2011; Yu & Egri, 2005). Therefore, we specifically focus on AC in our study.

AC mainly involves feelings of intrinsic motivation and self-determination and thus has stronger relationships with task performance and OCB than do normative commitment and continuance commitment (Brooks & Wallace, 2006; Grant et al., 2008; Johnson et al., 2010; Meyer, Stanley, Herscovitch, & Topolnytsky, 2002). AC, as a strong belief in terms of accepting and internalizing organizational goals, characterizes a

critical employee attitude that predicts a variety of employee behavioral out-
comes, ranging from decreased absenteeism and turnover intention to
increased prosocial organizational behaviour and job performance (e.g.
Brooks & Wallace, 2006; Fischer & Mansell, 2009; Harrison et al., 2006;
Johnson et al., 2010; Meyer et al., 2002; Riketta & Van Dick, 2005;
Williamson, Burnett, & Bartol, 2009).

Given that Allen and Meyer's (1990) three-component model of commitment (affective, continuance, and normative commitment) arguably
dominates relevant research, a plethora of studies measure AC referring to
their seminal eight-item scale or the revised version of the six-item scale
by Meyer, Allen, and Smith (1993) (e.g. Boxall, Ang, & Bartram, 2011;
Eisinga, Teelken, & Doorewaard, 2010; Grant et al., 2008; Tornikoski,
2011; Veitch & Cooper-Thomas, 2009; Yu & Egri, 2005). The original
eight-item AC measurement is composed of four items reflecting the positive feelings of employees towards their organizations such as: 'I really feel as
if this organization's' problems are my own' and four reversed items such as:
'I don't feel emotionally attached to this organization' while the revised version eliminates two reversed items. However, some scholars argue that one
item: 'I would be very happy to spend the rest of my career with the organization' of the AC scale by Allen and Meyer's (1990) and Meyer et al.
(1993) may contaminate the commitment measures because this item content overlaps a behaviour referent reflecting turnover intention rather than
the attitude or feeling of AC to the organization (Grant et al., 2008;
Pittinsky & Shih, 2004). Taking their suggestions into consideration, we
therefore excluded this reversed item and selected three of the rest of the
five items from Meyer et al. (1993) AC scale.

Meyer et al. (2002) confirm the strong psychometric properties of both
the above-mentioned eight- and six-item AC scales in their meta-analyses
and point out the importance of further examining cross-cultural invariance from the three-component commitment model derived from US
concepts. Sparked by this appeal, evidence of cross-cultural research shows
relatively small cross-cultural differences in three dimensions (Fischer &
Mansell, 2009; Meyer et al., 2012) and that, compared to the other two
dimensions, the AC dimension might be less susceptible to cultural influences (Wasti, 2003). Eisinga et al. (2010) use samples of university faculty
employees from six European countries, revealing that all three components of commitment exhibited strict factorial invariance outside the
United States. Despite the lack of research focusing specifically on testing
the cross-cultural invariance of the Western AC measurements by Allen

and Meyer (1990) in China, their indicators have been widely adopted in the Chinese context (e.g. Chen & Francesco, 2003; Fischer & Mansell, 2009) and were employed to investigate the mediating effect of Chinese traditionality on the association between AC and job satisfaction (Zhang & Zheng, 2009). Considering these arguments, the nature of the AC measure developed in the Western context seems to be etic rather than emic and therefore appropriate to be applied to link a Chinese notion (harmony) with a Western concept (AC) in HRM practices.

Culture as mental software (Hofstede et al., 2010) incorporating values, norms, and socially constructed realities is expected to significantly influence employee attitude towards their organizations. A large body of the literature has identified the great impact of cultural variables on employee attitude and behaviour at work (e.g. Adler, 2008; Sidle, 2009). Following this dominant view, it is reasonable to assume that AC levels differ across cultural groups (Fischer & Mansell, 2009; Wasti, 2003) and, more specifically, are susceptible to national cultural values (Zhang & Zheng, 2009). For instance, Randall (1993) argues that AC levels are higher in collectivist cultures than in individualistic cultures. The AC degrees of North American, West European, and Asian employees were found to be different by several studies (Fischer & Mansell, 2009; Meyer et al., 2002, 2012). Additionally, while most researchers agree on the significant association between AC and turnover, Fischer and Mansell (2009) show contradictory findings—that lower turnover among Japanese workers does not coincide with higher AC.

In the light of the arguments above, the effect of national culture is confirmed to be significantly related to the AC level despite the ambiguous results reported in the literature. As far as Chinese cultural variables go, employing the questionnaire derived from the 1987 Chinese Value Survey, Yu and Egri (2005) found that the Chinese cultural value of 'human-heartedness' was positively related to AC, while 'Confucian work dynamism', which emphasizes a future orientation as well as organizational identity and loyalty, was not significantly related to AC. Additionally, as mentioned earlier, using the identical scales of Chinese traditionality designed by Farh, Earley, and Lin (1997) and Zhang and Zheng (2009) discovered a positive relationship between Chinese traditionality and employee AC, while Farh et al. (2007) could not find the direct effect of Chinese traditionality on AC.

Since China is undergoing significant sociocultural transformation, its workforce values are in a complex scenario and increasingly diverse, ranging from traditionalist Chinese to those of the more DEs with a strong international cultural influence (Ralston et al., 2006). In this vein, although the construct of traditionality rooted in Confucianism is an indigenous cultural variable (Farh et al., 1997, 2007), it may not be satisfactory for delineating—in a way that can be communicated—the prominent cultural value orientations in current Chinese society. Comparatively, the cultural variable of harmony, which reflects the greatest values in both contemporary Chinese ideology and traditional Confucianism (Fung, 1948; Zhou, 2004), seems be more suitable for characterizing China's cultural values orientations.

Taken together, it is plausible to assume that the degree of harmony at the workplace may be particularly important for a Chinese employee to perform AC. Therefore, we suggest:

> **Hypothesis 1:** The level of harmony is positively related to individual AC to a Chinese organization.

### 5.3.2.4 Compliance Behaviour

The social psychological perspective indicates that attitudes influence behaviour (Ajzen & Fishbein, 1980). According to Ajzen and Fishbein's (1980) compatibility principle, an attitude impels behaviour only when the two constructs are compatible in their action, target, context, and time. Furthermore, the attitude–behaviour connection will become the strongest when the attitude is matched in specificity or generality to particular behaviour. Following the logic of this attitude–behaviour compatibility, AC as a potent indicator of job attitude is very likely to kindle a general force driving employees to perform specific (positive or negative) behaviours that are significantly related to AC (Harrison et al., 2006).

Compliance behaviour is often discussed in the OCB literature under different labels, including obedience and the following rules (e.g. Boxall et al., 2011; Den Hartog, De Hoogh, & Keegan, 2007). In general, compliance characterizes employee internalization and acceptance of organizational rules and procedures as well as adherence to and loyal compliance with them, even when there is no one watching or monitoring their behaviour (Boxall et al., 2011; Podsakoff et al., 2000). On the basis of the literature, Den Hartog et al. (2007) developed a three-item scale to measure compliance behaviour. Using their measurement, Boxall et al. (2011) discovered that employee compliance behaviour is a key factor linking HRM practices to employee cost-effective performance given that compliance helps employees to avoid being tardy, wasting company resources, and working as efficiently as possible. Many organizations are endeavouring to restructure and re-engineer to reduce costs and boost efficiency. Firms need to ensure employee compliance with changes. Therefore, we expect that employees with high levels of AC and experiencing high degrees of harmony within organizations may perform more compliance behaviours. This produces our next hypothesis:

> **Hypothesis 2a:** Individual AC positively relates to Chinese employee compliance behaviour.

> **Hypothesis 2b:** The level of harmony is positively related to individual compliance behaviour in a Chinese organization.

As noted, we argue that the 'degree of harmony' variable may have a positive relationship with AC, and AC may have a positive relationship with compliance behaviour. Following this logic, we further expect that the mediation effect of individual AC on the relationship between harmony and compliance behaviour may also exist. Thus, we hypothesize:

> **Hypothesis 3:** Individual AC mediates the positive relationship between the degree of harmony and employee compliance behaviour in a Chinese organization.

## 5.3.3 Methods

### 5.3.3.1 Sample Selection

About 50% of FDI into China has been in the manufacturing sector since the 1990s, making it vital in promoting fast economic growth over the past three decades, and China has the world's largest workforce. Thus, it is particularly suitable for investigating HR-related issues (Zhu, Cooper, Fan, & De Cieri, 2013). To ensure the clearness and correctness of the measures used in our research, we conducted in-depth interviews with several HR experts from China's manufacturing industry prior to conducting our formal survey. In these interviews, our hypotheses were presented and discussed at length. Their feedback was that the hypotheses were logical and consistent with their observations of the institutional setting.

Given that the Pearl River Delta region of Guangdong province is Southern China's manufacturing hub and has been the most densely populated area with a variety of migrant workers in China, collecting data from this region may help to obtain demographic diversification of our sample. Our survey was carried out between May and December 2013. We distributed 1000 questionnaires to randomly selected participants of 80 manufacturing firms (about 100–200 participants per firm), according to the membership lists of HR associations of the three largest manufacturing cities with the largest migrant labour force in the Pearl River Delta: GZ, Shenzhen, and Dongguang (ranked by GDP as the first, second, and fourth competitive cities, respectively (Chin, 2015). We also constrained the sample collection to full-time employees working in private firms in manufacturing to enhance comparability and to reduce extraneous sources of variation and measurement error (Batt & Colvin, 2011). Each questionnaire was accompanied by a note explaining the academic nature of the survey and assuring anonymity and confidentiality. In the end, we received 596 usable replies, a response rate of 59.6%. To assure data validity, we conducted follow-up telephone interviews shortly after the completed questionnaires were returned—about one-third were examined. On the telephone, we asked respondents to indicate their responses to a set of selected questions used in the questionnaire to reconfirm their participation.

Of the respondents, some 38.9% ($n = 232$) were male, 61.1% ($n = 364$) were female, and 64% had $<5$ years working experience. In all, 59.7% had senior high school or lower diplomas while 39.7% had a bachelor's, a 4-year college, or higher degrees. In total, 38.9% were 25 years old or younger, 46.8% were between 26 and 35 years old, and 13.7% were above 35. Their occupational backgrounds were: management (16.1%), technician/engineering (12.6%), marketing/sales (16.9%), administration/finance (19.3%), and manufacturing/others (33.9%).

### 5.3.3.2 Measures

We integrated three types of measures into our questionnaire to examine how the degree of harmony is related to two employee outcomes: AC and compliance behaviour. The instruments were measured using a six-point Likert-type scale ranging from (1) strongly disagree to (6) strongly agree. This was partly to prevent response bias because Chinese people (as do others, Rowley, 2003) tend to choose the midpoint of the scale regardless of their true feelings or attitudes (Cheng et al., 2003). The subsequent analyses used SPSS and LISREL software.

## The Degree of Harmony

As noted earlier, we adopted the harmony model developed by Chin and Mao (2010) to measure the level of harmony. This scale comprised eight factors, including 46 items in total (Cronbach's $\alpha = 0.971$), six items for harmony of employee self-harmony (Cronbach's $\alpha = 0.852$), with: six for harmony with employees (Cronbach's $\alpha = 0.894$), five for harmony with teams (Cronbach's $\alpha = 0.893$), five for harmony with supervisors (Cronbach's $\alpha = 0.894$), six for harmony with the management system (Cronbach's $\alpha = 0.901$), five for harmony with departments (Cronbach's $\alpha = 0.839$), six for harmony with the highest leader (Cronbach's $\alpha = 0.919$), and seven for harmony with internal and external organizations (Cronbach's $\alpha = 0.892$). To achieve the parsimony of the final mediating model, we followed the aggregation method suggested by Little et al. (2002) to reduce the number of parameter estimates and therefore averaged the eight sub-dimensions of the harmony model to form one composite score indicator to test hypotheses.

## AC

As mentioned above, referring to Meyer et al. (2002) and Grant et al. (2008) studies, we used a scale consisting of three items to measure employee AC to the company (Cronbach's $\alpha = 0.867$). Sample items included: 'This organization has a great deal of personal meaning for me'.

## Compliance Behaviour

We adapted Den Hartog et al. (2007) three-item measure to measure employee compliance behaviour (Cronbach's $\alpha = 0.867$). Sample items included: 'I don't take unnecessary breaks'.

## Control Variables

We controlled for three demographic variables, age (25 years old or younger $= 1$, others $= 0$), gender (male $= 1$, female $= 0$), and education level (senior high school or lower $= 1$, others $= 0$).

## Construct Validity and CMV

As noted, Cronbach $\alpha$ for each construct is above 0.8, indicating adequate reliability. Then we used LISREL 8.7 to further test the applicability and the construct distinctiveness of the eight-factor harmony model by a CFA method. Fit indexes indicated an acceptable fit $(\chi^2_{n=596} = 4805.63, P < .01; RMSEA = 0.08; SRMR = 0.057; CFI = 0.97; NNFI = 0.96)$ to the hypothesized eight-factor structure. Though research claimed that the value of about 0.05 or less for the RMSEA would indicate a goodness of model fit, it is also recommended that a 0.05 cut-off value may reject too many valid models in sample sizes smaller than 800, and therefore the value of about 0.08 or less would be acceptable (Chen, Curran, Bollen, Kirby, & Paxton, 2008). Hence, the results of CFA support the eight-factor framework, showing that the measures are reliable.

The statistical remedial approach recommended by Podsakoff et al. (2003) was employed to rule out the potential for CMV. We entered all 52 items into an exploratory factor analysis. If CMV was an issue, either a single factor will emerge from the factor analysis or one general factor will account for the majority of the covariance among the variables (Podsakoff et al., 2003). Our factor analysis showed nine distinct factors (an eigenvalue 41.0), accounting for 69.587% of the total variance, with no single factor accounting for a majority of the variance. Consequently, CMV is unlikely to be a concern in our data.

## 5.3.4 Results

According to Mackinnon et al. (2002) suggestion, the most commonly cited approach for testing mediation in HRM and relevant fields is the HMR procedure recommended by Baron and Kenny (1986). Despite its popularity, some studies demonstrate that using nonexperimental research designs to perform HMR may provide a relatively weak foundation for inferences about causal connections between variables, including those in assumed mediation models (Stone-Romero & Rosopa, 2008). Stone-Romero and Rosopa (2008) illustrate that the model specification problems in nonexperimental research result in the researcher's inability to make valid inferences about causality in testing mediation effects. However, considering the extensive usage of this HMR procedure, we used it to examine our assumed mediation model and then conducted a path model-based approach (the Sobel test) (Mackinnon et al., 2002; Sobel, 1988) to confirm our results.

Table 5.6 shows the descriptive statistics, including means, standard deviations, and correlations, for all variables. The degree of harmony had a positive relationship with AC ($P < .01$) and compliance behaviour ($P < .01$). The correlation coefficient between AC and compliance behaviour was also significant ($P < .01$).

Table 5.7 shows all regression results. In Model 1, we regressed the degree of harmony on AC. In Model 2, we regressed AC on compliance behaviour.

**Table 5.6** Means, SD, and Correlations

| | Mean | SD | 1 | 2 | 3 | 4 | 5 | 6 |
|---|---|---|---|---|---|---|---|---|
| Gender | 0.39 | 0.488 | 1 | | | | | |
| Age | 0.3912 | 0.48844 | 0.215** | 1 | | | | |
| Educational level | 0.6014 | 0.49003 | 0.056 | 0.269** | 1 | | | |
| Degree of harmony | 4.2676 | 0.83436 | 0.026 | 0.149** | 0.082 | 1 | | |
| AC | 3.9033 | 1.16459 | 0.107* | 0.098* | 0.024 | 0.466** | 1 | |
| Compliance behaviour | 4.9890 | 0.83668 | 0.031 | 0.039 | 0.083* | 0.462** | 0.367** | 1 |

Notes: $n = 596$. **,* Correlation is significant at the 0.01 and 0.05 levels (two-tailed), respectively.

**Table 5.7** Results of Regression Analysis

| | Model 1 AC (H1) | Model 2 Compliance Behaviour (H2) | Model 3 Compliance Behaviour | Model 4 Compliance Behaviour (H3) |
|---|---|---|---|---|
| Independent variables | | | | |
| Degree of harmony | 0.673*** | | 0.451*** | |
| | (0.057) | | (0.041) | |
| AC | | 0.268*** | | |
| | | (0.028) | | |
| Degree of harmony | | | | 0.334*** |
| | | | | (0.046) |
| AC | | | | 0.170** |
| | | | | (0.033) |
| Control variables | | | | |
| Gender | 0.128 | 0.129**** | 0.024 | 0.014 |
| | (0.099) | (0.069) | (0.071) | (0.069) |
| Age | 0.363** | 0.042 | 0.028 | 0.019 |
| | (0.103) | (0.071) | (0.075) | (0.074) |
| Educational level | 0.137 | 0.104* | 0.147* | 0.127**** |
| | (0.097) | (0.069) | (0.070) | (0.068) |
| Constant | 1.025*** | 3.927*** | 3.002*** | 2.855*** |
| | (0.254) | (0.126) | (0.181) | (0.180) |
| $R^2$ | 0.248 | 0.147 | 0.225 | 0.267 |
| $F$ value | 37.160*** | 23.743*** | 32.657*** | 32.199*** |

Notes: $n = 596$. Significance levels based on two-tailed tests. Unstandardized regression coefficients are reported; robust SEs are given in parentheses. * $P < .05$; ** $P < .01$; *** $P < .001$; **** $P < .10$.

In Model 3, compliance behaviour was entered as the dependent variable and the degree of harmony as the independent variable. In Model 4, we entered the degree of harmony and compliance behaviour together to test the mediating effect of AC. In all analyses, age, gender, and educational level were controlled for.

According to Models 1 and 3, the degree of harmony is a positive predictor of both employees' AC ($\beta = 0.484$, $P < .001$) and compliance behaviour ($\beta = 0.461$, $P < .001$). Hypothesis 1 and 2b are supported. Model 2 reports that AC is positively related to compliance behaviour ($\beta = 0.375$, $P < .001$). Hypothesis 2a is also supported. In Model 3, the relationship between the degree of harmony and compliance behaviour was significant. In Model 4, the regression coefficient of the degree of harmony on compliance behaviour was still significant ($\beta = 0.342$, $P < .001$), but the magnitude of the coefficient decreased ($\beta$ from 0.461 to 0.342). This indicates the existence of the mediating effect of AC. Thus, we performed the Sobel test (Mackinnon et al., 2002; Sobel, 1988) ($Z = 5.515 > 3.29$, $P < .001$) to examine it. The results confirm that AC partially mediates the relationship between the degree of harmony and compliance behaviour, supporting Hypothesis 3.

## 5.3.5 Discussion

Overall, our empirical findings provide evidence consistent with our hypotheses. First, our results suggest that the degree of harmony is significantly related to individual AC. More specifically, in situations where an employee perceives a lower level of harmony at work, their desire to become committed to the company may be diminished. In other words, maintaining harmony in the workplace could be seen as a means to foster loyal employees. Second, individual AC and the degree of harmony are both positively related to compliance behaviour. In this sense, the achievement of a higher level of harmony may not only help to strengthen employees' emotional attachment to their firms, but also motivate them to comply with policies, standards, procedures, and applicable laws and regulations at work in China. Third, the assumed mediation model that AC positively mediates the relationship between the degree of harmony and employee compliance behaviour was examined. This corroborates the point that AC can serve as an intervening variable through which cultural variables (e.g. Chinese harmony) affect employee behaviour, in response to Brooks and Wallace's (2006) suggestion for exploring the intervention effect of commitment. Related to this point, implicit in our mediation analysis is the indication that if employee AC is low, a higher level of harmony may not be effectively translated into an individual's exhibition of compliance behaviour.

With respect to the control variables, according to the regression analysis, our findings show that in China's manufacturing sector, females may engage in more compliance behaviour than males, while older workers seem to possess a higher level of AC towards their organizations. Additionally, compared with employees having higher education backgrounds, lower-educated employees are more likely to perform compliance behaviours.

### 5.3.5.1 *Contributions and Implications*

In sum, our research yields several unique contributions as follows. First, management is not universal, but subject to cultural differences (Hofstede et al., 2010; Rowley & Ulrich, 2014). One essential difference is that in the West, in general, management is viewed primarily as a science, whereas in the East, management is typically viewed as an art, even though Western management education is still valued (Tung, 2006). Despite the prevalence of using western scientific methodology to build management theories, an increasing number of researchers have tended to adopt a more Eastern perspective, using art-based approaches to discuss business issues, for example, learning courage to see reality and envision possibility from the arts (Adler, 2006; Taylor & Ladkin, 2009; Tung, 2006; Weick, 2007). In fact, after the 2008 global financial crisis and the 2010 European sovereign debt crisis, the ascendance of China and other EEs has offered a great opportunity for the West to challenge conventional wisdom on globalization and to more closely study and learn from Eastern managerial practices (Chen & Miller, 2010). The recent recession further highlights that the world is riddled with dynamically global interconnections and is sorely in need of fresh ideas and new perspectives on cross-cultural learning and theoretical development (Li, Mobley, & Kelly, 2013; Rhee, 2010).

In response to this, scholars have been encouraged to exert Asian traditional philosophies such as Confucianism, Daoism, or Buddhism in HRM practices, considering that the paucity of Asia-born management theories may impede the development of cross-cultural learning between the West and the East (McElhatton & Jackson, 2012; Rhee, 2010). Following this trend, our study identified the East–West cultural differences in the notion of harmony (art-based versus science-based views), investigating HRM issues in China through a newer and broader lens, namely a perspective of East–West integrative thinking. More specifically, using the eight-factor model decoded by the Eastern eight trigrams from a Western art-based method to measure organizational harmony, our study puts forward a novel framework demonstrating the mechanism between a Chinese cultural variable—harmony—and two well-established Western measures—AC and compliance behaviour. Viewed from this angle, our research is considered as a proactive step for advancing our knowledge in cross-cultural management, as well as for integrating Eastern with Western thought to build new mosaic-style theories connecting globally shared axioms to locally unique components (Li, 2012) that may be able to account for highly complicated HRM phenomena in a globalized world.

Second, many scholars have acknowledged that the existing US biased HRM models that dominate the literature may not be always adequate to meet the needs of workers in other countries due to the differences in cultural contexts (Hofstede et al., 2010; Rowley, 2003; Teagarden, 2010). Hence, context-sensitive research on China, a kind of indigenous study that seeks to find Chinese uniqueness to modify/compare Western theories or even build novel constructs/variables, has become a growing research stream (Li, 2012; Whetten, 2009).

Notwithstanding that Confucianism is recognized to play a critically important role in affecting employee attitude and behaviour in China (e.g. Chen & Miller, 2010; Chin & Mao, 2010; Farh et al., 1997, 2007; Hofstede et al., 2010), the way in which Confucian roots are reflected at workplaces is still a perplexity needing further investigation (Han & Altman, 2010). In view of this, our study, based on the Confucian canon *Yijing* identifying the distinctions between the Chinese and Western notions of harmony, provides a useful theoretical basis as well as a great potential for the future development of new models that are able to establish tighter links between Confucian codes and employee outcomes. In this sense, our study in some way answers calls for analysing context-specific implications to develop new context-sensitive constructs in the field of HRM (e.g. Rowley, 2016; Teagarden, 2010; Whetten, 2009).

The findings of our study also hold important implications for practitioners regarding possible solutions to HRM challenges. As mentioned at the beginning, in the face of turbulent and competitive global markets, it has become increasingly imperative to retain talent and lure skilled workers. The messages implied by our study suggest that since China is suffering severe labour shortages, managers may use workforce commitment to reduce high employee turnover by conducting harmonious labour relationships. Also, when implementing corporate restructuring or introducing new policies, companies could make good use of creating a harmonious work environment as a stepping stone to foster committed employees so as to ease resistance to organizational changes in the Chinese context.

Moreover, considering that the capability to manage cultural differences is one of the critical skills for global leaders (Li et al., 2013; Rowley & Ulrich, 2012a, 2012b; Teagarden, 2010), our study can acquaint non-Chinese entrepreneurs with the art-oriented, multidimensionally dynamic, and somewhat abstract notion of Chinese harmony at workplaces and thus deliver insights and boost a deep understanding of cross-cultural management. For instance, this understanding may help foreign managers to realize how to intensify the harmonious spirit of their organizations to enhance production efficiency via developing emotional ties with Chinese employees, given that the level of harmony would have stronger effects on employee compliance behaviour when people feel more connected to their firms.

Finally, China has been the world's fastest-growing and largest EE and was the wellspring for the traditional culture and civilization of numerous Asian countries. Thus, our results also provide certain theoretical and practical implications for many other EEs.

### 5.3.5.2 Limitation and Future Research

We acknowledge that our research is subject to limitations. First, since the research was conducted only in manufacturing organizations, generalizability might be limited. Future research could take different kinds of industries into consideration as well. Second, given that China has the largest population in the world and diversity within and across regions, our sample size is relatively small. Future studies could collect more comprehensive data in more regions of China. Third, owing to the dearth of some critical firm-level data as control variables, our study did not address the interrelationship of the eight separate subscales of the model on Chinese harmony with AC. Future research could further explore the relationships between the degree of harmony at the workplace and more employee outcome variables such as task performance and organizational identity. Moreover, given that we used subjective dependent variables, future research could also include objective outcome variables, such as employee turnover rates, to enrich research results.

### 5.3.5.3 Conclusion

Scholars have been encouraged to discover the heritage of classical Chinese philosophies and move towards a true sense of a melting pot by incorporating indigenous wisdom with the essential notions of US organization theories (Chen & Miller, 2010; Rhee, 2010). Likewise, the West, which used to traditionally favour a scientific, linear logic, has started to embrace art-oriented paradoxical strategies that are best embodied and espoused by the Eastern Yin–Yang principle (Li, 2012; Tung, 2008). This indicates some converging tendency between Eastern and Western management theories. Consistent with the above, Von Glinow and Teagarden (2009) claim that the future of Chinese HRM (see also Rowley, 2016) requires studies to encompass the wider spectrum of research from rigour to relevance, emic to etic, and exploration to exploitation, as well as any approaches in between. Hence, our study—which uncovered a previously unexplored mechanism among the Chinese notion of harmony, the Western concepts of AC, and compliance behaviour—brings about the potential for cross-fertilization and sophisticated integration of Chinese and Western management thinking, providing fresh avenues for future research to look into HRM-related issues in China as well as in many other EEs.

## 5.4 CONCLUSION

This chapter presented two empirical studies to help readers realize how Chinese harmonious culture characterized by *Yijing*'s eight-trigram model influences and shapes manufacturing workers' attitudes and behaviours at work. Culture—as an evolved capacity for adaptation and a system of shared values, rules, norms, and institutions at group level—is deeply ingrained in human mental processes (Hofstede et al., 2010). 'Deep' national culture learnt unconsciously from childhood is very difficult to change (Rowley, Benson, & Warner, 2004) but gradually evolves across generations, while relatively 'shallow' organizational culture learnt consciously in a specific organizational setting may be easily altered with internal control, such as leadership styles, or external pressures, such as economic conditions (Hofstede, 2015).

Whereas Chinese cultural values that construct employee mentality and work-related values are believed to be rather stable, it is vital for manufacturers in China, particularly FDI firms, to have a deeper and more comprehensive understanding of Chinese cultural ideology. Viewed from this angle, this chapter as a matter of fact displays a novel East–West integrative thinking, fostering an attitude of an openness to see the wisdom embedded in Chinese harmonious culture and to connect it to global HRM practices.

As mentioned in previous chapters, forming international JVs with local companies seems to be the easiest way for DE manufacturers to enter China in the early years of its reform and opening-up, that is, the 1990s. Evidence indicates that these international JVs created numerous jobs for rural migrant workers and contributed to China's social and economic growth. However, managing a local workforce has also raised a variety of HRM challenges as MNCs often simply applied Western developed policies and practices in their Chinese subsidiaries. After all, too often, pure Western HR techniques appear to be incompatible with Chinese harmonious culture and even cause context-specific labour problems. We will proceed to discuss further relevant issues around this point in the next chapter.

CHAPTER SIX

# Labour Dispute and Conflict Resolution: A Yin–Yang Harmony View

## 6.1 INTRODUCTION

### 6.1.1 The Rise of Blue-Collar Wages and Worker Activism

As indicated in previous chapters, fast-rising wages, an ageing population, and pervasive shortages of skilled labour have impacted on the workforce landscape of Chinese manufacturing. China has moved from an economy with a plentiful supply of cheap labour to one with more better paid and educated blue-collar workers. As shown in Fig. 6.1, from 2006 to 2015 the average annual salary in China's manufacturing sector doubled (from RMB 18,394 to 55,162, about US$2772 to 8314), signifying the end of the original extensive growth model which depended heavily on the vast number of low-cost, undereducated migrant workers. To use Krugman (1994) famous point about the 'Asian miracle' of the 20th century, there is a need to move from 'perspiration to inspiration'.

In order to increase profit margins for relieving cost pressure, the Chinese manufacturing industry has been gradually integrated with service functions and into an advanced manufacturing mode, namely service-oriented manufacturing (Zhen, 2012). However, this kind of structural change along the GVC often involves a profound and multifaceted transition from product-based to service- and value-based innovation (Lin, Pekkarinen, & Ma, 2015). Apart from training employees with new technical skills, it is therefore imperative for Chinese manufacturers to nurture a service-oriented culture that can enhance production workers' service awareness and their understanding of the significance to establishing

*The Future of Chinese Manufacturing*
https://doi.org/10.1016/B978-0-08-101108-9.00006-9

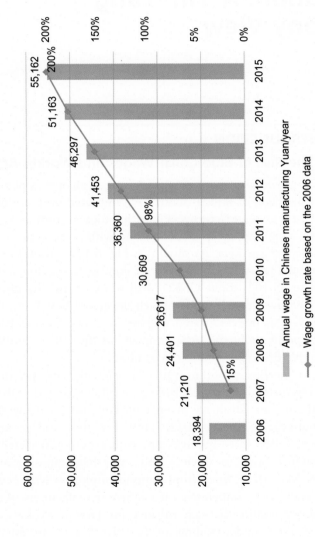

**Fig. 6.1** The changes of annual wage.

harmonious cooperation relationships with colleagues in marketing, sales, and relevant departments, as well as with customers.

Responding to the government's call for enhancing the support to front-line workers, an increasing number of Chinese manufacturers have devised new workforce development programmes (WDP) to provide professional skills training and service culture education in production line workers whereby the goal to engage in higher value activities within GVCs can be better accomplished. Unfortunately, evidence reveals that the implementation of such WDPs is usually not as successful as expected (Chin & Liu, 2014). This can be attributed to a variety of reasons. For example, the complexity and distinctiveness regarding the input–output architecture of different GVCs may perplex the evaluation standard of a WDP designed for a specific industry, while the governance systems in which the GVC is embedded could also diversify the upgrading trajectories by manufacturers in different industries. Moreover, employees often feel very stressed and thus express strong discontent in the process of upgrading. Overall, a WDP must incorporate a wide range of actors and stakeholders, ranging from public institutions (e.g. local and national government), quasi-public institutions (e.g. higher education), private firms, international associations, nongovernmental organizations (NGOs), and the like (Chin & Liu, 2014; Gereffi, 2009). Hence, when Chinese manufacturers undertake WDPs to facilitate upgrading along a GVC, they may simultaneously confront manifold challenges involving national, provincial, or industrial institutions and at individual, organizational, and societal levels.

As a result of the above, quite a few Chinese manufacturers opted to shut down their plants in China and shift labour-intensive production lines to other countries with lower workforce costs. Some chose to introduce a higher degree of automation or robots to replace traditional manual production processes. Under such conditions, it is not surprising that the number of labour dispute cases and work activism has increased sharply in recent years,[1] with 1.8 million registered labour disputes in 2016. In the following section, we will present research that deepens our understanding of how to resolve labour conflicts in a socialist market economy like China.

---

[1] https://www.statista.com/chart/10443/china-labor-disputes-on-the-rise/

## 6.2 UNDERSTANDING LABOUR CONFLICTS IN CHINESE MANUFACTURING: A YIN–YANG HARMONY PERSPECTIVE

### 6.2.1 Introduction

China has taken advantage of its cheap labour and low-cost production to play the role of 'the world's factory' for more than two decades. In recent years, currency appreciation, shortages of migrant workers, and minimum wage increases are among the factors leading to rising labour costs (Fang, Gunterberg, & Larsson, 2010). Many large MNC manufacturers, especially those which are export-oriented OEMs, feel the pressure to shut down factories and/or reduce production in China, shifting main manufacturing bases to other EEs with lower wage rates, such as Vietnam, Indonesia, Mexico, and India (Chin & Liu, 2014). In such a tough environment, manufacturing employment in China has been deteriorating, further incurring the associated labour issues of high turnover rates and recruitment difficulties.

In early 2014, many people were stunned when >30,000 workers engaged in a 2-week strike at the world's largest footwear factory complex in Dongguan, China. As one of the biggest labour strikes in recent history, this incident was caused by disputes about low pay and migrant workers' lack of social insurance and highlighted the rising conflicts between production employees and management in Chinese manufacturing.[1] In fact, a series of high-profile labour strikes have been occurring in China since the 2008 global financial crisis hit the OEM industry (Chan, 2012; Chin, 2015; Tang & Fitzsimons, 2013). Conflicts between production workers and management are now becoming a major concern for Chinese manufacturing.

However, the manner in which labour unrest is typically tackled in China has not been fully addressed (Nguyen & Yang, 2012; Posthuma, 2011). Scholars have underscored the critical role of cultural context in managing conflicts, arguing that the differences in language systems and thought patterns between Chinese and Western societies lead the Chinese to have their own ways of resolving workplace conflicts (Nguyen & Yang, 2012; Tjosvold & Sun, 2010). For instance, unlike Western people treating confrontations or conflict positively, Chinese workers tend to conduct passive resistance, rather than discussing disputes straightforwardly, and avoid saying 'No' directly to the other party to maintain interpersonal harmony in the workplace (Chin, 2014; Deng & Xu, 2014; Fang, 2014). In short, Western theories are unable to explain adequately the unique conflict-coping behaviours in China. It is still unclear how Chinese culture influences the resolution process of labour conflicts, and very few researchers have investigated how labour-intensive OEMs, especially those linked to MNCs, effectively deal with increasing disputes in this context. Hence, our study will advance our understanding of the impact of Chinese culture on conflict management.

Some scholars have identified the unique value of Yin–Yang thinking for indigenous research on Chinese management because it embodies the notion of Chinese harmony (Chin, 2015), offering a holistic, dynamic, and Chinese culture-specific approach to interpersonal problem-solving (Fang, 2014; Li, 2014). Considering the discussion above, a cultural perspective of Yin–Yang harmony seems to be particularly suitable for grounding our research. Hence, we propose the Yin–Yang harmony framework (5C model, as outlined earlier) for elucidating the conflict resolution process, which is distinctive from the predominant dual-concern model of Western assumptions (Yan & Sorenson, 2004). Furthermore, building on such a cultural perspective, our research team conducted an empirical study on a large Taiwan-invested OEM that had just experienced a large labour protest in China.

In sum, the main contribution of our study is to respond to appeals for context-specific research to analyse labour relations issues (Nguyen & Yang, 2012; Rowley, 2016; Zarankin, 2008). More specifically, by investigating a large labour-intensive manufacturer where a severe labour strike occurred, we propose an integrative, context-specific concern—concern for harmony in Chinese conflict management and illustrate the dynamic, contingent, and art-oriented nature of the circled harmonizing process (5C model) for resolving conflicts in China.

## 6.2.2 Theoretical Foundation

### 6.2.2.1 Overview of the History of Labour-Management Conflicts in China's Manufacturing Sector

China's spectacular industrialization and economic growth over the past three decades have been driven by export-oriented low-cost manufacturing and an undervalued currency (Chan, 2010; Pun, 2007). With its further advantages of an immense supply of low-educated and low-wage workers from rural areas, China has been quickly integrated into the GVC as the 'world's factory' and became the largest FDI recipient from 2002 to recently. Also, over 50% of the FDI has flowed into the labour-intensive manufacturing/OEM industry, in which most of the foreign-invested OEMs were initially located in China's coastal areas (Chan, 2012, 2014). Following this economic development trend, millions of rural workers from the impoverished central and western provinces moved to the coastal and urban regions, such as Guangdong, Fujian, and Shandong, to earn better wages in foreign-invested, export-oriented factories (Chan, 2014; Pun, 2007).

The aforementioned massive waves of rural migrants have formed a new working class of internal migrant labourers in China, namely the so-called 'peasant workers' (Chan, 2012) or *nong* min *gong* (农民工) in Chinese. However, unlike the Maoist working-class worker or *gongren* (工人) in Chinese, who carried the highest status, the peasant workers until most recently signified being a 'second-class citizen' with an inferior social status due to the government's distinctive, segregational *hukou* (household registration) system in Chinese (Zhu, 2004). *Hukou*, a very powerful and dominant sociopolitical instrument, enables the government to control the geographical mobility of the domestic population and labour, thus creating a two-tiered citizenship of rural and urban *hukou* residents (Chan, 2012; Yang, 2015). It excludes rural workers from applying for local/urban *hukou* as well as some social insurance and welfare services provided by the state in the cities where they migrated and work (Chan, 2014, 2010). Moreover, firms employing urban residents are usually required to pay much more in pensions and medical coverage than those employing migrant workers. In this vein, labour-intensive OEMs typically rely on hiring migrant workers as their competitive advantage in cost savings (Pun, 2007). For instance, as the principal OEM for Apple, Taiwan-invested manufacturer Foxconn employs >1.2 million workers in China, of whom over 85% of its employees in its Shenzhen factories are rural migrant workers aged between 16 and 29 years old (Chan, Pun, & Selden, 2013) with a single factory in GZ employing 250,000. The poor working conditions are shown in reports in the media of worker suicides in these sorts of factories.

Despite playing a vital role in sustaining the low labour costs for China's export-led OEM industry, peasant workers are vulnerable to mistreatment and exploitation by management due to their weak workplace bargaining power (Chan, 2010). Evidence indicates that factory workers have only enjoyed a very small proportion of the benefits of China's economic development given that their nominal income has lagged far behind the growth in GDP per capital (Chan, 2014). The contradiction of high economic growth and low pay of migrant workers has resulted in a growing number of labour protests since the early 2000s. Low wages, long working hours, unhealthy/ dangerous working environments, abusive management, and nonpayment of wages and social insurance are believed to be primary grievances among the peasant workers of labour-intensive OEMs in China (Pun, 2007; Yang, 2015; Zhu, 2004). Under such circumstances, a trend of mounting labour unrest in Chinese manufacturing has been reported.

### 6.2.2.2 All-China Federation of Trade Unions

Research revealed that 2008 was the year marking a major turning point for labour relations issues in Chinese manufacturing (Chan, 2014). The implementation of the Labour Contract Law in that year was an important event that signalled the reform of China's labour relations by establishing a legal basis for worker activism (Chan, 2014; Chang & William, 2013). This law has strengthened and legitimized the role of the All-China Federation of Trade Unions (ACFTUs) in helping migrant workers to protect their legal rights through union organizing. Hence, since the 2008 financial crisis triggered an economic downturn, the number of labour dispute cases in Chinese manufacturing going to court has been rising sharply because of numerous OEMs being shut down and workers being laid off (Chin & Liu, 2014).

The ACFTU, whose main functions are to mediate employee–employer conflicts, represents the only labour union in China formally recognized by the Chinese Communist Party (CCP). The formal structure of ACFTU was originally established in 1925, but its functions and structure were formalized after China's liberation in 1949. It consists of three interrelated elements: democratic centralism, top–down control, and a dual local and industrial structure (Metcalf & Li, 2007). More specifically, Chinese unions comply with a hierarchical system in which the ACFTU stands at the top, governing three sublevel unions (i.e. first tier: the provincial union, second tier: the local/city, county, and town union, and third tier: the workplace-based/ corporate union). According to the Trade Union Law 2001 and the Trade Union Constitution 2003, all workers in China enjoy the freedom to join a union but this union must be approved and supervised by the ACFTU, the only permitted official union organization (Metcalf & Li, 2007; Wang, 2011). Also, the union leaders of higher local levels (i.e. county, city, and province) are directly appointed by the CCP rather than elected by individual workers.

In this vein, the ACFTU usually chooses to work with employers to mitigate labour conflicts rather than promote confrontation between labour and management. Therefore, the ACFTU may not be considered as a potent defender of peasant workers. Evidence reports that many protesting factory workers view the ACFTU as ineffectual in protecting their interests (Chang & William, 2013). However, Chinese workers' legal knowledge and consciousness about challenging workplace unfairness are being strengthened (Chan, 2014).

Even though the ACFTU with its subordinate labour unions and their activities is seen as just another aspect of China's administrative structure, these institutions nevertheless provide a legal basis and a social foundation for the trade union movement in China (Chang & William, 2013). In the history of the international labour movement, the ACFTU indeed represents one of the most functional conceptions associated with the transition from a planned economy to a market economy and plays a crucial role in the appearance and development of an embryonic, grass-roots labour movement in China.

### 6.2.2.3 Major Differences in Conflict Management Between the Chinese and Westerners

A large body of research shows that differences in cultural context, language system, and thought patterns among the Chinese and Westerners led the Chinese to manage and resolve conflicts in their own unique ways, especially as reflected in their strong tendency to avoid direct/face-to-face conflicts and to value interpersonal relationships and harmony (e.g. Chin, 2015; Deng & Xu, 2014; Hofstede et al., 2010; Leung et al., 2011; Ndubisi, 2011; Tang & Fitzsimons, 2013). According to Friedman, Chi, and Liu (2006), the Chinese people reported more conflict avoidance than the Americans because they are inclined to interpret a direct or confrontational approach to conflicts as harmful to their relationships with others. Yuan (2010) discovered that in terms of handling conflicts in the workplace, Chinese employees are more likely to adopt avoidance, passive resistance, and third-party approaches than their American counterparts in US-based MNCs in China. In general, research suggests that the Chinese display overt conflict avoidance behaviour, preferring to deal with conflicts in a nonconfrontational, indirect, and even implicit manner.

Several studies further argue that the Chinese are particularly susceptible to contextual factors involved in conflict incidents and thus may alter their conflict-coping strategies, depending on distinctive situational cues regarding the conflict parties, such as differences in job positions, social hierarchies, work relations, and individual personalities (Fu, Yan, Li, Wang, & Peng,

2008). For example, although Chinese employees often use an avoidance strategy to handle conflicts with their supervisors, they may choose to adopt a direct confrontation strategy to resolve similar conflicts if the work relationships at stake with the other party are horizontal, for example, between colleagues (Nguyen & Yang, 2012). In this view, the Chinese seem to be more likely than Westerners to take a variety of circumstantial factors into consideration in terms of choosing conflict-handling strategies. Chinese employees may carry out multiple complex and/or interactive conflict-solving strategies according to the varying roles they play in organizations. These arguments explicitly shed light on the dynamic and contingent nature of Chinese conflict management and implicitly defy a simply 'Chinese' typology of favoured conflict-coping strategies/styles.

### 6.2.2.4 Beyond the Western Dual-Concern Model: Concern for Harmony

Two major characteristics of Chinese conflict resolution are identified through a literature review—the confrontation-avoidant and contingency-oriented propensities—both of which are attributable to the most palpable cultural idiosyncrasy of Chinese people, that is, the utmost concern in pursuit of harmony (Chin, 2015, 2014; Hofstede et al., 2010; Ndubisi, 2011). Harmony as the core value of the Chinese mental software (Hofstede et al., 2010) represents the desired means as well as the ideal goal/end in building and maintaining relationships in Chinese society (Chin, 2014; Fung, 1948). The Chinese are very inclined to pursue a unique harmonious settlement that may ultimately offer no explicit solution to disputes rather than to optimize the outcomes of the disputants.

Most research is still based on the Western dual-concern model of conflict management which posits that the choice of conflict-coping strategy is determined by rational decisions related to satisfying one's own concerns (assertiveness) and satisfying the other party's concerns (cooperativeness) (Thomas & Kenneth, 1976). However, it is recognized that conflict management conceptualizations developed in Western contexts should be adapted, or even revised, for non-Western cultural contexts (Yan & Sorenson, 2004). Consistent with this, a dual-concern model may be inadequate to account for the strong proclivity of Chinese people towards harmony in conflict resolution. Hence, we argue that there is a dominant concern transcending the Western dual concerns in China, that is, concern for harmony.

The core principle for the ACFTU to deal with labour conflicts also embodies this ultimate concern. As noted, unlike Western labour unions acting as the representatives of grass-roots workers, in China the ACFTU is an organ of the CCP. The ACFTU is not only mandated to represent the interests of the workers but also has clear goals on facilitating the government to ensure some degree of control and influence over private enterprises, particularly foreign-invested, and enhancing incentives of investment and economic growth (Bai, 2011; Wang, 2011). Arguably, with such a state-mandated nature, the ACFTU may not be able to best serve and protect the interests of workers, but rather the interests of the country (Wang, 2011). Metcalf and Li (2007) have indicated that when the conflicts show a conspicuous infringement of individual worker rights by management, Chinese unions are very willing to represent the interests of employees. However, when management infringes collective worker's rights, unions may conversely become much more cautious in taking sides. This is because the ACFTU is also mandated to avoid arousing group dissatisfaction and social disturbance to maintain the productivity of enterprises (Bai, 2011). As a result, the guiding ideology of concern for harmony leads the ACFTU to mostly perform mediation functions between labour and management, rather than negotiation functions on behalf of workers' interests.

It is worth recalling how the Chinese conceptualization of harmony is different from the Western definition of harmony. The Chinese notion of harmony, which originated from *Yijing*, is characterized by Yin–Yang dynamics. As noted earlier, the Yin–Yang frame has been recognized as a unique, superior approach to manage conflicting paradox in the Chinese context (Fang, 2014; Li, 2014, 2012). Accordingly, we use a Yin–Yang harmony perspective to ground our research.

### 6.2.2.5 The Harmonizing Process of Chinese Conflict Resolution: A Yin–Yang Harmony View

As mentioned above, the concepts of harmony exhibit prominent East–West cultural differences (Leung et al., 2011; Li, 2012). The Western ideal of harmony as derived from the classical Greek philosophy symbolizes a linear progressive model with a preset order, which is generally defined as 'a perfect unity of many mixed (elements), a satisfactory agreement between disagreeing (elements)', or 'a perfect accordance of the discordant', on the premise of solving conflicts of opposing forces in the world (Chin, 2014). Given that it is a clear quantitative tendency significantly related to the scientific logic of integration, the Western concept of harmony is thus viewed as a science, beginning with the identification and recognition of conflicts and contradictions and then moving on towards the final goal of pursuing a rational, satisfactory reconciliation, an absolute solution, or a perfect resolution of conflicts and contradictions (Chin, 2014).

In contrast, as manifested by Chin (2015, 2014), the Chinese notion of harmony, as originality from the most influential cultural canon, *Yijing*, is best understood as a holistic, dynamic but somewhat abstract expression of the harmonization process deciphered by all the combinations and permutations of Yin and Yang components, an art rather than a science in essence (Tung, 2006). Unlike the Western logic of harmony seeking an ultimate, absolute, and perfect noncontradictory resolution to conflicts, the Chinese ideal of harmony, with its peculiar art-oriented nature, suggests that people treat all conflicts and contradictions as permanently coexistent yet continuously interactive forms of two opposite elements, Yin and Yang, and thus embraces a unique paradoxical strategy questing for a 'temporarily balanced yet constantly changing status of harmony' in managing conflicts. For a better understanding, we briefly introduce the origin of Yin–Yang next.

As mentioned in Chapter 5, *Yijing* is commonly acknowledged as the source of all Chinese philosophical ideologies, especially for the two major mainstreams of Chinese philosophy, Confucianism and Taoism (Fung, 1948; Lai, 2008). The eight trigrams constitute the preliminary model of *Yijing*; by combining any two of the eight trigrams into one set (hexagram), the central paradigm of *Yijing* including 64 hexagrams in total emerged. The 64 hexagrams signify 64 types of transitional states instead of static conditions. Each hexagram, apart from its core meaning, denotes an entire set of associated concepts. In short, the eight-trigram model with its extension (the 64-hexagram paradigm) characterizes the basic framework of Chinese mental programming, that is, seeing the whole rather than only parts/pieces; seeing interrelationships and the interplay of things rather than merely things per se.

The foregoing arguments reflect the most conspicuous difference between Eastern and Western ways of thinking (Hofstede et al., 2010). Western analytical thinking focuses on the elements/components of a conflict, which tends to break apart the conflict problems first for determining the best strategies to completely resolve conflicts, whereas Eastern/Chinese synthetic thinking focuses on the holistic picture of a conflict, which tends to rely on intrinsic sense instead of instrumental rationality handling conflicts for achieving a 'tentatively balanced yet continuously dynamic harmonious settlement' (Chin, 2014, pp. 330). As a result, we argue that the Chinese way of conflict resolution is 'dynamic, contingent, and art-oriented in nature.' It is best characterized as a distinctive, circled harmonizing process of five primary stages—conflict, clash, communication, compromise, and consensus (5C model)—as in the changing sequence of *Yijing*'s eight trigrams interpreted by their respective combinations of Yin and Yang.

We further illustrate the changing pattern and sequence of the eight trigrams in greater detail as follows. As described above, the core attributes of trigrams could be characterized by eight essential nature forces. On the basis of the attributes of individual trigrams, King Wen, the founder of the Zhou dynasty (1099–1050 BCE), arranged the sequence of the eight trigrams (called the Later Heaven sequence in Chinese literature) to demonstrate the development course of life as well as the cyclical, recurrent process of change for all living entities in the world with time–space limitations (Lai, 2008; Miller, 1991; Zhou, 2004).

### 6.2.2.6 *The Harmonizing Process: 5C Model*

Considering the dynamic, contingent, and art-oriented characteristics of the harmonizing process, we used an art-based method (Tung, 2006; Taylor & Ladkin, 2009), using imagination to distil the semiotic and symbolic implications from the images of the eight trigrams in the Later Heaven sequence first and then applied them to decipher the five stages. For a better understanding, the Later Heaven sequence of the eight trigrams with our 5C model is shown in Fig. 6.2 referring to the Formal Interpretation of Yijing by Yingda Kong during the Tang dynasty (574–648 CE).

*Stage 1: Conflict.* This Later Heaven sequence starts with the Zhen trigram (Image: Thunder—the arousing) given that this trigram symbolizes the Spring, the 6th hour, and the East, indicating the beginning of provoking all kinds of latent energies or living entities, and stimulating them into movement (Miller, 1991). The Sun trigram is the next (Image: Wind—the gentle) because the aroused energies are shaped and entrenched when the gentle wind nurtures and guides (Lai, 2008; Zhou, 2004).

Hence, the first stage of the harmonizing process, conflict, is embodied by the Zhen and Sun trigrams because the most important task of this step is to identify and confirm the potential opposition or incompatibility that may trigger actual conflicts.

*Stage 2: Clash.* Being the third of the Later Heaven sequence, the Li trigram (Image: Fire—the clinging) symbolizes the Summer, the 12th

**Fig. 6.2** Later heaven sequence of the eight trigrams with the 5C model.

hour, and the South, expressing a strong tendency to cling together for attaining warmth, radiance, maturity, or a variety of specific goals, just like igniting a fire/flame of life (Fung, 1948; Miller, 1991; Zhou, 2004). Given that the second stage of the harmonizing process, clash, indicates the eruptions of actual conflicts or disputes, it can be best characterized by the Li trigram.

*Stage 3: Communication.* The Kun trigram (Image: Earth—the receptive) as the fourth in the sequence represents the spirit of generosity, receptiveness, and openness. That which is explored under the Li trigram is absorbed into the Kun trigram, thus being receptive to profound transitions from physical consciousness to spiritual consciousness, as well as from rational cognition to intuitive cognition (Miller, 1991; Zhou, 2004). The third stage, communication, refers to the crucial harmonizing phase in which the disputing parties finally break the Chinese habit/inertia of conflict avoidance, thus starting to honestly exchange information, receive different opinions, and enhance mutual understanding. In this vein, this stage could be well embodied by the Kun trigram.

*Stage 4: Compromise.* That which is assimilated through the Kun trigram moves further into the fifth trigram, the Dui (Image: Lake—the joyous), symbolizing the Autumn, the 18th hour, and the West, that is, the joyful time of celebrating harvest or watching the west down of the sunset, and then proceeds to access the six trigram, the Qian (Image: Heaven—the creative), symbolizing the creative inner strength that inspires deeper contemplation and positive movement towards a greater interconnection and omnipotent resonance (Fung, 1948; Miller, 1991).

The fourth stage of the harmonizing process, compromise, indicates the win–win resolution Chinese people often favour when handling conflicts, despite the fact that it may still contain a certain level of forbearance or dissatisfaction. Thus, it is adequately characterized by the Dui and Qian trigrams.

*Stage 5: Consensus.* The creative inner forces lead all living entities to overcome obstacles as a brave torrent, flowing and permeating into the deepest, almost unmeasurable essence of the being, just like the seventh trigram—the Kan (Image: Water—the abysmal) that represents the Winter, the midnight hour, and the North. Then the abysmal, yet temporary, stillness of the being boosts the steadfastness of inwardness incarnated by the Gen trigram (Image: Mountain—the resting).

As a result, given that the fifth stage of the harmonizing process, consensus, indicates reaching a kind of tentative agreement, closure, or balance between conflicting parties, it is thus best embodied by the Kan and Gen trigrams.

In conclusion, as explained in the Formal Interpretation of *Yijing* by Yingda Kong in the Tang dynasty (574–648 CE), life begins with the sign of Zhen and ends in the sign of Gen; the evolutionary nature and process of life will be recurring again and again. From the Chinese perspective, this cyclical, recurrent circle, delineating the principle of change in the universe, mirrors the harmonizing process (5C model) of conflict resolutions.

### 6.2.2.7 From a Yin–Yang Harmony View to Labour Conflicts in China

Following the discussion above, our research focuses on exploring how to activate the harmonizing process in practice to help Chinese manufacturers resolve labour conflicts. To achieve this goal, we used the Harmony scale developed by Chin, 2015, 2014) from a perspective of *Yijing* to investigate the world's biggest footwear OEM in China where a labour strike occurred. In summary, we intend to answer the following research questions (RQs):

1. What are the main/underlying unharmonious factors triggering increasing labour disputes in labour-intensive factories in China?
2. What and how do individual/demographic characteristics of workers influence their perceptions of harmony in the workplace, which reveal critical clues about the potential areas of labour-management conflicts?

3. Is the conflict-handling process the Chinese manufacturer conducted in line with the harmonizing process embodied by our 5C model?

## 6.2.3 Methods

### 6.2.3.1 Case Overview

Our case firm is a large Taiwan-invested OEM (hereafter 'the company'), which once had 175,000 employees and still employs >50,000 workers in China. Of them, around 75% are low-paid production line workers. Despite shutting down their plants in China from 2009, the company currently has seven factories with about 40,000 workers in southern China and about 15,000 workers in Eastern China. The company experienced a serious labour strike that began in early May 2014 and lasted for >10 days. The local police force had to maintain security. On 17 May, the provincial trade union under the leadership of the ACFTU assigned several representatives to facilitate negotiations between the company and protesters. On 29 May the strike finally ended. Given that the general manager claimed that the company was still unsure of the actual motives for the strike, our research team was invited to investigate in late May 2014. Under such tense circumstances, top management sought our help in discerning the root causes of the dispute so as to formulate possible remedies and coping strategies for re-boosting the morale among production workers.

### 6.2.3.2 An Explanatory Sequential Mixed Methods Design

This research project, including one round of pilot interviews and two lengthy field surveys, was conducted over 7 months from late May to early December 2014. The purpose of the pilot interviews was to facilitate our understanding of the background knowledge of the whole situation, based on which we could further modify the original questionnaire and harmony scale designed by Chin (2015, 2014) for the next formal quantitative survey.

Following Creswell's (2014) explanatory sequential mixed methods design, our formal research consisted of two phases (Study 1 and Study 2). We collected quantitative data and analysed the results in the first phase. Using this as a basis, we decided on the types of participants to be purposefully selected and the types of questions for the interviews in the second phase. To answer RQ3 for corroborating the 5C model, we referred to Sonenshein (2014), using a Grounded Theory approach (Charmaz, 2006) to gather and analyse the qualitative data. The details are shown below.

## 6.2.4 Study 1

### 6.2.4.1 Data Collection

We first carried out pilot interviews of 21 workers (two production managers, five production superintendents, two HR supervisors, and twelve full-time production workers) selected by the company over 1.5 days in early June. However, we were requested to talk with the respondents very cautiously to avoid stirring up negative feelings or resentment because the strike had just ended and many workers still felt agitated. As a result, we merely asked respondents to talk freely about the most critical unharmonious factors affecting the organization from their point of view and to share their opinions about their working conditions and experience. We discovered that most of their major concerns had been contained in our formal questionnaire.

Given the feedback from the pilot interviews, we carefully amended some word usages of the harmony scale (Chin, 2015, 2014) and then conducted a quantitative study in July 2014. This aimed to ascertain the dominant unharmonious factors resulting in the discontent of the factory workers and to examine the influence of respondents' individual characteristics (gender, age, education, etc.). Participants spent an average of about 40 min completing a questionnaire in a closed meeting room during working hours on approval of the factory general manager. It is worth noting that, given that most of the production workers were junior high graduates and below, the questionnaire would be read directly to those who were illiterate or encountered trouble understanding the items.

### 6.2.4.2 Participants

Referring to the demographic distribution characteristics of the factory, we randomly selected 400 production workers from the name list. Assisted by the company's HR team in arranging the time and venue during working hours, 363 workers responded to our questionnaire. Respondents were: 55.9% female, 76.9% married, 44.7% older than 35 years, 47.6% from Hunan province, 64.7% junior high or polytechnic educated, and 36.3% had worked in the factory for between 1 and 5 years. In total, 82.6% of respondents were full-time production workers at the grass-roots level.

### 6.2.4.3 Instrument

#### The Harmony Scale

Our study used a Yin–Yang harmony perspective to disclose the underlying unharmonious factors that might trigger labour conflicts. Hence, the harmony model developed by Chin, (2015, 2014) from the view of *Yijing* appeared to be particularly appropriate for detecting the key unharmonious elements.

As noted, the original harmony scale had been modified in adaption to the low-morale, poststrike workplace. This modified instrument was measured using a six-point scale ranging from 1: strongly disagree to 6: strongly agree to prevent response bias, given that Chinese people (and others) often seem to prefer choosing the midpoint of scales regardless of their true feelings (Chin, 2015). It comprised eight factors with 32 items in total: three items for harmony with the highest leader, for example, 'Top management accommodates different opinions from us' (Cronbach's = 0.767), three for harmony of employees, for example, 'Colleagues also maintain good relationships after work' (Cronbach's = 0.767), three for harmony with own team, for example, 'My team has a cooperative spirit' (Cronbach's = 0.710), three for self-harmony, for example, 'I cherish my work environment' (Cronbach's = 0.770), three for harmony with direct boss, for example, 'Direct boss does not steal contributions from me' (Cronbach's = 0.741), three for harmony of internal and external organizations, for example, 'My factory values communication with clients' (Cronbach's = 0.713), three for harmony of departments, for example, 'I often participate in cross-department meetings' (Cronbach's = 0.800), and three for harmony with corporate system, for example, 'My factory has a sound employee benefits plan' (Cronbach's = 0.705).

### 6.2.4.3.1 Reliability and Validity of the Harmony Scale

As described above, Cronbach's for each dimension of the harmony scale is above 0.70, indicating adequate reliability. Then we used AMOS 21.0 to test the validity of the constructs. The results of confirmatory factor analysis provided an adequate model fit ($\chi^2_{n=363} = 503.488$, $df = 182$, $\chi^2/df = 2.766 < 3$, $P < .001$, CFI = $0.911 < 0.90$, IFI = $0.914 > 0.90$, RMSEA = $0.070 < 0.08$) (Hair, Black, Babin, Anderson, & Tatham, 2005). According to Hair et al. (2005), we then further compared the above hypothesized eight-factor model with two alternative, more parsimonious models in which we set the following items of different dimensions to load on a single factor: 'harmony of internal and external organizations' and 'harmony with own team' (a seven-factor construct) ($\chi^2_{n=363} = 595.412$, $df = 196$, $\chi^2/df = 3.038 > 3$, $P < .001$, CFI = $0.889 < 0.90$, IFI = $0.892 < 0.90$, RMSEA = $0.075 < 0.08$); 'harmony of internal and external organizations', 'harmony with the highest leader', and 'harmony with own team' (a six-factor construct) ($\chi^2_{n=363} = 766.969$, $df = 203$, $\chi^2/df = 3.778 > 3$, $P < .001$, CFI = $0.844 < 0.90$, IFI = $0.848 < 0.90$, RMSEA = $0.088 > 0.08$). As a result, the assumed eight-factor structure displayed a better fit to the data, showing an acceptable level of construct validity. Moreover, except two items, all values of the factor loadings were higher than 0.5, indicating an acceptable convergent validity (Hair et al., 2005). Hence, the reliability and the validity of the harmony scale were examined.

## 6.2.5 Findings of Study 1

The data were analysed by SPSS 17. Table 6.1 displays the Pearson correlation matrix and the means of all measured variables in our study. The correlations among the eight factors of harmony are positive and statistically significant, except the correlation between 'self-harmony' and 'harmony with own team'. Despite all values being higher than 4, 'harmony with corporate system' (4.094), 'harmony of departments' (4.302), and 'harmony with firm leader' (4.358) were the top three with the lowest scores. The results imply that these three factors might be the underlying unharmonious factors triggering the labour dispute, which is in response to RQ1.

Table 6.2 presents the results of one-way analysis of variance with the least studentized difference (LSD) approach. This illustrates whether the following demographic characteristics of workers may affect the levels of their perceived harmony in organizations.

### 6.2.5.1 Gender

Gender was found to influence employee perceptions of 'self-harmony' and 'harmony with corporate system'. Females scored higher than males in both dimensions at significant levels.

### 6.2.5.2 Age

Age was identified as affecting employee perceptions of harmony in the four dimensions at significant levels. Respondents aged equal to or above 36 years old scored the highest, while respondents aged between 26 and 35 years old scored the lowest in terms of 'harmony with firm leader', 'harmony with own team', and 'harmony of departments.' With respect to 'self-harmony', respondents aged between 26 and 35 years old scored higher.

### 6.2.5.3 Marital Status

Married individuals gained higher scores than singles in both dimensions: 'harmony with firm leader' and 'harmony with own team' at significant levels.

### 6.2.5.4 Job Positions

Grass-roots workers were found to score lower than employees with managerial positions in four dimensions: 'harmony with firm leader', 'harmony

**Table 6.1** Person Correlations Matrix

| Variable | Mean | SD | 1 | 2 | 3 | 4 | 5 | 6 | 7 | 8 | 9 | 10 | 11 | 12 | 13 | 14 | 15 |
|---|---|---|---|---|---|---|---|---|---|---|---|---|---|---|---|---|---|
| 1. Gender | 0.44 | 0.49 | 1 | | | | | | | | | | | | | | |
| 2. Marital status | 0.22 | 0.41 | 0.26** | 1 | | | | | | | | | | | | | |
| 3. Age | 2.21 | 0.79 | −0.15** | −0.61** | 1 | | | | | | | | | | | | |
| 4. Province | 1.87 | 0.90 | 0.01 | 0.19** | −0.13* | 1 | | | | | | | | | | | |
| 5. Education level | 1.30 | 0.52 | 0.13** | 0.04 | 0.01 | −0.10 | 1 | | | | | | | | | | |
| 6. Tenure | 2.02 | 0.79 | 0.02 | −0.35** | 0.50** | −0.09 | 0.20 | 1 | | | | | | | | | |
| 7. Job position | 0.82 | 0.37 | 0.07 | 0.21** | −0.34** | 0.09 | −0.49 | −0.53*** | 1 | | | | | | | | |
| 8. With firm leader | 4.35 | 0.93 | 0.06 | 0.09 | 0.10* | 0.03 | 0.14 | 0.14** | −0.19** | 1 | | | | | | | |
| 9. Of employees | 4.69 | 0.83 | 0.03 | 0.07 | 0.05 | 0.06 | −0.15 | −0.17** | 0.31** | 0.41** | 1 | | | | | | |
| 10. With own team | 4.69 | 0.87 | 0.04 | 0.16** | 0.20** | 0.00 | 0.21 | 0.21** | −0.37** | 0.50** | 0.28** | 1 | | | | | |
| 11. Self-harmony | 4.70 | 0.79 | 0.09 | 0.08 | 0.08 | 0.05 | −0.17 | −0.25** | 0.43** | 0.21** | 0.59** | 0.10 | 1 | | | | |
| 12. With direct boss | 4.40 | 1.02 | 0.00 | 0.01 | 0.04 | 0.03 | 0.17 | 0.09 | −0.20** | 0.47** | 0.26** | 0.55** | 0.12* | 1 | | | |
| 13. Internal and external organizations | 4.53 | 0.91 | 0.00 | 0.02 | 0.07 | 0.01 | 0.03 | 0.05 | −0.04 | 0.41** | 0.29** | 0.44** | 0.31** | 0.31** | 1 | | |
| 14. Of departments | 4.30 | 0.99 | 0.02 | 0.04 | 0.12* | 0.05 | 0.12 | 0.04 | −0.11* | 0.41** | 0.28** | 0.40** | 0.27** | 0.49** | 0.39** | 1 | |
| 15. With system | 4.09 | 0.97 | 0.10 | 0.02 | 0.03 | 0.07 | 0.14 | −0.13** | 0.33** | 0.46** | 0.52** | 0.30** | 0.47** | 0.31** | 0.46** | 0.38** | 1 |

Notes: ** Correlation is significant at the 0.01 level (two–tailed); * correlation is significant at the 0.05 level (two–tailed).

**Table 6.2** One-Way ANOVA Results

| Harmony Scale | Demographic Characteristic | F-Value | Significance | LSD Post Hoc Test |
|---|---|---|---|---|
| Harmony with firm leader | Gender | 1.35 | 0.24 | |
| | Age | 2.99 | 0.05* | Older and equal to 36-year old (4.49) > younger and equal to 25-year old (4.27)<br>Older and equal to 36-year old (4.49) > between 26 and 35 (4.23) |
| | Marital status | 3.56 | 0.06* | Married (4.40) > single (4.18) |
| | Province | 0.26 | 0.76 | |
| | Education level | 4.28 | 0.01** | High school (4.59) > junior high and below (4.27) |
| | Years worked | 4.85 | 0.00*** | Greater and equal to 5 years (4.57) > greater and equal to 1 year to less than 5 years (4.26)<br>Greater and equal to 5 years (4.57) > less than 1 year (4.24) |
| | Group | 13.91 | 0.00*** | Managers (4.76) > employees (4.27) |
| Harmony of employees | Gender | 0.39 | 0.52 | |
| | Age | 0.68 | 0.50 | |
| | Marital status | 2.23 | 0.13 | |
| | Province | 1.05 | 0.34 | |
| | Education level | 4.46 | 0.01** | Junior high and below (4.76) > high school (4.52)<br>Junior high and below (4.76) > college (4.24) |
| | Years worked | 6.25 | 0.00*** | Less than 1 year (4.85) > greater and equal to 5 years (4.48)<br>Greater and equal to 1 to less than 5 years (4.75) > greater and equal to 5 years (4.48) |
| | Group | 38.59 | 0.00*** | Employees (4.81) > managers (4.13) |

**Table 6.2** One-Way ANOVA Results—cont'd

| Harmony Scale | Demographic Characteristic | F-Value | Significance | LSD Post Hoc Test |
|---|---|---|---|---|
| Harmony with own team | Gender | 0.61 | 0.43 | |
| | Age | 8.00 | 0.00*** | Older and equal to 36-year old (4.87) > between 26 and 35 (4.62) |
| | | | | Older and equal to 36-year old (4.49) > younger and equal to 25-year old (4.43) |
| | Marital status | 10.47 | 0.00*** | Married (4.77) > single (4.42) |
| | Province | 0.10 | 0.90 | |
| | Education level | 8.79 | 0.00*** | College (5.39) > junior high and below (4.58) |
| | | | | High school (4.92) > junior high and below (4.58) |
| | Years worked | 13.24 | 0.00*** | Greater and equal to 5 years (5.02) > less than 1 year (4.56) |
| | | | | Greater and equal to 5 years (5.02) > greater and equal to 1 year to less than 5 years (4.50) |
| | Group | 57.75 | 0.00*** | Managers (5.41) > employees (4.54) |
| Self-harmony | Gender | 3.55 | 0.06* | Female (4.77) > male (4.61) |
| | Age | 3.19 2.51 | 0.04** | 26–35 (4.84) > older and equal to 36-year-old (4.59) |
| | Marital status | 2.51 | 0.11 | |
| | Province | 0.591 | 0.55 | |
| | Education level | 6.95 | 0.00*** | Junior high and below (4.79) > high school (4.44) |
| | Years worked | 12.55 | 0.00*** | Less than 1 year (4.92) > greater and equal to 5 years (4.42) |
| | | | | Greater and equal to 1 year to less than 5 years (4.77) > greater and equal to 5 years (4.42) |
| | Group | 81.14 | 0.00*** | |

*Continued*

**Table 6.2** One-Way ANOVA Results—cont'd

| Harmony Scale | Demographic Characteristic | F-Value | Significance | LSD Post Hoc Test |
|---|---|---|---|---|
| Harmony with direct boss | Gender | 0.00 | 0.94 | |
| | Age | 0.33 | 0.71 | |
| | Marital status | 0.12 | 0.72 | |
| | Province | 0.31 | 0.73 | |
| | Education level | 5.62 | 0.00*** | College (5.03) > junior high and below (4.30) High school (4.64) > junior high and below (4.30) |
| | Years worked | 4.15 | 0.00*** | Greater and equal to 5 years (4.61) > greater and equal to 1 year to less than 5 years (4.23) |
| | | 5.62 | 0.00*** | |
| | Group | 15.12 | 0.00*** | Managers (4.87) > employees (4.31) |
| Of internal and external organizations | Gender | 0.00 | 0.95 | |
| | Age | 1.69 | 0.18 | |
| | | 0.33 | 0.71 | |
| | Marital status | 0.15 | 0.69 | |
| | | 0.12 | 0.72 | |
| | Province | 0.08 | 0.92 | |
| | | 0.31 | 0.73 | |
| | Education level | 0.46 | 0.63 | |
| | Years worked | 0.61 | 0.53 | |
| | Group | 0.81 | 0.36 | |
| Of departments | Gender | 0.13 | 0.71 | |
| | Age | 2.95 | 0.05* | Older and equal to 36-year old (4.44) > between 26 and 35 (4.21) Older and equal to 36-year old (4.44) > younger and equal to 25-year old (4.16) |
| | Marital status | 0.77 | 0.37 | |
| | | 0.12 | 0.72 | |
| | Province | 0.59 | 0.55 | |
| | | 0.31 | 0.73 | |
| | Education level | 2.91 | 0.05* | College (4.81) > junior high and below (4.23) |
| | Years worked | 1.20 | 0.30 | |

**Table 6.2** One-Way ANOVA Results—cont'd

| Harmony Scale | Demographic Characteristic | F-Value | Significance | LSD Post Hoc Test |
|---|---|---|---|---|
| | Group | 4.97 | 0.02** | Managers (4.57) > employees (4.25) |
| With system | Gender | 3.82 | 0.05* | Female (4.18) > male (3.98) |
| | Age | 0.22 | 0.80 | |
| | | 0.33 | 0.71 | |
| | Marital status | 0.15 | 0.69 | |
| | | 0.12 | 0.72 | |
| | Province | 1.87 | 0.15 | |
| | | 0.31 | 0.73 | |
| | Education level | 4.50 | 0.01** | Junior high and below (4.18) > high school (3.83) |
| | Years worked | 3.55 | 0.03** | Less than 1 year (4.26) > greater and equal to 5 years (3.92) |
| | Group | 46.46 | 0.00*** | Employees (4.24) > managers (3.37) |

Notes: *** Significant at the 0.01 level (two tailed); ** significant at the 0.05 level (two tailed); * significant at the 0.10 level (two tailed).

with own team', 'harmony with direct boss', and 'harmony of departments'. Grass-roots workers scored higher in three dimensions: 'harmony with corporate system', 'harmony of employees', and 'self-harmony', with differences at significant levels.

### 6.2.5.5 Educational Level
Educational level was found to influence seven dimensions at significant levels. Junior high/polytechnic graduates scored the lowest in terms of 'harmony with firm leader', 'harmony with own team', 'harmony of departments', 'harmony with direct boss', and 'with corporate system' but scored the highest in terms of 'harmony of employees' and 'self-harmony.'

### 6.2.5.6 Tenure
Tenure affected employee perceptions of harmony in six dimensions at significant levels. As far as 'harmony with own team' and 'harmony with direct boss', respondents with one to five working years scored the lowest. Respondents with five or more working years scored the lowest in terms of 'harmony with corporate system', 'harmony of employees' and

'self-harmony.' However, they scored the highest in 'harmony with own team', 'harmony with firm leader', and 'harmony with direct boss'. In contrast, respondents with <1 working year tenure scored the highest in 'harmony with corporate system', 'harmony of employees', and 'self-harmony'.

The foregoing findings reveal how differences in key demographic characteristics of workers (i.e. age, gender, marital status, job position, educational level, and tenure) influence their levels of perceived harmony at the workplace. This indicates the critical clues for the emergence of employee grievance and the potential areas of labour-management conflict, thus responding to RQ2. More specifically, when we integrated the quantitative results, we discovered that lower-educated grass-roots workers aged between 26 and 35 years old or with 1–5 working years tenure appeared to be an important source of grievance and resentment. Therefore, we chose the subjects for the follow–up qualitative survey based on the foregoing criteria.

## 6.2.6 Study 2

We reported the results of study 1 to the company in late October 2014. After intensive discussion with the company's chief HR director, we were finally allowed to conduct 11 in–depth, comprehensive interviews with four critical groups of employees who were directly involved in the labour strike, two HR and two production managers representing the company to deal with the protestors, three production foremen as the strike advocates/leaders, and four production grass-roots workers as the strike participants. To avoid disturbing workers at this sensitive period, all interviewees were chosen by the HR team, whereby the selection bias was also reduced. Then we spent 2 days interviewing, which typically lasted 40 min on average, in a closed meeting room of the company. We recorded most interviews and had them professionally transcribed. Interview questions broadly focused on discussing the following 5 broad topics and their opinions, views, and perceptions of: (1) dissatisfaction and grievance against the company; (2) use of strike as a means to voice discontent; (3) how and why the strike happened and ended; (4) how and why the conflict was resolved; and (5) predictions about the possibility of the occurrence of labour protests in the future. However, the questions changed somewhat as our informants guided our inquiries through the stories they told (Charmaz, 2006; Sonenshein, 2014). We were also interested in their demographic information, position, and tenure in the job. Table 6.3 contains an overview of our interview data.

**Table 6.3** Overview of Interview Data for Study 2

| No. | Name/Province | Gender | Age | Tenure | Department | Position | Monthly Wage (Excluding Social Insurance) (RMB/USD) |
|-----|---------------|--------|-----|--------|------------|----------|-----------------------------------------------------|
| 1 | David (Taiwan) | M | 40 | 15 | HR | Top management | Over 20,000/3256 |
| 2 | Eric (Fujian) | M | 31 | 10 | HR | Team director | About 5000/814 |
| 3 | Lisa (Hubei) | F | 37 | 18 | Production | Worker | About 2400/391 |
| 4 | Jack (Hunan) | M | 30 | 5 | Production | Worker | About 2500/407 |
| 5 | Peter (Hunan) | M | 34 | 9 | Production | Worker | About 2500/407 |
| 6 | John (Sichuan) | M | 32 | 5 | Production | Worker | About 2500/407 |
| 7 | Mary (Hunan) | F | 41 | 20 | Production | Line supervisor | About 5000/814 |
| 8 | Steve (Hubei) | M | 29 | 4 | Production | Foreman | About 3300/537 |
| 9 | Mark (Hunan) | M | 29 | 5 | Production | Foreman | About 3500/570 |
| 10 | Helen (Hubei) | F | 43 | 25 | Production | Manager | About 13,000/2117 |
| 11 | Sherry (Hunan) | F | 44 | 25 | Production | Manager | About 13,000/2117 |

Apart from the interviews, we also tried to gather additional data through the internet and other public sources, including a variety of archival materials such as newspapers, journal articles, and internal reports. Unfortunately, owing to strict control over all media outlets in China, we got limited evidence about relevant labour unrest. Hence, we relied on an important personal contact from the third party who introduced our research team to the company to serve as one of our key informants. He frequently provided us with in-depth, informative updates throughout the study.

### 6.2.6.1 Data Analysis

As mentioned earlier, we used a Grounded Theory approach (Charmaz, 2006; Sonenshein, 2014) to code data that involved three primary steps. First, we used initial coding to sort data from the interview transcripts and field notes, classifying repeated and similar codes into first-order categories. In this phase, we continued reading and rereading data until there were no new insights yielded by them. Second, we used second-order or axial coding searching for relationships within and between the initial codes, converting them into second-order categories. Third, with a deeper understanding of second-order themes, we eventually matched them with the five aggregate theoretical dimensions of our 5C model, as noted above. We went back and forth between the developed model and the data, making several refinements along the way. Fig. 6.3 illustrates the relationships between first-order categories, second-order themes, and our aggregate five dimensions.

To ensure the credibility of our data, we tested our interpretations by reviewing all of the data again and again, looking for both confirming and disconfirming evidence (Sonenshein, 2014). Moreover, we used member checking with key informants, asking for feedback about whether our interpretations and theoretical accounts were convincing. Finally, we depended on peer debriefing by discussing the identified model with colleagues and experts not involved in this research project.

## 6.2.7 Findings of Study 2

Referring to Fig. 6.3, we further unpacked our findings in greater detail following the pattern of the 5C model that structures the harmonizing process in China.

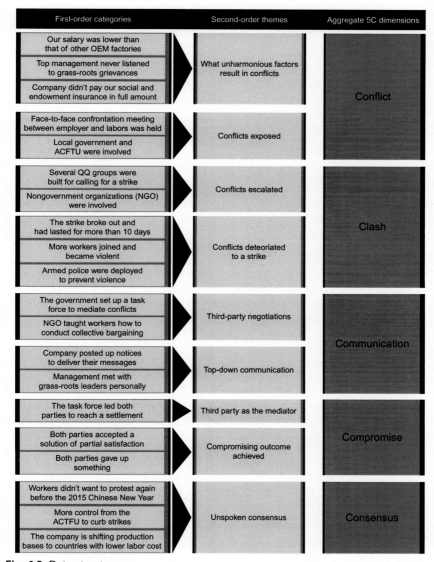

| First-order categories | Second-order themes | Aggregate 5C dimensions |
|---|---|---|
| Our salary was lower than that of other OEM factories | What unharmonious factors result in conflicts | Conflict |
| Top management never listened to grass-roots grievances | | |
| Company didn't pay our social and endowment insurance in full amount | | |
| Face-to-face confrontation meeting between employer and labors was held | Conflicts exposed | |
| Local government and ACFTU were involved | | |
| Several QQ groups were built for calling for a strike | Conflicts escalated | Clash |
| Nongovernment organizations (NGO) were involved | | |
| The strike broke out and had lasted for more than 10 days | Conflicts deteoriated to a strike | |
| More workers joined and became violent | | |
| Armed police were deployed to prevent violence | | |
| The government set up a task force to mediate conflicts | Third-party negotiations | Communication |
| NGO taught workers how to conduct collective bargaining | | |
| Company posted up notices to deliver their messages | Top-down communication | |
| Management met with grass-roots leaders personally | | |
| The task force led both parties to reach a settlement | Third party as the mediator | Compromise |
| Both parties accepted a solution of partial satisfaction | Compromising outcome achieved | |
| Both parties gave up something | | |
| Workers didn't want to protest again before the 2015 Chinese New Year | Unspoken consensus | Consensus |
| More control from the ACTFU to curb strikes | | |
| The company is shifting production bases to countries with lower labor cost | | |

**Fig. 6.3** Data structure.

### 6.2.7.1 Stage 1: Conflict

The dispute was aroused by an incident in the news. A production superintendent who had worked in the company for >20 years retired in 2013 but only got a pension of just RMB 650 (about US$106) per month. This news spread quickly in the factory, causing various rumours and anxieties among production workers. A lot of veteran workers felt that the company had not paid their social insurance premiums in full and began to complain about their low wages and worry about their pensions. As indicated by our informant Peter (5):

> I have worked here for 9 years with 10-12 working hours a day; however, my average monthly take-home pay is only RMB 2,500 (about US$407), which is too low to support my family. All top managers are enjoying good houses, great cars, and dining in good restaurants, but never listened to our voice [...]. I deserved a higher wage!

Hence, some workers went to check their social security accounts but found that the balance of their accounts was zero. Many workers thus became very agitated. To ease the discontent of workers, the company immediately hosted a face-to-face confrontation meeting in late April 2014 to explain that the discrepancy was due to an official system's error. David (1), on behalf of the company, responded that:

> We have started to invest in the factory complex in China since 1990 and the social insurance law was just enacted at that time. However, the government didn't actually executed that law until 2005 [...]. In fact, to attract more foreign direct investment, the local government officials even orally promised us to enjoy the social insurance fee waiver until 2005 [...]. Unfortunately, the new official overthrew the previous oral agreement [...] this is why that retired superintendent's pension was so little because the payment years were less than his actual working years.

The local labour bureau and local trade union also attended the meeting and confirmed the company's statement by issuing a formal red-head document.[2] Nevertheless, most workers did not believe this. Jack (4) described this situation emphatically:

> The collusion between government officials and employers were very common in China. The representative of our corporate labor union was also appointed by the government. Hence, the local government and trade union definitely defended the employer's interests, helping the company to make fools of us. The company should return us our money to our insurance accounts immediately!

Obviously, at the first harmonizing stage, conflict, the critical unharmonious factors that may trigger the strike action were identified.

### 6.2.7.2 Stage 2: Clash
Since the end of April 2014, several NGOs, including Hong Kong-, New York-, and domestic-based labour NGOs, have been very concerned about

---

[2] A colloquial term of formal, official documents in China.

this matter and have even provided advisory opinion provoking workers to take stronger action in bargaining with the employer. In the meantime, at least seven QQ (the largest microblog community with the best instant messaging service in China)[3] groups were built for networking and organizing disgruntled workers. As noted by David (1):

> [...] some workers took the informal leading role of all discontented employees, planning to carry out a strike via QQ groups. Workers supporting the company's side were not allowed to join their QQ groups and the labor-management conflict had escalated.

On 5 May, China News Service abruptly reported that there would be a wildcat strike by the company's workers in the vicinity of the main plant. Although the news was dismissed as mere rumour and the QQ group lord (the appellation of the QQ blog owner) disseminating this rumour was soon arrested and interrogated by the police, many workers seemed to feel more provoked and were indeed planning to stage a strike. As illustrated by Helen (10):

> After the incident on May 5, we perceived that many production workers were very low in morale and some people were preparing big banners and amplifiers- a sign for conducting a street demonstration!

On May 14, the strike broke out. In the beginning, thousands of workers stopped work to participate in the protest, some of whom held banners demanding their due benefits. The protest leaders kept using QQ groups to call for workers from all the plants in the company in southern China to support them. Then more and more workers joined, and finally >25,000 workers were on strike. They demanded that the company grant wage rises of 30%, catch up on all overdue social benefits that should have been paid since 1998, and allow workers the right to pick their own union. Hundreds of police officers were sent to the scene to help keep order.

Given that the company still failed to agree on their demands on 16 May, the protesting workers became very agitated and violent. On the morning of 17 May, some workers rushed into the residential area of Taiwanese cadres (i.e. expatriate executives from Taiwan), threatening to beat the people who had humiliated and tortured China workers. David (1) described it:

> Those workers just broke into the dormitory area of Taiwanese cadres and shouted. They claimed to "kill the chickens to frighten the monkeys!" (In

---

[3]  https://www.tencent.com/en-us/abouttencent.html

*Chinese, it means to punish someone as a warning to others not accept their demands). In this vein, most of Taiwanese workers did not dare to leave their apartments. As a result, the company was forced to ask for the government's protection and evacuated part of female Taiwanese workers and relatives back to Taiwan.*

On the afternoon of 17 May, the whole situation deteriorated. The protesting workers even beat up the workers who did not want to continue with the strike. The majority of the local police force (60%) was therefore deployed to guard against further violence. The strike allowed a long-lasting feeling of anger among production workers to be pushed to the surface, which is consistent with the second harmonizing stage, clash.

### 6.2.7.3 Stage 3: Communication

After experiencing the severe unrest between 14 and 17 May, a special task force consisting of >80 labour bureau officials, trade union executives, lawyers, police officers, and labour experts was urgently set up by the government to mediate. The members of the task force frequently met worker representatives, listening to their requests, and organized negotiations between labour and the employer. It is worth noting that during the strike several international and local NGOs had close contact with the workers' representatives and offered them guidance to bargain with the company. As Eric (2) recalled:

*The NGOs were helpful. They taught us how to carefully avoid any activity that might be viewed as illegal or a political challenge to the government. The ACFTU was unable to give us such assistance.*

However, as far as this case is concerned, too much NGO intervention might have complicated the negotiation situation because the task force had been officially designated to conciliate. As David (1) described it:

*Some NGOs had intended to speak on behalf of workers and even spread untruthful rumors about the company [...] Fortunately, the government immediately stopped them.*

Given that the riot had just happened and the workers' QQ groups still forbade access from people supporting the employer, the company's management chose to post notices on the plant walls to deliver their messages. Apart from face-to-face talks with production foremen and superintendents, through the help of the aforementioned task force, management held several multilateral meetings with the representatives of protesting workers and the representatives of local and corporate trade unions. The action of top-down communication to a certain extent pacified tension between labour and the employer. This was mentioned by Steve (8):

> *I have worked here for four years but this was the first time our Taiwanese Deputy General Manager talked to me in person. He was very friendly and nice.*

At the third harmonizing stage, communication, the involvement of the third party created a foundation of mutual understanding and a platform for further progress.

### 6.2.7.4 Stage 4: Compromise

After the official task force became deeply involved in this issue, the provincial trade union played a particularly important role in driving both parties to reach an agreement. The protesting workers were persuaded to give up their demand for a 30% wage rise, while the company was requested to catch up on the full amount of the unpaid social benefits since 1999. The chairman of the local ACFTU acted as a key mediator in this negotiation, rejecting any proposal in favour of one side and demanding that both sides use maximum respect to devise a settlement.

On 21 May, the company agreed that they would increase grass root worker monthly wages by about RMB 230 (US$37) and compensate for the unpaid social insurance premiums as long as employees applied to the company, while the corporate trade union (a union branch established and guided by the local ACFTU) led some protestors to write an initiative encouraging all protesting workers to resume work. On 25 May, most protesting workers had returned to work.

Facilitated by the mediator, namely the official task force, the protesting workers and management ultimately accepted a solution that actually provided incomplete satisfaction of both parties' concerns. This embodies the distinguishing characteristic of the fourth harmonizing stage, compromise.

### 6.2.7.5 Stage 5: Consensus

On 29 May, production was largely back to normal, despite the fact that the morale among grass-roots workers was still low. In early June, the company claimed that they suffered losses of US$27 million during the strike and future payments for offsetting worker social security debt since 1999. Additionally, the company faced falling orders from global brands for their

Chinese factories due to the looming risks of future strikes and accompanying production shutdowns. David (1) described it seriously:

> Due to the increasing labor cost, our parent company in Taiwan has decided to close most of our China factories and quicken the pace to move our production basis to South East Asia where the labor lost is lower.

Some workers were also aware of the negative impact induced by the strike at the company and were thus inclined to avoid such aggressive confrontation in the future. Lisa (3) noted:

> My three family members and I have worked here for more than 18 years and this seems to be the worst situation. Our factory has been receiving falling orders and struggling with the crunch of reducing profit margins. I will not support a strike because I don't want them to close down this factory!

However, some workers seemed to feel that a strike was the most effective way to improve their conditions. As John stated (5):

> Our employer had earned a lot of money but we were the toiling mass with poor income. I think there will be no protest again until the Chinese New Year, but some workers may plan to do it again for raising wages after the vocation.

The provincial labour union led by the ACFTU was very concerned with this situation. To curb further labour unrest, the provincial union was elevated to act more expediently as the 'transmission belt' of the party. Since June 2014, the officials of the provincial labour union instructed the company to rebuild their corporate trade union, forming a new type of 'joint corporate trade union' where six independent, grass-roots trade unions with their own suborganizations were set up to monitor the six plants of the company, helping to enhance workplace management and maintain harmonious relationships between labour and employers.

In sum, it is apparent that consensus was reached among labour, management, and government as follows: (1) no strike until the 2015 Chinese New Year (the promise of the workers); (2) more control from the ACTFU (the promise of the government); and (3) the reallocation of the production basis (the promise of the company). Nevertheless, consistent with our 5C model, the consensus stage may just mean an ephemeral harmonious status given that the actual labour–management relationship of the company is still highly uncertain, tense, and contingent, constantly changing according to the shift in the external economic environment.

According to the foregoing findings, our 5C model has been well examined.

## 6.2.8 Discussion

Leung et al. (2011) have claimed that conflict and harmony are really two sides of the same coin and that harmony maintenance should be considered as a response to conflict from a Chinese point of view. Chin (2014) further underscores the importance of understanding the Chinese notion of harmony to resolving conflicts/contradictions in China from the perspective of *Yijing*. Following this viewpoint, our study therefore explored the fundamental and hidden causes of the increasing labour-management conflicts in Chinese manufacturing with a unique harmony approach, providing evidence on what and how the demographic variables of factory employees affect their perceptions of harmony in the workplace. Our major findings are discussed in depth in the following summary.

Given that 'harmony with corporate system', 'harmony of departments', and 'harmony with firm leader' were found to be the top three lowest scores in the eight dimensions of harmony, it is plausible to view them as the three vital factors that could arouse serious labour grievance and trigger aggressive employee disputes, such as labour strikes. Consistent with our findings and as reported in the news, the factory workers participating in the strike indeed expressed strong discontent at the corporate system and its top echelon. Employees thought that the corporate compensation and benefit systems were very unfair and unsatisfactory and that top management did not listen to the voices of grass-roots employees. However, as shown in our case, it is surprising that under such a post-strike, low-morale, and uncertain working environment, the scores of the three factors remained higher than 4, indicating that Chinese employees indeed tend to avoid direct criticism and confrontation publicly when answering questionnaires (Leung et al., 2011; Nguyen & Yang, 2012).

The characteristics of employees such as age, gender, marital status, education level, tenure, and position were identified as significantly influencing employee perceptions on the level of harmony in the workplace. For example, females mainly scored higher than males, while married workers mostly scored higher than unmarried ones, in accordance with the common recognition (e.g. Pun, 2007) that males or unmarried employees (including both male and female ones) are often more aggressive, but that females or married employees with family burdens are prone to hold relatively conservative attitudes. Employees with a lower educational level seemed to emphasize more on self-harmony, whereas those with higher educational qualifications were more concerned with their teams and direct supervisors/bosses. Employees with managerial positions agreed more on the leader and their own team, whereas grass-roots workers agreed more on self-harmony and colleagues. This may be because managers generally have a better understanding of the importance of teamwork as well as the responsibilities and duties held by managerial staff. Employees older than 35 years old generally scored higher, indicating a higher tolerance of disharmony and disagreement in the workplace. It is worth noting that in terms of 'harmony with corporate system', the dimension with the lowest score, males (3.981), high school graduates (3.839), employees with more than five working years (3.922), and managerial positions (3.376), gave relatively low evaluations.

The results of the case study corroborate the explanatory power of the 5C model in elaborating the unique harmonizing way that the Chinese people tend to handle labour conflicts. According to our findings, the company's misconduct on social insurance as the root cause of the labour strike can, to a certain extent, be attributed to the institutional void at the embryo stage of China's fast economic growth in the 1990s. At that time, the government loosened the implementation of labour laws to attract FDI. Despite the government deciding to move towards a more market-oriented economy, the strong intervention of the ACFTU in this case confirmed the critical role of the government in facilitating business operations in China. Taking a deeper look at the behaviour of the provincial trade union in our case, we discovered that their strategic actions to a certain extent mirrored the core spirit of Yin–Yang harmony and the 5C model. Despite supporting workers to effectively voice their worries and grievances, the union was not able to completely represent the interests of workers because its eventual goal was to maintain harmonious labour relations and stable productivity for the factory due to its political role in safeguarding the interests of the country (Chan, 2014; Wang, 2011).

Scholars suggest that the growing labour unrest in the manufacturing sector is actually a product of China's transition in its economic and regulative system. While China is at a critical stage of developing a unique socialistic market economic system with the coexistence of socialist and market-based capitalist characteristics, labour protection with associated labour relation issues will draw increasing attention (Chang & William, 2013; Liu & Li, 2014). However, research demonstrates that many of today's factory employees are migrant/peasant workers who remain exploited as they are subject to long working hours, low pay, and monotonous jobs and are often denied even basic individual rights (Chan, 2010; Liu & Li, 2014; Tang & Fitzsimons, 2013). If so, the number of labour strikes at China's manufacturers may escalate in the future. Our findings therefore can be considered as a feasible cue or guidance for OEMs in China to help limit strikes and protests. Additionally, our study is particularly useful for non-Chinese managers to better comprehend the unique harmonizing process of Chinese conflict resolution that is distinctive from the way of solving conflicts in Western societies.

In short, our study yields several important contributions. First, it advances our understanding of how labour-intensive OEMs cope with increasing employee–employer conflicts, in answer to the call for exploring the roles of specific contexts in managing conflicts (Nguyen & Yang, 2012; Zarankin, 2008). Second, in terms of theoretical implications, given that harmony is considered as the core value of the humanistic spirit in China (Chin, 2015, 2014), we extend the Western dual-concern model, proposing a dominant, context-specific concern–concern for harmony in this context. Most importantly, on the basis of the perspective of Yin–Yang harmony, we elucidate the dynamic, contingent, and art-based nature of Chinese conflict management, and put forward our 5C model delineating the unique harmonizing process for resolving conflicts in China. Third, we applied conflict management theories to business practices, which can be seen as an exciting step forward in bridging the common academic-practitioner divide.

## 6.2.9 Limitations and Future Research

Although our study contributes to an initial understanding of applying the cultural perspective of Yin–Yang harmony to Chinese conflict management, its limitations and constraints should be noted. First, the sample only involved one Taiwan-based manufacturing giant in a country with >130 million migrant workers in manufacturing. Future studies could collect more comprehensive data in more diversified regions of China. Second, despite new potential research avenues that can be drawn from our study, it is still exploratory in essence and only offers implicit suggestions on possible directions rather than explicit solutions to labour-management contradictions. Hence, future research could focus on further analysing how the 5C model of the harmonizing process can actually be applied to conflict-coping strategies in China.

Overall, the same episode of conflict may denote distinctive meanings or be perceived differently across diversified cultures, and the ongoing social and economic transformation makes Chinese people's conflict management styles even less predictable (Oetzel, Garcia, & Ting-Toomey, 2008; Yan &

Sorenson, 2004). Considering that the appreciation of the Chinese currency and worsening shortages of skilled labour have slowed down export growth in China's OEM industry, the government has claimed that China will be moving from a production-based to a more innovation-oriented economy. The export-led OEM business is expected to be even less competitive and profitable in China and the relocation of labour-intensive OEMs from China to other developing countries with cheaper labour is becoming a phenomenon (Chin & Liu, 2014; Fang et al., 2010). Hence, manufacturing employment could be further reduced and conflicts may raise increasing concerns in the Chinese market. It is imperative to collect more first-hand data by probing into relevant labour relations issues in depth in this context.

## 6.3 CONCLUSION

This chapter illustrates the seriousness of manufacturing employment problems in China. According to the news, China's job market seemed to have become stable in 2016 and 2017 as the urban unemployment rate was brought gradually under control.[4] However, China Labour Bulletin (a Hong Kong-based NGO), claimed that there were nearly 1400 labour strikes recorded in 2014, many of which happened in the manufacturing sector, and the number rose to over 2700 in 2015 and 2016.[5]

One of the fundamental causes of industrial relations conflicts lies in the inconsistency between employer and employee points of view on corporate welfare and benefit issues. From an employer's perspective, China's labour cost has increased to the extent that most labour-intensive manufacturers have problems. In contrast, from a production employee's perspective, blue-collar workers have never shared the fruits of China's growth, but rather were exploited, so the government, trade unions, and employers should better protect their legally mandated benefits and do more to secure their jobs.

Another fundamental cause of industrial relations conflict is the unbalance and contradiction between labour demand and supply. Under the pressure to upgrade and automate production lines, many manufacturing firms attempt to increase recruitment of more technical personnel and decrease recruitment of low-educated migrant workers. However, the younger

[4] http://www.chinadaily.com.cn/business/2017-01/23/content_28032614.htm

[5] http://edition.cnn.com/2016/03/28/asia/china-strike-worker-protest-trade-union/index.html

generation with advanced technology knowledge may prefer to develop their careers in service-oriented industries or start their own business directly after graduation.

Considering the varied, yet entrenched, stances taken by employers and employees, it seems difficult to settle labour conflicts in Chinese manufacturing in a short period of time. Moreover, in response to the government's 'One Belt One Road' initiative, an increasing number of Chinese manufacturers are establishing production bases in the South Asia region and thus employing a more multinational workforce. Thus, the problems of labour disputes will be made more complex. Hence, in the next chapter, we will advance to discuss the job-related and employment issues in the Chinese manufacturing industry from a cross-cultural perspective.

CHAPTER SEVEN

# Cross-Cultural Management: A Globalized Production Network

## 7.1 INTRODUCTION

### 7.1.1 The Increasingly Important Role of Culture in Manufacturing Transformation

Along with the pervasive trend to establish geographically dispersed production bases for cost advantages, the ability to communicate with a multinational or diversified workforce has become a prerequisite and competitive strength. In other words, having an understanding of the host countries' local culture and business environment is of great significance for managers to develop cross-cultural management abilities and skills. Furthermore, whereas MNCs are often multilingual, how to manage effectively language and translation-related activities turns out to be a critical challenge for Chinese manufacturers with globalization. Hence, in the next section, we first use a case story to highlight the importance of cultivating cultural sensitivity for managers of MNE manufacturers to cope with workforce diversity. Then we introduce a study that presents why MNE manufacturers should be concerned more about lingua franca and related translation activities in the course of manufacturing transition.

### 7.1.2 A Story About Working From Home: Awesome or Demotivated?

After 7 years of working in a large American-invested electronics component manufacturer (an international JV) in GZ, China, Mark Zhang,[1] a male Chinese aged 35, was promoted as a supply chain development manager in charge of several main products procurement. His former direct supervisor was Sam Wang, a Chinese American who often invited subordinates to hang out together after work, enjoying KTV or just having casual chats about a

[1]All names in this story are disguised.

*The Future of Chinese Manufacturing*
https://doi.org/10.1016/B978-0-08-101108-9.00007-0

variety of topics, such as kids or personal issues. In addition, Sam had maintained very good and close *guanxi* with local clients and suppliers, some of whom used to pay visits to Mark's team at their office with some cookies, cakes, or small gifts. Having a close and harmonious relationship with his colleagues, Mark felt quite happy with his company until his current boss, Pietro Trocchi, a Frenchman, came to work in China for the first time.

The story above describes that building of harmonious *guanxi* with co-workers and suppliers indeed affects Chinese employee motivation towards work not only at the front line, but also at middle and top levels. Echoing the former two chapters, this case explicitly highlights the impact of harmonious culture on Chinese employee attitudes and behaviours, and implicitly indicates the crucial role of cross-cultural management for manufacturers in an increasingly competitive international arena.

### 7.1.3 Cross-Cultural Communication in Manufacturing

As noted above, the pivotal role that language and translation play in GVCs has been widely acknowledged. However, relatively little attention has been paid to elucidating relevant issues (Chidlow, Plakoyiannaki, & Welch, 2014; Piekkari, Welch, Welch, Peltonen, & Vesa, 2013). As such, this chapter presents research that proposes a novel, indigenous model delineating the dynamic and vital role of translation as a boundary-spanning tool in cross-border knowledge transfer within the intra-organizational networks of Chinese manufacturing firms.

## 7.2 CROSS-CULTURAL KNOWLEDGE TRANSFER IN A CHINESE MANUFACTURING MNE: THE ROLE OF TRANSLATION

### 7.2.1 Introduction

MNCs dominate the business landscape and account for over 90% of world trade (McGuinness, Demirbag, & Bandara, 2013). Given that MNCs are multilingual in nature, some critical language issues, such as language barriers in the headquarters (HQs)—subsidiary relationship (Harzing, Koster, & Magner, 2011), language and cultural skills (Barner-Rasmussen, Ehrnrooth, Koveshnikov, & Makela, 2014), and corporate language strategies within MNCs (Brannen & Doz, 2012), have been drawing increasing attention in recent years (Harzing & Pudelko, 2013; Barner-Rasmussen & Aarnio, 2011). In contrast, the corresponding translation activities, despite the day-to-day reality for MNCs of handling language diversity, seem to remain 'the forgotten factor' or are subsumed under the topics of language and cultural differences in the narrow, often inward-looking, silo of international business (IB) literature (Chidlow et al., 2014; Holden & Michailova, 2014).

A possible explanation for neglecting the indispensable role of translation is that most scholars still consider it a mundane, peripheral yet technical activity in the MNC context (Piekkari et al., 2013) and generally detach the act of translation from sociocultural context. However, some words may be culturally salient and thus inherently untranslatable between different languages (Blenkinsopp & Pajouh, 2010). For instance, if adopting English as the corporate lingua franca within MNCs, it will be difficult to literally translate the Russian word '*upravleniye*' (Holden & Michailova, 2014) and the German word '*schadenfreude*' (Blenkinsopp & Pajouh, 2010) into English. The Chinese word *guanxi* (关系) offers another obvious example. Although *guanxi* has been widely translated as relationships or networking in English, the term actually contains far more connotations beyond its literal meaning that are 'lost in translation'.

Research indicates that MNCs owe their very existence to superior ability on transferring valuable cross-cultural knowledge through their internal business units, that is, subsidiaries (Peltokorpi & Vaara, 2014) and external value chains, that is, customers, suppliers, and strategic alliance partners (Johanson & Vahlne, 2009). Specifically, knowledge transfer enables MNCs to form unique competitive advantages and inspire innovation via learning within their existing business networks, namely globally distributed subsidiaries, suppliers, and clients (Logemann & Piekkari, 2015; McGuinness et al., 2013). Language differences may thus be considered an obstacle restricting such knowledge flows. In some cases, the HQ may exercise its power by introducing a corporate-mandated language and imposing it on its global business network in an attempt to accelerate cross-national knowledge transfer. Moreover, expatriate managers or people with language skills often need to perform an intermediary position, responsible for translating messages and information within an MNC's network relationships (Harzing et al., 2011; Peltokorpi & Vaara, 2014). As a result, this translation issue about lack of semantic equivalence between two languages may become even more critical when involving the vital process of knowledge transfer in an MNC context (see Rowley & Poon, 2011).

However, despite the fact that translation is widely recognized as a key element of conveying knowledge across countries (Welch & Welch, 2008), it has mostly been perceived as a technical instrument (Usunier, 2011) and its mediating function in knowledge spillover has not been fully understood or addressed yet. To bridge this gap, our study considers the act of translation as a strategic tool for cross-border knowledge transfer. It investigates how individuals as boundary spanners handle the translation requirements associated with the procedure of knowledge transfer in a multilingual environment. More specifically, we conduct an exploratory case study to demonstrate how MNC employees with translation tasks engage in significant interactions on transferring knowledge across China, Germany, Russia, and the United States within two large Chinese MNCs. Consistent with Piekkari et al. (2013), translation is defined as the process of moving communication in any form (verbal or written) from one language to another and it is used in an overarching way, covering both written and oral communication.

Integrating previous research (Barner-Rasmussen et al., 2014; Johnson & Duxbury, 2010), our study establishes a research framework with five dimensions to characterize the typical boundary-spanning functions regarding translation in the knowledge transfer process of an MNC's business network in China (i.e. Exchanging, Linking, Manipulating, Facilitating, and Intervening). Scholars have called for greater interdisciplinary research in the IB area, to enrich theory development and enhance practical contributions (Holden & Michailova, 2014; Piekkari et al., 2013; Rowley, 2014). Following this call, our research includes three notions from the linguistics and translation literature—semantic equivalence, cultural interference, and ambiguity—to analyse our results.

The main theoretical contribution of our research is to put forward a novel (three-dimensional) 3D–hierarchical framework that reveals the multifaceted and contingent nature of the translation activities for cross-cultural knowledge transfer within a Chinese MNC's global network. Translation needs to be recognized as more than a transmission device for the transfer of meaning from one language to another. It needs to be recognized as an act of knowledge creation per se.

## 7.2.2 Theoretical Foundation
### 7.2.2.1 Translation and Knowledge Transfer in an MNE Context
The outcomes of cross-cultural knowledge transfer significantly relate to a firm's innovation, learning, and performance in a globalized world. Scholars argue that the transfer of knowledge within units belonging to the same organization (Criscuolo & Narula, 2007) or value chain (Johanson & Vahlne, 2009; Li, Li, et al., 2010; Li, Wei, et al., 2010) seems easier to achieve than that between unrelated organizations. Hence, the knowledge

transmission and spillover between the relationships of HQ–subsidiary and of supplier–client are widely regarded as important factors enhancing an MNC's overall knowledge base as well as sustainable competitive advantage (McGuinness et al., 2013; Spender, 2014; Zander, Mockaitis, & Harzing, 2011).

Early literature in the area was mainly built on the home-centric view of MNCs, where knowledge flows from the HQ to subsidiaries or from high value-added branding companies to low-end sources or manufacturing suppliers. However, more recent literature has detailed the significance of strategically leveraging the knowledge transferred from subsidiaries to parent companies (Criscuolo & Narula, 2007; Mudambi et al., 2014) or from local suppliers to global well-known brands (Li, Li, et al., 2010; Li, Wei, et al., 2010). In other words, the MNC that possesses the ability to mobilize valuable knowledge resources across borders can not only gain cross-national information on market dynamics and technical updates, but can also enter into novel fields of technology through integrating geographically dispersed, culturally diverse knowledge sources.

It is worth noting that knowledge transfer within an MNC requires an articulation or externalization process to enable personally held tacit knowledge to be more explicit and accessible to others who speak different languages (Bordia & Bordia, 2015; Peltokorpi & Vaara, 2014; Spender, 2014). As a result, language commonality plays an important role in promoting knowledge transmission in such a multilingual environment (Peltokorpi & Vaara, 2014).

According to Barner-Rasmussen and Bjorkman's (2007) study of 164 Chinese and Finnish subsidiaries, language commonality indeed had a positive effect on two antecedents of knowledge transfer: shared vision and perceived trustworthiness. Welch and Welch (2008) further highlighted that translators often perform a crucial role in encoding and decoding the messages to and from foreign subsidiaries, influencing the effectiveness of knowledge sharing and diffusion in MNCs. Brannen and Doz (2012) claimed that knowledge transfer in a multiethnic and multilingual workplace requires far more than simple language translation, whereas knowledge may imply different associated meanings in different contexts. Piekkari et al. (2013) proposed that the translation process should be seen as part of an MNC's language absorptive capacity and the central translation department is merely a partial solution because there are much more informal paths in terms of knowledge transfer (see Rowley & Poon, 2011). Overall, the act of translation has been commonly recognized as a key intermediary that helps break down language barriers hindering the knowledge flow within an MNC's business network.

However, despite its essential role in the process of transferring knowledge, translation and how MNCs cope with relevant issues remains a topic that has received scant attention in IB research (Bordia & Bordia, 2015; Chidlow et al., 2014). It may be because numerous MNEs used to view translation as a technical exercise where the major focus is on whether a source text is correctly and precisely rendered from one language to another (Blenkinsopp & Pajouh, 2010). Nevertheless, this mechanical perspective largely ignores that translation in MNCs' knowledge transfer involves much more than the decoding of a linguistic signal; it is actually intertwined with the cultural and socio-economic backgrounds of people participating in interunit communications.

As shown by Usunier (2011), the Chinese concept 'face' (面子, *mianzi* in Chinese) is experienced differently in the East and in the West because this word associates varied cognitive linkages embedded in Eastern and Western mindsets. 'Face' in Chinese is a rather complicated concept as it can not only represent a concrete term of face in English, but it can also refer to the need of a person to maintain a positive self and public image (Leung, Chen, Zhou, & Lim, 2014). However, it is quite difficult to find a better single English translation replacing face to semantically fit *mianzi*. In addition, while undertaking oral translation, the choice of active or passive voice by translators may also influence the results of translation. Hence, simply knowing the lexical equivalence of words may not be sufficient. To convey equivalent experiential meanings, translators need to have some understanding of cultures regarding both the source and target languages while engaging in the process of knowledge sharing (Bordia & Bordia, 2015; Brannen, Piekkari, & Tietze, 2014). More than a simple, neutral mediator through whom knowledge is transferred between different business units, the role of a translator may result in multifaceted effects on knowledge transfer that pertain to communication, network, cultural identity, and power in international settings (Peltokorpi & Vaara, 2014).

### 7.2.2.2 Translation and Its Boundary-Spanning Functions in MNCs

Many organizations are increasingly establishing an international presence. Thus, it has become more and more important for MNCs to rely on organizational members with language/translation skills to support the inter-unit information flow across different countries and to exert outward control over clients, suppliers, partners, and others in their business-related activities

(Richter, West, Dick, & Dawson, 2006; Schomaker & Zaheer, 2014). Given that the functions of boundary spanning are significantly involved with knowledge sharing, transferring, and creation between different players in MNC network relationships, the effectiveness of performing such functions has become a basic determinant factor for MNCs to develop a distinctive advantage.

A review of the relevant literature shows that boundary spanning concerning language translation in an MNC context actually encompasses various types of activities (Barner-Rasmussen et al., 2014; Johnson et al., 2010; Richter et al., 2006). With the emergence of MNCs, scholars have proposed many different models delineating how people with necessary language skills perform the role of boundary spanning in international settings. However, much of the previous research did not pay attention to addressing how such boundary spanners behave and function differently in terms of adaptations according to situational changes (Au & Fukuda, 2002; Thomas, 1994). To fill this gap, Johnson et al. (2010) integrated previous conceptualizations of boundary spanners, putting forward a comprehensive framework capturing the nine central elements of the boundary-spanning role played by multilingual professionals on expatriate assignments. These are: relationship building, shaping, intelligence gathering, delivering, coordinating/negotiating, guarding, information gathering, representing, and between the boundary spanners' perception of the external change and their responses to that change. This thus aligns the micro-level boundary construct with the macro-level environmental uncertainty (Johnson et al., 2010). The unique strength and advantage of this typology is to characterize the boundary spanning role from a broader perspective, which, however, can also be seen as a major weakness because some respective functions of the nine dimensions may overlap with each other. For example, some activities defined as 'intelligence gathering' may also be categorized under the dimension of 'information gathering'. Hence, it may be better to aggregate the nine dimensions into a more simplified construct.

Grounded in Johnson et al. (2010) work, Barner-Rasmussen et al. (2014) suggest an integrative, sequential model that synthesizes different types of boundary-spanning activities concerning intra-MNC knowledge flows. This uses four categories:

**(1)** Exchanging, which refers to individual employees engaging in the exchange of information and knowledge with actors in other units on behalf of their own units. This includes the dimensions of: 'delivering', 'intelligence', and 'information gathering' in Johnson et al. (2010) model.

**(2)** Linking, which refers to utilization of personal networks to enable previously unconnected actors to link up across boundaries, bridging and brokering the structural holes in MNCs. This contains the: 'intermediary' and 'relationship building' dimensions of Johnson et al. (2010) model.

**(3)** Facilitating, which refers to personal engagement and assistance in facilitating others' cross-boundary transactions. This covers: 'delivering'; 'coordinating/negotiating'; 'shaping'; and 'relationship building' in Johnson et al. (2010) model.

**(4)** Intervening, which refers to personal active intervention in interunit interactions for creating positive outcomes, such as resolving misunderstandings and conflicts and helping to build interunit trust, effective relations, and cooperative spirit. This encompasses the dimensions of: 'relationship building', 'delivering', 'shaping', 'coordination/ negotiation', 'intermediary', and 'representing' in Johnson et al. (2010) model.

The foregoing arguments lead us to conclude that in comparison with Johnson et al. (2010) and Barner-Rasmussen et al. (2014) model is more concise and feasible. In particular, this model elucidates the sequence of the four boundary-spanning functions in order of increasing complexity and sophistication. However, owing to the sole focus of this model on knowledge flows between the HQ and subsidiaries, it fails to include the important 'guarding activities' that pertain to knowledge transfer occurring in an MNC's global network.

Following the literature (Au & Fukuda, 2002; Johnson et al., 2010; Thomas, 1994), this guarding function indicates an opposite behaviour relative to other boundary spanning functions. Contrary to propelling knowledge transmission across borders, this function represents the acts of refusal, obstruction, or hindrance about closing the flow of news and knowledge between players in MNC business networks to protect confidential knowledge of the firm (e.g. advanced R&D technology or market information). As far as China is concerned, this guarding function may become even more important given that it maintains one of the most pervasive and sophisticated regimes of information control in the world (Chin et al., 2015) and the Chinese people tend to employ an implicit, rather than explicit, approach to exchanging information (Chin et al., 2015; Chin, 2014, 2015). From the viewpoint of the Chinese government, social stability is a paramount precondition for economic growth, modernization, and prosperity (Chin et al., 2015). Therefore, it is imperative to censor all types of information across borders. Indeed, such stability rules underpin many of China's regulations and policies on public and national security (Liu, 2011).

In this vein, such a control mechanism, when performed in the Chinese context, may go beyond the guarding function, but refers to personnel awareness and actions of manipulating the flow of news and knowledge for protecting confidential information. This embodies the cross-disciplinary characteristic of our study because the concept of 'manipulating' is derived from translation science (Hermans, 2014; Lefevere, 2004). More specifically, when transferring knowledge, translators may reconstruct and distort the information to varying degrees, by omitting or altering some facts due to the company's interests or according to the translator's knowledge of the target or recipient culture (Hermans, 2014). Therefore, translators, as a matter of fact, play a decisive role in manipulating an appropriate linguistic and textual environment during the process of knowledge transfer, with the goal of preventing misunderstandings and creating a favourable context for the company. In view of this, we add the above-mentioned guarding/controlling function to our model but also make a further advancement by terming it 'manipulating' according to the nature of such activities in China.

Scholars suggest that different disciplines can illuminate analyses in a valuable and unexpected manner because some phenomena may be seen in contorted and partial ways if only one disciplinary lens is used (Rowley, 2016). This partiality and bias situation will be exacerbated as increasingly complex problems that cannot be dealt with by mono-disciplinary approaches (Rowley, 2016). As such, in response to calls for considering linguistic relatedness in discussing relevant IB topics (Schomaker & Zaheer, 2014), our study applies three notions from the disciplines of linguistics and translation studies—semantic equivalence, cultural interference, and ambiguity—to build the conceptual framework. According to Holden and Michailova (2014), the definitions of these three notions are:

**(1)** Lack of equivalence: equivalent fundamental words and expressions cannot be found in translation.

**(2)** Cultural interference: translation can be influenced by a translator's own language and cultural background, which may cause misunderstandings.

**(3)** Ambiguity: ambiguity can be introduced into a text when a translator misunderstands a word in the original and the translation may present multiple meanings, making it unclear or confusing.

On the basis of the above discussion, our study first proposes a conceptual framework to delineate the five major types of boundary spanning activities regarding translation in the knowledge transfer process within a MNC business network, that is, Exchanging, Linking, Manipulating, Facilitating, and Intervening. The uniqueness of this model is its hierarchical structure wherein the upper-level function is posited to contain the lower-level function. In other words, the Intervening function covers the activities of Exchanging, Linking, Manipulating, and Facilitating, while the linking function includes the exchanging activities (see Fig. 7.1). Building on this framework, we conducted case studies to investigate two large Chinese MNCs to answer two RQs:

**(1)** How do individuals as boundary spanners handle the translation requirements associated with the procedure of knowledge transfer in an MNC's business network?

**(2)** Can our 3D–hierarchical model mirror the characteristics of the role of such boundary spanning?

## 7.2.3 Methodology

### 7.2.3.1 Sample Selection

Our research used a case study method given that this is particularly appropriate for probing into a relatively new phenomenon or topic

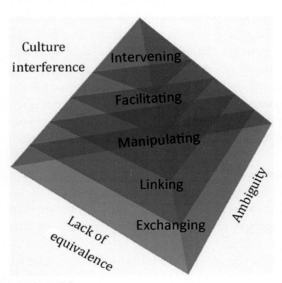

**Fig. 7.1** A conceptual model.

underestimated in the past (Chin et al., 2015; Yin, 2009). Whereas the construct of the boundary spanning role has not been well examined (Johnson et al., 2010), we conducted a qualitative, interview-based multiple case study to explore how individual boundary spanners engage in translation activities associated with the knowledge transfer process in MNC business networks. Moreover, referring to previous research (Charmaz, 2006; Sonenshein, 2014), we used a Grounded Theory approach to code the raw data following our initial orienting framework and model (see Fig. 7.1). This data coding technique allowed us to substantiate explicitly our conceptual research framework.

In alignment with the foregoing research design, we used purposeful sampling, which seeks to identify cases that may offer a more transparent and less cluttered view of the dynamics of theoretical interest (Yin, 2009). Given our core questions, we were concerned with finding Chinese MNCs where a certain proportion of employees possess the translation skills required to perform the boundary-spanning role in transferring knowledge. As a result, two MNCs were judgementally—not randomly—selected: Company A (listed on the Shenzhen Stock Exchange), headquartered in China's southern GZ city, provides OEM services for global water faucet brands and has more than 30,000 employees in China, Germany, and the United States. Company B, headquartered in the southern Dongguan city, is one of the world's leading electronic manufacturers with more than 100,000 employees globally.

### 7.2.3.2 Data Collection

The data were collected by a team of eight people who were fluent in both Chinese and English in March 2015. To obtain robust data, the triangulation method of qualitative research was used to ensure that multisource information was gathered, for example, interview records, archival materials, and company internal documentation (Chin et al., 2015; Yin, 2009). However, the critical data still came from the face-to-face interviews. With strong support from top managers of the MNCs, the research team spent 2 days at each company, gathering data through semistructured interviews (conducted mainly in Chinese) with 12 (six each from Company A and B) specially selected informants who had experience and good records in performing translation tasks. Table 7.1 presents an overview of the interviewee demographic information.

The interviews focused on the linkages between knowledge transfer and translation activities and on issues relevant to our RQs (see the Appendix).

**Table 7.1** Informants

| Name | Title | Gender | Age | Tenure | Education | Team size |
|------|-------|--------|-----|--------|-----------|-----------|
| Company A | | | | | | |
| Robert | Vice General Manager | Male | 60 | 30 years | PhD from China | More than 90 in total |
| Henry | Secretary to the General Manager | Female | 27 | 6 months | Master's degree from Germany | Unknown |
| Tank | Manager of Marketing Center | Female | 32 | 9 years | Bachelor's degree from China | 40 in total |
| Mary | Head of Division 1, Marketing Center | Female | 38 | 12 years | Bachelor's degree from China | 7 members |
| Lily | Member of Division 2, Marketing Center | Female | 30 | 7 years | Bachelor's degree from China | 5 members |
| Amy | Member of Division 3, Marketing Center | Female | 37 | 16 years | Bachelor degree's from China | 17 members |
| Karl | Director of Translation Center | Male | 48 | 18 years | PhD from China | 300 in total |
| William | Project Leader, Translation Center | Male | 37 | 8 years | Master's degree from United Kingdom | 20 |
| Zach | Project Leader, Translation Center | Male | 34 | 10 years | Master's degree from China | 15 |
| Zoe | Senior Translator, Translation Center | Female | 36 | 11 years | Master degree's from China | 12 |
| Simon | Product Manager | Male | 45 | 18 years | Master degree's from China | 20 |
| John | Senior Engineer | Male | 40 | 14 years | Bachelor's degree from China | 8 |

The interviewees were requested to give as many practical examples as possible. The interviews lasted 60–90 min each and were conducted by at least three researchers, where one handled interview questions and the other two took notes and made observations. All interviews were tape-recorded and the recorded data were then transcribed word for word.

In accordance with the study by Barner-Rasmussen et al. (2014), the role of boundary spanning as the core theme of our research was not directly addressed during the interviews but emerged during the interview process and was consequently elaborated upon through an 'abductive' process. Importantly, we tried to elicit informants' own narratives rather than direct informants to an a priori classification (i.e. our five-dimension model). Hence, when informants described their boundary spanning episodes, we prompted and interrupted only in instances where informants might provide insufficient details germane to our RQs.

### 7.2.3.3 Data Coding

As noted above, we used the analytic technique of data coding derived from Grounded Theory (Sonenshein, 2014). As indicated by Charmaz (2006), coding is the pivotal link between data collection and developing an emergent theory to explain the data, which helps us to grapple with what the data really mean. The data coding method requires researchers to move iteratively between raw data, emerging concepts, and the orienting framework. Furthermore, specifying an initial orienting framework sensitizes researchers to focus on observations of the raw data that are closely related to the variables of interest (Johnson et al., 2010).

Given that our study proposed the initial orienting framework of our five-dimension conceptual model, we followed Barner-Rasmussen et al. (2014) suggestion to code the data. First, we created simple, first-order descriptions based on the data's manifest content in relation to our research topic. Then we used second-order or axial coding searching for relationships within and between the initial codes, converting them into second-order categories, namely the five aggregate theoretical dimensions. Finally, we further considered the latent content of the data, integrating the three critically influential factors on the quality and reliability of translation—lack of equivalence, cultural interference, and ambiguity—into the coding. Examples of data coding are provided in Tables 7.2–7.6.

To ensure the credibility of our data, we tested our interpretations by repeatedly reviewing all of the data, looking for both confirming and disconfirming evidence (Sonenshein, 2014). Moreover, we compared the

**Table 7.2** Example of Exchanging

| | |
|---|---|
| *Case 2-1* | |
| Interviewee | Lily |
| Interview excerpt | 'We will pass on the latest market information on customers' needs and fashion trends in North America to headquarter' |
| Interpretation | Lily states that they will be responsible for passing on information from North America to headquarter |
| Coded as | One piece of evidence of the *exchanging function* recorded for Lily |
| Most frequently encountered difficulties | Lack of equivalence |
| *Case 2-2* | |
| Interviewee | Zoe |
| Interview excerpt | 'When the R&D managers need to communicate with the engineers in our German lab on technological issues, we will help them translate the documents, including emails and letters' |
| Interpretation | Zoe states how he helps the R&D managers to communicate with foreign engineers |
| Coded as | One piece of evidence of the *exchanging function* recorded for Zoe |
| Most frequently encountered difficulties | Lack of equivalence, cultural interference |
| *Case 2-3* | |
| Interviewee | John |
| Interview excerpt | 'Whenever our company asked for my advice on purchasing material from a new supplier, I usually had some discussions with my colleagues in our overseas R&D centre first' |
| Interpretation | Johan states that he has exchanged views with overseas colleagues |
| Coded as | One piece of evidence of the *exchanging function* recorded for William |
| Most frequently encountered difficulties | Lack of equivalence |

resultant data across the MNCs and found no differences concerning the overall distribution of the five boundary spanning functions beyond what might be expected owing to the different situations of the companies. Coding accuracy was also confirmed by triangulation between primary data (interview records), secondary data (observations and field notes), and archival materials (e.g. news and the companies' internal reports).

**Table 7.3** Example of Linking

| | |
|---|---|
| *Case 3-1* | |
| Interviewee | Amy |
| Interview excerpt | 'If a marketing manager of our client would like to give suggestions and feedbacks to our R&D engineers, there is actually no other way than communicating through me' |
| Interpretation | Amy is responsible for linking the persons of her clients to the counterpart/responsible personnel of her company |
| Coded as | One piece of evidence of the *linking function* recorded for Tank |
| Most frequently encountered difficulties | Lack of equivalence |
| *Case 3-2* | |
| Interviewee | Mary |
| Interview excerpt | 'Given the German company regularly assigned experts from Germany to audit our factory in China we had to link the auditor to the production personnel each time' |
| Interpretation | Mary states that her team helps to connect German auditor to communicate with the specific responsible personnel of her company |
| Coded as | One piece of evidence of the *linking function* recorded for Mary |
| Most frequently encountered difficulties | Lack of equivalence, Cultural interference |
| *Case 3-3* | |
| Interviewee | Zach |
| Interview excerpt | 'In respond to the demands of different departments, I will reallocate their works to the most suitable translator with professional knowledge in relevant field' |
| Interpretation | He states how he selects and links the most suitable subordinate to the person who apples for the translation service in Company B |
| Coded as | One piece of evidence of *linking function* is recorded for Zach |
| Most frequently encountered difficulties | Cultural interference |

**Table 7.4** Example of Manipulating

| | |
|---|---|
| *Case 4-1* | |
| Interviewee | Tank |
| Interview excerpt | 'The people of marketing centre sometimes are required to monitor the communication between the R&D staffs and the customers, in order to prevent unexpected information leakage. We have to tell the R&D people what they should say, and what they should not say' |
| Interpretation | Tank describes how she and her team play a role in manipulating the information outflows and inflows during the communication between company and customers |
| Coded as | One piece of evidence of the *manipulating function* recorded for Tank |
| Most frequently encountered difficulties | Cultural interference |
| *Case 4-2* | |
| Interviewee | William |
| Interview excerpt | 'For example, given the military background, our firm often participated in national security projects. We had to carefully prevent the release of such information while translating and introducing relevant projects to our foreign clients because some confidential information may still appear in our internal reports' |
| Interpretation | William states that they will control some information about national security when introducing projects to foreign clients |
| Coded as | One piece of evidence of the *manipulating function* recorded for William |
| Most frequently encountered difficulties | Cultural interference |

## 7.2.4 Results

As mentioned above, we sorted out the representative boundary spanning activities performed by the translators we had interviewed in the first-order coding and then classified the data into the five dimensions of our conceptual model in the second-order coding. In this vein, we dealt with our qualitative analysis in the light of the ordering of the boundary spanning functions in Fig. 7.1 (i.e. Exchanging, Linking, Manipulating, Facilitating, and Intervening). The key results are addressed in greater detail in the following tables.

**Table 7.5** Example of Facilitating

| *Case 5-1* | |
|---|---|
| Interviewee | Mary |
| Interview excerpt | 'I often help our technical engineers to communicate with our customer service department overseas for solving practical technical problems [...]. I need to play like a loop in-between, delivering messages back and forth' |
| Interpretation | Mary describes how she interprets messages between different units to facilitate communication |
| Coded as | One piece of evidence of the *facilitating function* recorded for Mary |
| Most frequently encountered difficulties | Lack of equivalence, cultural interference |
| *Case 5-2* | |
| Interviewee | William |
| Interview excerpt | 'When our CEO sounded too tough in his expression and we believed this may influence the company–client relationship, we may rephrase his words by softening the uncompromising and solid feeling when interpreting and translating his words from Chinese to English' |
| Interpretation | William states that to facilitate the relationship between the company and its clients, sometimes they may change the sentence patterns while interpreting their CEO's tough words from Chinese to English |
| Coded as | One piece of evidence of the *facilitating function* recorded for William |
| Most frequently encountered difficulties | Lack of equivalence, cultural interference |

### 7.2.4.1 Exchanging

As indicated above, this dimension involved delivery and gathering of information and knowledge in response to the demands of external stakeholders (e.g. buyers or suppliers) and those of internal business units in different countries. One of the most effective boundary spanners was Lily in Company A (see Table 7.1). She majored in English literature and minored in IB and had been an exchange student for a year in the United Kingdom. On graduation, she was recruited by Company A and is now responsible for serving several critical clients in North America. Lily described it as follows:

**Table 7.6** Example of Intervening

| | |
|---|---|
| *Case 6-1* | |
| Interviewee | Karl |
| Interview excerpt | 'Given that one of our key clients in Germany decided to build their own factory in China and thus requested us to help transfer relevant production knowledge to this new factory, I had to accompany our general manager who is not good at English to go to Germany for negotiating this new arrangement as well as future orders' |
| Interpretation | Karl illustrates how he intervenes in the negotiation between the company and its client |
| Coded as | One piece of evidence of the *intervening function* recorded for Karl |
| Most frequently encountered difficulties | Lack of equivalence, cultural interference, ambiguity |
| *Case 6-2* | |
| Interviewee | Tank |
| Interview excerpt | 'Recently our company and one of our key clients in North America were tangled with a quality dispute caused by a Canadian customer's claim [...]. When I helped to translate our arguments about why our company should not bear the sole liability from Chinese to English, I tried to put it in a more polite manner to avoid direct conflicts. [...]' |
| Interpretation | Tank describes how she intervenes in the negotiation between the company and its key client |
| Coded as | One piece of evidence of the *intervening function* recorded for Tank |
| Most frequently encountered difficulties | Lack of equivalence, cultural interference, ambiguity |

*The most important part of my team's job is to pass on the latest and daily market Information from our foreign customers to the company. It has been easy since I am good at English and very familiar with translating professional and fashion terminologies from English into Chinese.*

The boundary spanning role played by Lily in exchanging knowledge between Company A and its key foreign clients was strongly supported by her proficiency in both Chinese and English, outstanding translating skills, and a potent knowledge base of international trade terms. It is worth noting that exchanging seemed to be the most frequently performed function because all 12 participants mentioned their experience in playing this role.

### 7.2.4.2 Linking

This dimension underscored the importance of establishing interpersonal networks in linking people from different business units or enterprises across borders for the purpose of transforming valuable knowledge or information. Amy appears to be a prominent boundary spanner in terms of this function. She had worked in Company A for 16 years and thus was acquainted with almost every key person there (see Table 7.1). She often helped to connect managers at her clients' companies to the correct counterpart/responsible personnel of her organization and vice versa. As Amy recalled:

> Our team is like a bridge that links the interior to the exterior of the company. Hence, we often brokered introductions between my colleagues and external people who might need to work together for mutual interests. For instance, if a marketing manager of our client wants to contact and give feedbacks to our R&D engineers, there is actually no other way than communicating through our department (refer to Table 7.3, case 3-1).

However, although for most of the time Amy as a boundary spanner handled the translation tasks quite well, she pointed out that translation difficulties due to a lack of equivalent words are often encountered and sometimes might be pretty knotty. This is similar to the points noted by her colleague, Mary (Table 7.1):

> It is always not easy to translate the corporate jargons from Chinese to English. We had encountered a variety of clear examples of lack of equivalence. Once I had racked my brain to search for proper English words whose meanings were equivalent to the Chinese jargon "踩内存" (pronounced as Cai Nei Cun) but failed. Eventually, a senior engineer suggested me to use "memory leakage" to represent this technical jargon because this translation could express close semantic fit.

### 7.2.4.3 Manipulating

The manipulating function generally involved avoiding and refusing another party's requests and refers to effectively limiting the inward or outward flow of specific information between actors. William in Company B could be considered a typical boundary spanner who often performed this manipulating role in knowledge transfer. He had lived in the United Kingdom for about 3 years, obtaining his master's degree in economics. As a project leader at the translation centre, he led a team of 20 professional translators responsible for translating important documents from English to Chinese (and vice versa) for the R&D divisions, providing oral interpretation services and preparing the English drafts of speeches and press releases for top management. As William notes:

> Given the strong military background, our top leader preferred to use military terms in his speech which sometimes contained hostile messages against America and might cause misunderstandings to foreign media. To avoid misunderstanding, we often needed to modify the expression and omit politically sensitive phrases when interpreting his speech (Table 7.4, case 4-2).

Notably, William's job was quite demanding. To perform effectively the function of manipulating, he was required not only to speak fluent English and be familiar with the leader's speaking style, but also to have a good command of cultural and political knowledge. On the premise of adapting to the different cultural backgrounds of the audiences, he knew well how to manipulate the translation to better promote knowledge transfer.

### 7.2.4.4 Facilitating

The functional purpose of the facilitating activities was to enable other colleagues or different internal units, as well as external partners of an MNC's global network, to be more willing to coordinate and collaborate with each other during knowledge transfer. Mary seemed to be an outstanding example of this because, with 12 years' experience of working in the same division of Company A, she was widely praised for maintaining good interpersonal relationships within the organization as well as with foreign clients. As Mary recalled:

> I often help our technical engineers to communicate with our customer service department overseas for solving practical technical problems....Given the engineers, in general, are not good at dealing with customers, I need to play like a loop in-between, delivering messages back and forth. Also, I have to give feedback about when you should say this and when you should say that [...]. Of course, I need to be very patient (please see Table 7.4, case 5-1).

William in Company B also gave an example about the facilitating role:

> Due to his military background, our CEO often sounds too tough in expression. If we directly translate or interpret his words from Chinese to English, it may influence our clients' perception of our company and ruin the company–client relationship. Hence, we usually make some adjustments; e.g., when he says a narrative or imperative sentence, we will make it a rhetorical question to soften the tone (Table 7.4, case 5-2).

The above examples shed light on the fact that the translator's textual understandings of both the source and target texts indeed play a more pivotal role in translation when engaging in higher-level boundary-spanning functions.

Karl, the director of the translation centre in Company B, shared with us a typical example, illustrating how cultural interference influenced the translation results when he facilitated the R&D and marketing teams to translate the instruction book of a household appliance product:

> Based on the Chinese version of the instruction book, we used to choose the sentence "the testing of the alert function is completed" to articulate the end of the auto-testing process of such function (警报功能测试到此结束 in Chinese). However, recently, an Indian product manager proposed that it would be much clearer if we add one sentence "no further action is required" to avoid possible misunderstanding in Western markets. As a result, we decided to adopt his suggestion (Table 7.6, case 6-1).

### 7.2.4.5 Intervening

As the highest boundary spanning function, the intervening role mostly involved more extensive and complicated activities in which the parties concerned may be more diversified. Tank, in Company A, majored in finance and economics at a famous university in southern China. On graduation, she was recruited by Company A and was a marketing manager in charge of orders from several critical clients in Germany and North America. As a leader managing 40 boundary spanners, she offers a typical example for illustrating the boundary-spanning function of intervening:

> Recently our company and one of our key clients, a famous distributor in North America, were tangled with a quality dispute caused by a Canadian customer's claim. This customer complained about how our product (i.e. a water tap) resulted in tremendous damage on her luxurious furniture [...]. She requested for a compensation of USD 40,000 for her loss from the local distributor but the distributor thought our company as the producer should be liable for this [...]. As a result, I had to help my boss to negotiate with this client.
>
> When I helped to translate our arguments about why our company should not bear the sole liability from Chinese to English, I tried to put it in a more polite manner like "I do not think this issue was simply caused by our product quality, the local installer seemed to fail to follow our product instruction to assemble components" [...] [...]. To protect the interest of my company, I was requested to argue with our client but simultaneously avoid misunderstandings and direct conflicts" (Table 7.6, case 6-2).

The foregoing example explicitly characterizes the nature of the function of intervening, revealing that boundary spanners have to actively interact with all parties concerned and make efforts to create positive outcomes by resolving misunderstandings, managing conflicts, and building trust. Moreover, this example also implicitly highlights that it is of great importance for a translator to be well versed in legal technical terms because there may be more opportunities for them as boundary spanners to cope with knowledge transfer pertaining to humanistic and law-related knowledge. It is noticeable that the facilitating and intervening functions were performed by significantly fewer individuals—only three people in managerial positions mentioned this.

## 7.2.5 Discussion

Our findings demonstrate that from time to time translators indeed play vital roles in the following aspects: cross-border knowledge exchanging, linking persons with crucial knowledge, facilitating the cross-cultural interaction of various knowledge sources, intervening to prevent misunderstandings, and manipulating the flow of knowledge for the purpose of protecting confidentiality. More importantly, the unique sequential and hierarchical structure of our five-dimension hierarchical model was fully supported with the upper-level functions covering the lower-level functions, as was displayed in Tables 7.2–7.6. Our results also highlight that the typical challenges in translation science of lack of equivalence, culture interference, and ambiguity (Holden & Michailova, 2014) were generated throughout the entire translation procedure and were intertwined with all boundary spanning activities concerning knowledge transmission.

In sum, our research illustrates that the boundary spanning functions in cross-cultural knowledge transfer performed by individuals with translation skills within an MNC's business network can be well characterized by our conceptual framework (see Fig. 7.1). Hence, RQ1 and RQ2 have been answered explicitly. Taking a closer look at our findings, we discovered that within an MNC's global network, cross-cultural knowledge exchange most frequently takes place through individuals who interact with each other to do their job on behalf of their respective organizations. Thus, it is plausible to suggest that this function forms the fundamental part of the boundary spanning activities for translators in knowledge transfer, as delineated by our five-dimension model (see Fig. 7.1).

In terms of linking, one of the main determinants for Amy to perform this function well was her acquaintance with lots of people in her company. Evidence showed that building a harmonious source–recipient relationship in knowledge transfer was of particular importance in cultures where business relationships are mediated by personal relationships (Chin, 2014, 2015; Johnson et al., 2010; Peltokorpi & Vaara, 2014). Thus, our findings corroborate such arguments that in the Chinese context harmonious interpersonal ties are indeed critical for being a competent boundary spanner.

The function of manipulating, as expected, embodies the institutional rule about restricting free flow of knowledge by adaptation, alteration, distortion (if not destruction), and even omission of the source text (Hermans, 2014; Lefevere, 2004). Information control between domestic firms and their foreign partners is identified as crucial in forming cross–nation strategic alliances in China given that the party-state elite is decisive in preventing local firms from leaking out any sensitive or confidential information to foreign organizations to maintain social stability (Liu, 2011). Consistent with this viewpoint, our findings confirm that knowledge transfer across borders must be carried out very cautiously in the Chinese context (Table 7.4, Cases 4–1 and 4–2).

In terms of the upper-level functions, namely facilitating and intervening, the translational action seems to be more heavily reliant on the expert judgement of the boundary spanner as to what translation is more appropriate in the target culture. Hence, equivalence may no longer be the main objective and the source text may need to be 'dethroned' (Chidlow et al., 2014) because the problem of cultural interference can lead to poor results with a good translation of the source text. Translation activities therefore evolve to be a highly situated, context-bound practice, rather than an interpretation of meaning from one language to another.

It is also worth noting that our findings implicitly underscore the main differences between the two functions of facilitating and intervening. The scope of facilitating is to create positive outcomes through delivering and interpreting cross-cultural messages. Intervening, despite containing the facilitating function, may sometimes relate to negative or unpleasant outcomes according to the essence of the conciliation, conflict, and negotiation that the boundary spanners involve (Table 7.4, Cases 6–1 and 6–2).

## 7.2.6 Theoretical and Practical Implications

Overall, the main theoretical contribution of our research is a novel 3D–hierarchical model that reveals the multifaceted and contingent nature of translation activities concerning the cross–cultural knowledge transfer process within MNC business networks in China. The causes of such translation work are too varied contextually and linguistically, thus meriting study as a stand-alone topic in the IB and management fields.

Consistent with previous research (Chidlow et al., 2014; Schomaker & Zaheer, 2014), our research reflects the significance of cross-linguistic communication on knowledge transfer within MNC global networks. Without translation, the knowledge from source to recipient is static, namely the state in which it is left. Knowledge sources expressed in different languages are dependent on translation to activate originally static information into feasible and available resources. As shown in our findings, the translation process regarding the cross-cultural knowledge flow actually consists of multiple decision points determined by the subjectivities and comprehension of the individuals concerned. Viewed from this angle, our study contributes to the IB literature by elucidating that the translation procedure per se can also be seen as a source of knowledge transfer rather than a neutral transmission device because it contains unique cultural and historical embedding, as well as the understanding of philosophical hermeneutics.

As far as the practical implications are concerned, our results indicate that the higher the boundary spanning level, the more the spanning functions are involved and the more the translation difficulties of cultural interference and ambiguity are encountered. This might be due to the fact that while engaging in the higher order boundary spanning functions in the process of knowledge transfer, translation activities may move beyond a 'technical linguistic transcoding', but convey more information about the true content of a text under a specific sociocultural environment. As claimed by Venuti (2008), the translator is not just a neutral transmitter of the meaning of the source text, but rather is the active co-producer of the target context. Hence, it is particularly important for individuals to develop a high level of relevant cultural skills to perform better the boundary-spanning roles.

This new construct on the role of translation in cross-cultural knowledge transfer also engenders implications for performance appraisal, a core area of HRM. The multidimensionality and level of this model brings to our attention the wide range of translation activities necessary for MNC employees to be successful in language skills. In particular, this model characterizes the Chinese cultural tendency of manipulating hostile messages and sensitive information to avoid direct confrontation/conflict in the process of knowledge transfer (Chin, 2014; Chin et al., 2015). As a result, this novel hierarchical construct might be very suitable for use as a performance indicator to evaluate employee capability in terms of cross-border communication in China.

## 7.2.7 Limitations and Future Research

Our study is subject to several limitations that should be taken into account in future research. First, since our data were restricted to only two large

MNCs in the manufacturing sector, the generalizability of the results might be limited. Future research could take different types of industries into consideration and expand the sample size. Second, although our case study research provided some intriguing evidence, our proposed model needs more empirical verification and could be further tested in more regions of China. Third, given that knowledge transmission, unlike goods transfer, is liable to be affected by individual factors, such as motivation, work attitude, and personality, future research may also take into account the contributions of individual psychological characters in the performance of the boundary spanning role.

### 7.2.8 Conclusion

In summary, our study proposed a novel 3D–hierarchical model about the role of translation in cross-cultural knowledge transfer in Chinese MNEs' business networks and provided insightful implications for MNCs to treat translation as a significant 're-codification' rather than a mundane task. Indeed, knowledge transfer within MNCs involves not only knowledge regarding products, technology, and operations but also whole organizations, including business models, organizational visions, missions, and strategies. Despite the lack of specific focus in the past, the interface of translation and knowledge transfer in the MNC context is drawing increasing attention in the IB and other fields. Our results are an exciting step towards corroborating the notion that language is a container of contexts and the translation procedure in MNCs is actually dynamic and contingent in nature. Thus, the main value of our study is to advance our current thinking and practice, identifying fertile avenues for future research to further deal with relevant topics.

## 7.3 CONCLUSION

This chapter pointed out the strategic role translation plays in breaking communication gaps between employees from diverse language backgrounds, as well as in transmitting explicit and tacit knowledge (see Rowley & Poon, 2011) through a manufacturer's international production and marketing networks. Considering the recent trends to relocate labour-intensive production to EEs and to set up cross-border R&D alliances, it is imperative for Chinese manufacturers to improve the foreign language proficiency of employees and to develop a global management cadre who can better accommodate cultural differences and avoid errors in cross-cultural communication and negotiations.

Hence, it is apparent that cross-cultural management will be of greater significance to HRM practice for Chinese manufacturing firms. While cross-cultural learning can foster innovation and creativity, managers in the 21st century are required to possess the ability to manage workforce diversity and linguistic complexity whereby they can digest diversified knowledge obtained from various institutional and cultural contexts. In this vein, it is also expected that the career development path of production workers will change, while job crafting as 'the physical and cognitive changes individuals make in the task or relational boundaries of their work' (Wrzesniewski & Dutton, 2001, p. 179) may become a critical issue among manufacturing employees.

## APPENDIX: INTERVIEW QUESTIONS

- Please elaborate on your job duties. Does translation play an important role in your work?
- Can you tell us about the role translation plays in your company's business network (i.e., the networks between the parent and subunits and those among the players in the same value chain)?
- Please illustrate the mechanisms/process of cross-cultural knowledge transfer within your company's global network? Did translation play a role in this process?
- How were the visions and values of your parent company transferred to global subsidiaries?
- Can you describe the translation skills that people have in your company?
- What impact would you say a lack of translation skills have on daily operations or cooperation?
- In what ways do translation skills affect one's position or status in the company?
- What kind of difficulties would you usually meet while translating?
- Could you manifest how you perceive the cultural differences in general between China and another specific country (e.g., Germany, Russia, or America)?
- Dose the company take some measures to solve the problem caused by cultural differences?

# CHAPTER EIGHT

# Conclusion: Reflection

Evidence shows that the average annual wage of manufacturing employees has doubled during the past 10 years (see Fig. 6.1). Faced with decreasing profit margins, quite a few world-class brands like Nike, Panasonic, and Adidas have therefore shifted their production hubs from China to emerging economies (EEs) with cheaper labour such as Vietnam, Indonesia, and India (Chin et al., 2016; Das 2012), while more manufacturers in China opted to invest in digitalization and automation replacing human jobs with robots with artificial intelligence (AI) and machines. Accordingly, the skill criteria and job requirements in manufacturing have evolved into more complex, diversified forms, as the relocation of production bases and the implementation of high-tech automation push firms to recruit multinational and knowledgeable workers.

In recent years, accelerated urbanization has narrowed the urban–rural gap and reduced regional disparities. Encouraged by government policy, a vast number of peasant workers have thus been returning to work at their hometowns from the coastal cities with numerous industrial parks. Furthermore, the younger generation of migrant workers seems to prefer to look for jobs in the fast-growing, booming service-oriented industries than in the relatively declining manufacturing sectors. As a result, the original equipment manufacturing (OEM) model that used to rely on the rural mass migrant workforce to achieve an astonishing growth in the past cannot be sustained.

Taking the above contentions together, this book draws our attention to how and why a prominent factor—the fast-rising labour costs—triggered the upgrading of China's manufacturing sector and its impact on human resource management (HRM). From Chapters 2 to 4, incorporating HR, resource-based, and capability theories into the GVC framework, we comprehensively elaborate on how the Chinese manufacturing industry—that capitalized on the vast supplies of cheap labour and outstanding capabilities of technological imitation to serve as the world's workshop—spent 30 years growing to be one of the global economic leading powers. The dominant role of the Chinese Communist Party (CCP) and the intertwined functions of local governments, foreign direct investment (FDI), and informal

*The Future of Chinese Manufacturing*
https://doi.org/10.1016/B978-0-08-101108-9.00008-2

institutions that constitute the distinctive, multiplex manufacturing land-scape of China are described in depth.

From Chapters 5 to 7, echoing Rowley (2016) divergence perspective on the future direction of Chinese HRM, we illustrate how harmonious culture as a socially constructed concept (Redding, 2005) engenders context-specific effects on labour-related issues and shapes the behaviours and attitudes of manufacturing employees in China. Through a cultural lens, this book not only examines the existence of Chinese traditional values in modern management practices, but also makes sense of the intricate inter-play of multiple economic actors in the Chinese manufacturing industry. We also elucidate the evolving role of cross-cultural management in knowl-edge transfer among multinational workforces.

While this book has delineated the 30-year development trajectories of China's manufacturing industry in the past and the present, we also propose three themes on the employment and labour-related challenges for the future:

1. Sustainable career and innovation

According to many reports in the media, a large number of low-educated migrant workers in China who used to engage in simple and repetitive works are encountering difficulties in terms of developing a sustainable career path as their jobs are vulnerable to replacement by computers and robots. For example, some workers need to operate com-puterized production equipment and electronic devices, while some need to obtain relevant qualification licences such as the ISO auditor cer-tificate to execute quality testing as prescribed in international trade reg-ulations. Those might not have been part of their job descriptions several years ago. More specifically, in the current period of trying to pivot towards a more innovation-driven economy, China's production employees must continually update their knowledge and abilities to per-form new and more complex job requirements. Some proactive workers may even actively perform a crafting behaviour to reorganize and shape their prescribed jobs by changing the scopes, tasks, or working relation-ships so that the jobs can better fit their motives, strengths, and passions.

In short, while the category of job characteristics is changing and evolving, the related term of person-job fit should also be re-conceptualized accordingly. In order to prove their own value under such a tough situation of diminishing job opportunities, it is imperative for production employees to release their creative potential and to thrive on innovation, whereby they can more easily adjust their task boundaries with new, dynamic working processes towards creating a sustainable career.

2. Shrinking and ageing workforce

The working age population in China—defined as people between 16 and 60—is expected to decline modestly from about 853.7 million in 2015 to 848.9 million by 2020, but then drop sharply to 781.8 million by 2030, 743 million by 2040, and 650.9 million in 2050. This poses a considerable challenge to organizations in terms of recruiting new and qualified employees from a shrinking workforce, while the situation in the manufacturing industry seems more austere, as its contribution to the national gross domestic product (GDP) has been declining since 2011 (see Fig. 2.1 in Chapter 2).

Moreover, while the service- and consumer-oriented industries are booming in China, manufacturing jobs and related career identification may not be so attractive to the younger generation. To deal with an ageing labour force, manufacturing firms in China should pay more attention to understanding how to motivate older workers and to allocating resources to prepare for pension funds.

3. Multinational HRs and acculturation

As indicated, to sustain competitiveness, MNCs will continue to move manufacturing jobs to establish labour-intensive production lines in EEs with lower-cost labour. It thus becomes critically vital for production mangers to enhance their intercultural knowledge and communication competences so as to effectively manage a diversified and multicultural workforce composed of employees from different ethnic groups and function well under different cultural contexts (see Rowley and Bhopal, 2002, 2005, 2006). More specifically, manufacturing professionals will need to work across culturally diverse, geographically spread, and even linguistically distinct subsidiaries. They must become flexible enough to adapt to various working environments and institutional conditions.

In summary, since the 2008 global financial crisis, China's manufacturing employment has been riddled with a variety of uncertainties such as high turnover rates, recruitment difficulties, shortages of skilled workers, and labour strikes, as this recession marked a new phase of the restructuring of the global manufacturing sector. Foxconn, the world's largest contract electronics manufacturer, is executing a new automation project that aims to eliminate the intensive usage of low-wage labourers and thus had laid off more than 60,000 workers in their

China factories between 2016 and 2017. Without doubt, manufacturers in China are obliged to accept the upcoming end of low-cost production and a huge migrant workforce and to confront the imminent challenges arising from the development of a globally competitive human capital. The increasing prevalence of green technology, digitalization, and AI has changed the global manufacturing landscape, pushing firms to transform their production modes and tasks in adaptation to new demands for ecological protection and innovation in the 21st century. While more and more production tasks will be fulfilled by high-tech machines and industrial robots, the manufacturing processes, and corresponding job design are inevitable to be altered in adaptation to the changes in production modes, there seem to be fewer manufacturing job vacancies for human beings, while the jobs left for applicants often have enlarged responsibilities and high skill variety. It is thus particularly meaningful to analyse contemporary employment and labour issues in China during the course of its industrial upgrading from an interdisciplinary, cross-cultural, and integrative perspective. This is actually the main contribution of this book.

# References

Acquaah, M. (2012). Social networking relationships, firm-specific managerial experience and firm performance in a transition economy: a comparative analysis of family owned and nonfamily firms. *Strategic Management Journal, 33*(10), 1215–1228.

Adler, N. J. (2006). The arts & leadership: now that we can do anything, what will we do? *Academy of Management Learning & Education, 5*, 486–499.

Adler, N. J. (2008). *International dimensions of organizational behavior* (5th ed.). Mason, OH: South-Western.

Ajzen, I., & Fishbein, M. (1980). *Understanding attitudes and predicting social behavior.* Englewood Cliffs, NJ: Prentice Hall.

Allen, N. J., & Meyer, J. P. (1990). The measurement and antecedents of affective, continuance, and normative commitment to the organization. *Journal of Occupational Psychology, 63*, 1–18.

Anderson, A., Dodd, S., & Jack, S. (2010). Network practices and entrepreneurial growth. *Scandinavian Journal of Management, 25*(2), 121–133.

Anderson, J. C., & Gerbing, D. W. (1988). Structural equation modeling in practice: a review and recommend two-step approach. *Psychological Bulletin, 103*(3), 411–423.

Au, K., & Fukuda, J. (2002). Boundary spanning behaviors of expatriates. *Journal of World Business, 37*(4), 285–296.

Augier, M., Guo, J., & Rowen, H. (2016). The Needham puzzle reconsidered: organizations, organizing and innovation in China. *Management and Organization Review, 12*(1), 5–24.

Autio, E., George, G., & Alexy, O. (2011). International entrepreneurship and capability development-qualitative evidence and future research directions. *Entrepreneurship Theory and Practice, 25*, 11–37.

Bai, R. (2011). The role of the all China federation of trade unions: implications for Chinese workers today. *Journal of Labor and Society, 14*(1), 19–39.

Barner-Rasmussen, W., & Aarnio, C. (2011). Shifting the faultlines of language of language: a quantitative functional-level exploration of language use in MNC subsidiaries. *Journal of World Business, 46*(3), 288–295.

Barner-Rasmussen, W., & Bjorkman, I. (2007). Language fluency, socialization and inter-unit relationships in Chinese and Finnish subsidiaries. *Management and Organization Review, 3*(1), 105–128.

Barner-Rasmussen, W., Ehrnrooth, M., Koveshnikov, A., & Makela, K. (2014). Cultural and language skills as resources for boundary spanning within the MNC. *Journal of International Business Studies, 45*(7), 886–905.

Barney, J. B. (1991). Firm resources and sustained competitive advantage. *Journal of Management, 17*(1), 99–120.

Baron, R. M., & Kenny, D. A. (1986). The moderator-mediator variable distinction in social psychological research: conceptual, strategic, and statistical considerations. *Journal of Personality and Social Psychology, 51*(6), 1173–1182.

Baron, R. A., & Tang, J. (2009). Entrepreneurs' social skills and new venture performance: mediating mechanisms and cultural generality. *Journal of Management, 35*(2), 282–306.

Batt, R., & Colvin, A. J. S. (2011). An employment systems approach to turnover: human resource practices, quits, dismissals, and performance. *Academy of Management Journal, 54*, 695–717.

Benson, J., & Rowley, C. (2003). Changes in Asian HRM—implications for theory and practice. *Asia Pacific Business Review, 9*(4), 186–195.

Bergeron, D. M. (2007). The potential paradox of organizational citizenship behavior: good citizen at what cost? *Academy of Management Journal, 32*, 1078–1095.

Blenkinsopp, J., & Pajouh, M. S. (2010). Lost in translation? Culture, language and the role of the translator in international business. *Critical Perspectives on International Business, 6*(1), 38–52.

Bordia, S., & Bordia, P. (2015). Employees' willingness to adopt a foreign functional language in multilingual organizations: the role of linguistic identity. *Journal of International Business Studies, 46*(4), 415–428.

Boxall, P., Ang, S. H., & Bartram, T. (2011). Analysing the 'black box' of HRM: uncovering HR goals, mediator, and outcomes in a standardized service environment. *Journal of Management Studies, 48*(7), 1504–1532.

Brannen, M. Y., & Doz, Y. L. (2012). Corporate languages and strategic agility: trapped in your jargon or lost in translation? *California Management Review, 54*(3), 77–97.

Brannen, M. Y., Piekkari, R., & Tietze, S. (2014). The multifaceted role of Language in international business: unpacking the forms, functions and features of a critical challenge to MNC theory and performance. *Journal of International Business Studies, 45*(5), 495–507.

Brooks, G. R., & Wallace, J. P. (2006). A discursive examination of the nature, determinants and impact of organizational commitment. *Asia Pacific Journal of Human Resources, 44*(2), 222–239.

Brown, R. L. (1997). Assessing specific meditational effects in complex theoretical models. *Structural Equation Modeling, 4*, 142–156.

Bruton, G. D., Ahlstrom, D., & Li, H. -L. (2010). Institutional theory and entrepreneurship: where are we now and where do we need to move in the future? *Entrepreneurship Theory and Practice, 34*(3), 421–440. https://doi.org/10.1111/j.1540-6520.2010.00390.x.

Cannone, G., & Ughetto, E. (2014). Born globals: a cross-country survey on high-tech startups. *International Business Review, 23*(1), 272–283.

Cardoza, G., Fornes, G., Li, P., & Xu, S. (2015). China goes global: public policies' inflence on small-and medium-sized enterprises international expansion. *Asia Pacific Business Review, 21*(2), 188–210.

Chan, K. W. (2010). A China paradox: migrant labor shortage amidst rural labor supply abundance. *Eurasian Geography and Economics, 51*(4), 513–530.

Chan, C. K. (2012). Class or citizenship? Debating workplace conflict in China. *Journal of Contemporary Asia, 42*(2), 308–327.

Chan, C. K. (2014). Constrained labor agency and he changing regulatory regime in China. *Development and Change, 45*(4), 685–709.

Chan, J., Pun, N., & Selden, M. (2013). The politics of global production: Apple, Foxconn and China's new working class. *New Technology, Work and Employment, 28*(2), 100–115.

Chang, K., & Smithikrai, C. (2010). Counterproductive behavior at work: an investigation into reduction strategies. *The International Journal of Human Resource Management, 21*, 1272–1288.

Chang, K., & William, B. (2013). The transition from individual to collective labor relations in China. *Industrial Relations Journal, 44*(2), 102–121.

Charmaz, K. (2006). *Constructing grounded theory: A practical guide through qualitative analysis.* Thousand Oaks, CA: Sage.

Chen, C. C., Chen, X. -P., & Huang, S. (2013). Chinese Guanxi: an integrative review and new direction for future research. *Management and Organization Review, 9*(1), 167–207.

Chen, F., Curran, P. J., Bollen, K. A., Kirby, J., & Paxton, P. (2008). An empirical evaluation of the use of fixed cutoff points in RMSEA test statistic in structural equation models. *Social Methods and Research, 36*(4), 462–494.

Chen, G., Firth, M., & Xu, L. (2009). Does the type of ownership control matter? Evidence from China's listed companies. *Journal of Banking & Finance, 33*(1), 171–181.

Chen, Z., & Francesco, A. (2003). The relationship between the three components of commitment and employee performance in China. *Journal of Vocational Behavior, 62*(3), 490–510.

Chen, M., & Miller, D. (2010). West meets east: toward an ambicultural approach to management. *Academy of Management Perspectives, 24*, 17–24.

Cheng, C. (2006). Toward constructing a dialectics of harmonization: harmony and conflict in Chinese philosophy. *Journal of Chinese Philosophy, 33*((1), 25–59.

Cheng, C. Y. (2011). The Yijing: The creative origin of Chinese philosophy. In W. Edelglass & J. L. Garfield (Eds.), *The Oxford handbook of world philosophy*. New York, NY: Oxford University Press.

Cheng, B., Jiang, D., & Riley, J. H. (2003). Organizational commitment, supervisory commitment, and employee outcomes in the chinese context: proximal hypothesis or global hypothesis? *Journal of Organizational Behavior, 24*, 313–334.

Chidlow, A., Plakoyiannaki, E., & Welch, C. (2014). Translation in cross-language international business research: beyond equivalence. *Journal of International Business Studies, 45*(5), 1–21.

Child, J. (2016). Building the innovation capacity of SMEs in China. In A. Y. Lewin, M. Kenny, & J. P. Murmann (Eds.), *China's innovation challenge: Overcoming the middle-income trap*. Cambridge: Cambridge University Press.

Child, J., & Rodrigues, S. B. (2005). The internationalization of Chinese firms: a case for theoretical extension. *Management and Organization Review, 1*, 381–410.

Chin, T. (2010). An Empirical Study on Harmonious Organizations. *Journal of Sun Yat-sen University, 50*, 164–174 [in Chinese].

Chin, T. (2012). Harmony in Chinese organizations: from the perspective of national culture. *Journal of Strategy and Decision-Making, 3*(5), 42–50 [in Chinese].

Chin, T. (2013). An exploratory study on upgrading by FDI OEMs in China. *International Business Research, 6*(1), 199–210.

Chin, T. (2014). Harmony as means to enhance affective commitment in a Chinese organization. *Cross Cultural Management: An International Journal, 21*(3), 326–342.

Chin, T. (2015). Harmony and organization citizenship behavior in Chinese organizations. *International Journal of Human Resource Management, 26*(8), 1110–1129.

Chin, T., & Liu, R. (2014). An exploratory study on workforce development strategies by Taiwan-invested OEMs in China. *Asian Social Science, 10*(4), 233–240.

Chin, T., & Liu, R. H. (2015). Understanding labor conflicts in Chinese manufacturing: a Yin-Yang harmony perspective. *International Journal of Conflict Management, 26*(3), 288–315.

Chin, T., & Liu, R. -h. (2017). Critical management issues in China's socio–economic transformation: multiple scientific perspectives to strategy and innovation. *Chinese Management Studies, 11*(1), 12–18.

Chin, T., Liu, R. -h., & Yang, X. (2015). Reverse internationalization in Chinese firms: a study of how global startup OEMs seek to compete domestically. *Asia Pacific Business Review, 22*(2), 201–219.

Chin, T., Liu, R. -H., & Yang, X. (2016). Reverse internationalization in Chinese firms: a study of how global startup OEMs seek to compete domestically. *Asia Pacific Business Review, 22*(2), 201–219.

Chin, T., & Mao, Y. (2010). *Understanding harmonious spirit, the humanistic-caring value in Chinese organizational behavior. Paper presented at the Academy of Management Annual Meeting, Montreal, August 6–10*. Available at:http://program.aomonline.org/2010/submission.asp?mode=ShowSession&SessionID=1544.

Chin, T., Tsai, S., Zhu, W., Yang, D., Liu, R. -h., & Tsuei, R. T. (2016). EO–performance relationships in reverse internationalization by Chinese global startup OEMs: social networks and strategic flexibility. *PLoS One*. https://doi.org/10.1371/journal.pone.0162175.

China Statistical Yearbook (2010), Ministry of Commerce and the State Statistics Bureau of China, Beijing, China.

Chiu, S., & Chen, H. (2005). Relationship between job characteristics and organizational citizenship behavior: the mediating role of job satisfaction. *Social Behavior and Personality*, *33*, 523–540.

Chou, T. L., Chang, J. Y., & Li, T. C. (2014). Government support, FDI clustering and semiconductor sustainability in China: case studies of Shanghai, Suzhou ad Wuxi in the Yangtze Delta. *Sustainability*, *6*(9), 5655–5681.

Cohen, J., Cohen, P., Stephen, F. W., & Leona, S. A. (2003). *Applied multiple regression/correlation analysis for the behavioral sciences* (3rd ed.). Mahwah, NJ: Lawrence Erlbaum Associates.

Covin, J., & Wales, W. (2012). The measurement of entrepreneurial orientation. *Entrepreneurship Theory and Practice*, *36*(4), 677–702.

Coyne, I., & Ong, T. (2007). Organizational citizenship behavior and turnover intention: a cross-cultural study. *The International Journal of Human Resource Management*, *18*, 1085–1097.

Creswell, J. W. (2014). *Research design: Qualitative, quantitative, and mixed methods approaches* (4th ed.). London: Sage.

Criscuolo, P., & Narula, R. (2007). Using multi-hub structures for international R&D: organisational inertia and the challenges of implementation. *Management International Review*, *47*(5), 639–660.

Curevo-Cazurra, A., Inkpen, A., Musacchio, A., & Ramaswamy, K. (2014). Governments as owners: state-owned multinational companies. *International Environmental Agreements Politics Law and Economics*, *14*(2), 125–127.

Dai, L., Maksimov, V., Gilbert, B., & Fernhaber, S. (2014). Entrepreneurial orientation and international scope: the differential roles of innovativeness, proactiveness, and risk-taking. *Journal of Business Venturing*, *29*(4), 511–524.

Das, D. K. (2012). How did the Asian economy cope with the global financial crisis and recession? A revaluation and review. *Asia Pacific Business Review*, *18*(1), 7–25.

Davies, D., & Liang, W. (2011). *Human resource management in China: Cases in HR practice*. Oxford: Chandos Publishing.

Den Hartog, D. N., De Hoogh, A. H. B., & Keegan, A. E. (2007). The interactive effects of belongingness and charisma on helping and compliance. *Journal of Applied Psychology*, *92*(4), 1131–1139.

Deng, Y., & Xu, K. (2014). Chinese employees negotiating differing conflict management expectations in a US-based multinational corporation subsidiary in Southwest China. *Management Communication Quarterly*, *28*(4).

Drauz, R. (2013). In search of a Chinese internationalization theory: a study of 12 automobile manufacturers. *Chinese Management Studies*, *7*(2), 281–309.

Du, X., & Luo, J. H. (2016). Political connections, home formal institutions, and internationalization: evidence from China. *Management and Organization Review*, *12*(1), 103–133.

Eapen, A. (2012). Social structure and technology spillovers from foreign to domestic firms. *Journal of International Business Studies*, *43*(3), 244–263.

Eisenberger, R., Cummings, J., Aremeli, S., & Lynch, P. (1997). Perceived organizational support, discretionary treatment, and job satisfaction. *Journal of Applied Psychology*, *82*, 812–820.

Eisenhardt, K. M., & Graebner, M. E. (2007). Theory building from cases: opportunities and challenges. *Academy of Management Journal*, *50*(1), 25–32.

Eisinga, R., Teelken, C., & Doorewaard, H. (2010). Assessing cross-national invariance of the three-component model of organizational commitment: a six-country study of European university faculty. *Cross-Cultural Research*, *44*(4), 341–372.

Eng, T. -Y., & Spickett-Jones, J. G. (2009). An investigation of marketing capabilities and upgrading performance of manufacturers in Mainland China and Hong Kong. *Journal of World Business*, *44*(4), 463–475. https://doi.org/10.1016/j.jwb.2009.01.002.

Euwema, M. C., Wendt, H., & van Emmerik, H. (2007). Leadership styles and group organizational citizenship behavior across cultures. *Journal of Organizational Behavior, 28,* 1035–1057.

Evans, W. R., Davis, W. D., & Frink, D. D. (2011). An examination of employee reactions to perceived corporate citizenship. *Journal of Applied Social Psychology, 41,* 38–964.

Fang, T. (2014). Understanding Chinese culture and communication: The Yin Yang approach. In B. Gehrke & M. -T. Claes (Eds.), *Global Leadership Practices* (pp. 171–187). London: Palgrave Macmillan.

Fang, T., Gunterberg, C., & Larsson, E. (2010). Sourcing in an increasingly expensive China: four Swedish cases. *Journal of Business Ethics, 97*(1), 119–138.

Farh, J. L., Earley, P. C., & Lin, S. C. (1997). Impetus for action: a cultural analysis of justice and organizational citizenship behavior in Chinese society. *Administrative Science Quarterly, 42,* 421–444.

Farh, J. L., Hackett, R. D., & Jian, L. (2007). Individual-level cultural values as moderators of perceived organizational support-employee outcome relationships in China: comparing the effects of power distance and traditionality. *Academy of Management Journal, 50,* 715–729.

Farh, J. L., Zhong, C. B., & Organ, D. W. (2004). Organizational citizenship behaviour in the People's Republic of China. *Organization Science, 15,* 241–253.

Fischer, R., & Mansell, A. (2009). Commitment across cultures: a meta-analytical approach. *Journal of International Business Studies, 40,* 1339–1358.

Foss, N. J., & Lindenberg, S. (2013). Microfoundations for strategy: a goal-framing perspective on the drivers of value creation. *Academy of Management Perspectives, 27*(2), 85–102.

Franklin, J. C. (2002). Harmony in Greek and Indo-Iranian cosmology. *Journal of Indo-European Studies, 30*(1–2), 1–25.

Friedman, R., Chi, S. C., & Liu, L. A. (2006). An expectancy model of Chinese-American differences in conflict-avoiding. *Journal of International Business Studies, 37,* 76–91.

Fu, P. P., Yan, X. H., Li, Y., Wang, E., & Peng, S. (2008). Examining conflict-handling approaches by Chinese top management teams in IT firms. *International Journal of Conflict Management, 19*(3), 188–209.

Fuentes-Fuentes, M., Bojica, A., & Ruiz-Arroyo, M. (2015). Entrepreneurial orientation and knowledge acquisition: effects on performance in the specific context of women-owned firms. *International Entrepreneurship and Management Journal, 11,* 695–717.

Fung, Y. L. (1948). In D. Bodde (Ed.), *A short history of Chinese philosophy.* New York: Free Press.

Fung, Y. L. (1997). *A short history of Chinese philosophy.* New York, NY: Free Press.

Gallagher, K. S. (2006). Limits to leapfrogging in energy technologies? Evidence from the Chinese automobile industry. *Energy Policy, 34*(4), 383–394.

Gan, L. (2003). Globalization of the automobile industry in China: dynamics and barriers in greening of the road transportation. *Energy Policy, 31*(6), 537–551.

Gao, G. Y., Murray, J. K., Kotabe, M., & Lu, J. (2010). A "strategy tripod" perspective on export behaviors: evidence from domestic and foreign firms based in an emerging economy. *Journal of International Business Studies, 41*(3), 37–70.

Gelfand, M. J., Erez, M., & Aycan, Z. (2007). In M. I. Posner & M. K. Rothbart (Eds.), *Annual review of psychology: Vol. 58. Cross-cultural organizational behavior* (pp. 479–514). Palo Alto, CA: Annual Reviews.

Gereffi, G. (2009). Development models and industrial upgrading in China and Mexico. *European Sociolgical Review, 25*(1), 37–51.

Gereffi, G., Humphrey, J., & Sturgeon, T. J. (2005). The governance of global value chain. *Review of International Political Economy, 12*(1), 78–104.

Gerschewaki, S., Elizabeth, L. R., & Lindsay, V. J. (2015). Understanding the drivers of international performance for born global firms: an integrated perspective. *Journal of World Business, 50*(30), 558–575.

Gong, Y., Chang, S., & Cheung, S. (2010). High performance work system and collective OCB: a collective social exchange perspective. *Human Resource Management Journal, 20,* 119–127.

Gonzalez, J. V., & Garazo, T. G. (2006). Structural relationships between organizational service orientation, contact employee job satisfaction and citizenship behavior. *International Journal of Service Industry Management, 17*(1), 23–50.

Grant, A. M., Dutton, J. E., & Rosso, B. D. (2008). Giving commitment: employee support programs and the prosocial sensemaking process. *Academy of Management Journal, 51*(5), 898–918.

Gu, M. D. (2005). The Zhouyi (Book of Changes) as an open classic: a semiotic analysis of its system of representation. *Philosophy East and West, 55,* 257–282.

Hacklin, F., & Wallnofer, M. (2012). The business model in the practice of strategic decision making: insights from a case study. *Management Decision, 50*(2), 166–188.

Hair, J. F., Black, W. C., Babin, B. J., Anderson, R. E., & Tatham, R. L. (2005). *Multivariate data analysis* (6th ed.). Upper Saddle River, NJ: Prentice-Hall.

Han, Y., & Altman, Y. (2010). Confucian moral roots of citizenship behaviour in China. *Asia-Pacific Journal of Business, 2*(1), 35–52.

Harrison, R. T., Leitch, C. M., & Chia, R. (2007). Developing paradigmatic awareness in university business schools: the challenge for executive education. *Academy of Management Learning & Education, 6,* 332–343.

Harrison, D. A., Newman, D. A., & Roth, P. L. (2006). How important are job attitudes? Meta-analytic comparisons of integrative behavioral outcomes and time sequences. *Academy of Management Journal, 49,* 305–325.

Harzing, A. -W., Koster, K., & Magner, U. (2011). Babel in business: the language barrier and its solutions in the HQ-subsidiary relationship. *Journal of World Business, 46*(3), 279–287.

Harzing, A. -W., & Pudelko, M. (2013). Language competencies, policies and practices in multinational corporations: a comprehensive review and comparison of Anglophone, Asian, Continental European and Nordic MNCs. *Journal of World Business, 48*(1), 87–97.

Hermans, T. (2014). In: T. Hermans (Ed.), *The manipulation of literature: Studies in literary translation.* London: Routledge.

Herrigel, G., Wittke, V., & Voskamp, U. (2013). The process of Chinese manufacturing upgrading: transitioning from unilateral to recursive mutual learning relations. *Global Strategy Journal, 3,* 109–125.

Hofstede, G. (2015). Culture's causes: the next challenge. *Cross Cultural & Strategic Management, 22*(4), 545–569.

Hofstede, G., & Bond, M. H. (1988). The confucius connection: from cultural roots to economic growth. *Organizational Dynamics, 16,* 5–21.

Hofstede, G., Hofstede, G. J., & Minkov, M. (2010). *Culture and organizations.* New York: McGraw-Hill.

Hofstede, G., & Minkov, M. (2010). Long- vs short-term orientation: new perspectives. *Asia Pacific Business Review, 16*(4), 493–504.

Holden, N. J., & Michailova, S. (2014). A more expansive perspective on translation in IB research: insights from the Russian handbook of knowledge management. *Journal of International Business Studies, 45*(2), 906–918.

Horng, C., & Chen, W. (2008). From contract manufacturing to own-brand management: the role of learning and cultural heritage identity. *Management and Organization Review, 4*(1), 109–133.

Huang, T. J. (2008). *Zhou Yi Bian Yuan.* Guangzhou: Guangdong Renmin [in Chinese].

Huang, K. -P., & Wang, K. Y. (2013). The moderating effect of social capital and environmental dynamism on the link between entrepreneurial orientation and resource acquisition. *Quality and Quantity, 47,* 1617–1628.

Hughes, M., & Morgan, R. (2007). Deconstructing the relationship between entrepreneurial orientation and business performance at the embryonic stage of firm growth. *Industrial Marketing Management*, *36*(5), 651–661.

Humphrey, J., & Schmitz, H. (2004). Globalized localities: Introduction. In H. Schmitz (Ed.), *Local Enterprises in the Global Economy*. Cheltenam/Northampton: Edward Elgar.

Ivarsson, I., & Alvstam, C. G. (2011). Upgrading in global value-chains: a case study of technology-learning among IKEA-suppliers in China and Southeast Asia. *Journal of Economic Geography*, *11*, 731–752.

Jia, N. (2016). Political strategy and market capabilities: evidence from the Chinese private sector. *Management and Organization Review*, *12*(1), 75–102.

Johanson, J., & Vahlne, J. -E. (1977). The internationalization process of the firm: a model of knowledge development and increasing foreign market commitments. *Journal of International Business Studies*, *8*(1), 23–32.

Johanson, J., & Vahlne, J. E. (2009). The Uppsala internationalization process model revisited: from liability of foreignness to liability of outsidership. *Journal of International Business Studies*, *40*(9), 1411–1431.

Johnson, R. E., Chang, C., & Yang, L. (2010). Commitment and motivation at work: the relevance of employee identity and regulatory focus. *Academy of Management Review*, *35*(2), 226–245.

Johnson, K. L., & Duxbury, L. (2010). The view from the field: a case study of the expatriate boundary-spanning role. *Journal of World Business*, *45*(1), 29–40.

Jones, M. V., Coviello, N., & Tang, Y. K. (2011). International entrepreneurship research (1989–2009): a domain ontology and thematic analysis. *Journal of Business Venturing*, *26*, 632–659.

Jones, D. A., Willness, C., & Madey, S. (2014). Why are job seekers attracted by corporate social performance? Experimental and field tests of three signal-based mechanisms. *Academy of Management Journal*, *57*(2), 383–404.

Kabasakal, H., Dastmalchian, A., & Imer, P. (2011). Organizational citizenship behavior: a study of young executives in Canada, Iran, and Turkey. *International Journal of Human Resource Management*, *22*, 2703–2729.

Kaplinsky, R., Readman, J., & Memedovic, O. (2009). *Upgrading strategies in global furniture value chain*. Vienna: United Nations Industrial Development Organization.

Keister, L. A., & Zhang, Y. L. (2009). 8 Organizations and management in China. *The Academy of Management Annuals*, *3*(1), 377–409.

Kim, L. (1999). Building technological capability for industrialization: analytical frameworks and Korea's experience. *Industrial and Corporate Change*, *8*(1), 257–263.

Kiss, A., & Danis, W. (2008). Country institutional context, social networks, and new venture internationalization speed. *European Management Journal*, *26*(6), 388–399.

Kiss, A. N., Danis, W. M., & Tamer Cavusgil, S. (2012). International entrepreneurship research in emerging economies: a critical review and research agenda. *Journal of Business Venturing*, *27*, 266–290.

Kollmann, T., & Stockmann, C. (2012). Filling the entrepreneurial orientation-performance gap: the mediating effects of exploratory and exploitative innovations. *Entrepreneurship: Theory and Practice*, *38*(5), 1001–1026.

Kouzes, J. M., & Posner, B. Z. (2007). *The leadership challenge*. San Francisco: John Wiley and Sons.

Kraus, S., Rigtering, J., Hughes, M., & Hosman, V. (2012). Entrepreneurial orientation and the business performance of SMEs: a quantitative study from the Netherlands. *Review of Managerial Science*, *6*, 161–182.

Kreiser, P., Marino, L., Kuratko, D., & Weaver, K. (2013). Disaggregating entrepreneurial orientation: the non-linear impact of innovativeness, proactiveness and risk-taking on SME performance. *Small Business Economics*, *40*, 273–291.

Krugman, P. (1994). The myth of Aisa's miracle. *Foreign Affairs*, *73*(6), 62–78.

Krug, B., & Hendrischke, H. (2012). Market design in Chinese market places. *Asia Pacific Journal of Management*, *29*(3), 525–546.

Kuivalainen, O., Saarenketo, S., & Puumalainen, K. (2012). Startup patterns of internationalization: a framework and its application in the context of knowledge-intensive SMEs. *European Management Journal*, *30*(4), 372–385.

Kuvaas, B., & Dysvik, A. (2010). Exploring alternative relationships between perceived investment in employee development, perceived supervisor support and employee outcomes. *Human Resource Management Journal*, *20*, 138–156.

Kwon, Y. -C. (2011). Relationship-specific investments, social capital, and performance: the case of Korean exporter/foreign buyer relations. *Asia Pacific Journal of Management*, *28*(4), 761–773.

Lai, K. L. (2008). *An introduction to Chinese philosophy*. Cambridge: Cambridge University Press.

Lam, T., Baum, T., & Pine, R. (2001). Study of managerial job satisfaction in Hong Kong's Chinese restaurants. *International Journal of Contemporary Hospitality Management*, *13*, 35–42.

Lam, S. S. K., Chun, H., & Law, K. S. (1999). Organizational citizenship behavior: comparing perspectives of supervisors and subordinates across four international samples. *Journal of Applied Psychology*, *84*, 594–623.

Lau, C. M., & Bruton, G. D. (2008). FDI in China: what we know and what we need to study next. *Academy of Management Perspectives*, *22*(4), 30–44.

Lefevere, A. (2004). *Translation, rewriting and the manipulation of literary fame*. Shanghai: Shanghai Foreign Language Education Press.

Leung, K., Brew, F. P., Zhang, Z., & Zhang, Y. (2011). Harmony and conflict: a cross-cultural investigation in China and Australia. *Journal of Cross-Cultural Psychology*, *42*(5), 795–816.

Leung, K., Chen, Z., Zhou, F., & Lim, K. (2014). The role of relational orientation as measured by face and rengqing in innovative behavior in China: an indigenous analysis. *Asia Pacific Journal of Management*, *31*(1), 105–126.

Leung, K., Koch, P. T., & Lu, L. (2002). A dualistic model of harmony and its implications for conflict management in Asia. *Asia Pacific Journal of Management*, *19*, 201–220.

Li, C. (2008). The ideal of harmony in ancient Chinese and Greek philosophy. *Dao*, *7*, 81–98.

Li, P. P. (2012). Toward an integrative framework of indigenous research: the geocentric implications of Yin-Yang balance. *Asia Pacific Journal of Management*, *29*, 849–872.

Li, X. (2014). Can Yin-Yang guide Chinese indigenous management research? *Management and Organization Review*, *10*(1), 7–27.

Li, X., & Brødsgaard, K. E. (2013). SOE reform in China: past, present and future. *The Copenhagen Journal of Asian Studies*, *31*(23), 54–78.

Li, Y., Li, P. P., Liu, Y., & Yang, D. (2010). Learning trajectory in offshore OEM cooperation: transaction value for local suppliers in the emerging economies. *Journal of Operations Management*, *28*(3), 269–282.

Li, M., Mobley, W. H., & Kelly, A. (2013). When do global leaders learn best to develop cultural intelligence? An investigation of the moderating role of experiential learning style. *Academy of Management Learning & Education*, *12*(1), 32–50.

Li, Y., Wei, Z., & Liu, Y. (2010). Strategic orientations, knowledge acquisition, and firm performance: the perspective of the vendor in cross-border outsourcing. *Journal of Management Studies*, *47*(8), 1457–1482. https://doi.org/10.1111/j.1467-6486.2010.00949.x.

Lian, H., Brown, D. J., Ferris, D. L., Liang, L. L., Keeping, L., & Morrison, R. (2014). Abusive supervision and retaliation: a self-control framework. *Academy of Management Journal*, *57*, 116–139.

Lim, K., & Cu, B. (2012). The effects of social networks and contractual characteristics on the relationship between venture capitalists and entrepreneurs. *Asia Pacific Journal of Management, 29*, 573–596.

Lin, L. -H., & Ho, Y. -L. (2010). Guanxi and OCB. *Journal of Business Ethics, 96*, 285–298.

Lin, H., & Hou, S. (2010). Managerial lessons from the East: an interview with Acer's Stan Shih. *Academy of Management Perspectives, 24*(4), 6–16. https://doi.org/10.5465/AMP.2010.55206380.

Lin, Y., Pekkarinen, S., & Ma, S. (2015). Service-dominant logic for managing the logistics-manufacturing interface: a case study. *The International Journal of Logistics Management, 26*(1), 195–214.

Little, T. D., Bovaird, J. A., & Widaman, K. F. (2006). On the merits of orthogonalizing powered and product terms: implications for modeling latent variable interactions. *Structural Equation Modeling, 13*, 479–519.

Little, T. D., Cunningham, W. A., & Shahar, G. (2002). To parcel or not to parcel: exploring the question, weighing the merits. *Structural Equation Modeling, 9*, 151–173.

Liu, S. (2011). Structuration of information control in China. *Cultural Sociology, 5*(3), 323–339.

Liu, M., & Li, C. (2014). Environment pressures, managerial industrial relations ideologies and unionization in Chinese enterprises. *British Journal of Industrial Relations, 52*(1), 82–111.

Liu, X., Wang, C., & Wei, Y. (2009). Do local manufacturing firms benefit from transactional linkages with multinational enterprises in China? *Journal of International Business Studies, 40*, 1113–1130.

Lockstrom, M., Schadel, J., Harrison, N., Moser, R., & Malhotra, M. K. (2010). Antecedents to supplier integration in the automobile industry: a multiple-case study of foreign subsidiaries in China. *Journal of Operations Management, 28*(3), 240–256.

Logemann, M., & Piekkari, R. (2015). Localize or local lies? The power of language and translation in the multinational corporation. *Critical Perspectives on International Business, 11*(1), 30–53.

Lu, Y., Zhou, L., Bruton, G., & Li, W. (2010). Capabilities as a mediator linking resources and the international performance of entrepreneurial firms in an emerging economy. *Journal of International Business Studies, 41*(3), 419–436.

Lumpkin, G., & Dess, G. (1996). Clarifying the entrepreneurial orientation construct and linking it to performance. *Academy of Management Review, 21*, 135–172.

Luo, Y., & Child, J. (2015). A composition-based view of firm growth. *Management and Organization Review, 11*(3), 379–411.

Luo, Y., Huang, Y., & Wang, S. (2011). Guanxi and organizational performance: a meta-analysis. *Management and Organization Review, 8*, 139–172.

Luo, Y., & Tung, R. L. (2007). International expansion of emerging market enterprises: a springboard perspective. *Journal of International Business Studies, 38*(4), 481–498.

Lyles, M. A., & Park, S. H. (2013). The life cycle of internationalization. *Business Horizons, 56*, 405–410.

Ma, S., & Trigo, V. (2011). The 'country-of-origin effect' in employee turnover intention: evidence from China. *International Journal of Human Resource Management.* https://doi.org/10.1080/09585192.2011.579923.

Ma, Z., Yu, M., Gao, C., Zhou, J., & Yang, Z. (2015). Institutional constraints of product innovation in China: evidence from international joint ventures. *Journal of Business Research, 68*(5), 949–956.

Mackinnon, D. P., Lockwood, C. M., Hoffman, J. M., West, S. G., & Sheets, V. (2002). A comparison of methods to test mediation and other intervening variable effects. *Psychological Methods, 7*(1), 83–104.

Makadok, R. (2001). Toward a synthesis of there source-based and dynamic-capability views of rent creation. *Strategic Management Journal, 22*(5), 387–401. https://doi.org/10.1002/smj.158.

Malik, O. R., & Kotabe, M. (2009). Dynamic capabilities, government policies, and performance in firms from emerging economies: evidence from India and Pakistan. *Journal of Management Studies*, *46*(3), 421–450.

Matthews, J. A. (2006). Dragon multinationals. *Asia Pacific Journal of Management*, *23*, 5–27.

McElhatton, E., & Jackson, B. (2012). Paradox in harmony: formulating a Chinese model of leadership. *Leadership*, *8*(4), 441–461.

McGuinness, M., Demirbag, M., & Bandara, S. (2013). Towards a multi-perspective model of reverse knowledge transfer in multinational enterprises: a case study of Coats plc. *European Management Journal*, *31*(2), 179–195.

McKeever, E., Anderson, A., & Jack, S. (2014). Entrepreneurship and mutuality: social capital in processes and practices. *Entrepreneurship and Regional Development*, *25*(5–6), 453–477.

McNiff, S. (1998). *Art-based research*. London: Jessica Kingsley.

Metcalf, D., & Li, J. (2007). Chinese unions: an Alice in wonderland dream world. *Advances in Industrial and Labor Relations*, *15*, 213–268.

Meyer, J. P., Allen, N. J., & Smith, C. (1993). Commitment to organizations and occupations: extension and test of a three-component conceptualization. *Journal of Applied Psychology*, *78*, 538–551.

Meyer, J. P., Stanley, D. J., Herscovitch, L., & Topolnytsky, L. (2002). Affective, continuance, and normative commitment to the organization: a meta-analysis of antecedents, correlates, and consequences. *Journal of Vocational Behavior*, *61*(1), 20–52.

Meyer, J. P., Stanley, D. J., Jackson, T. A., McInnis, K. J., Maltin, E. R., & Sheppard, L. (2012). Affective, normative, and continuance commitment levels across cultures: a meta-analysis. *Journal of Vocational Behavior*, *80*(2), 225–245.

Miller, D. (1983). The correlates of entrepreneurship in three types of firms. *Management Science*, *29*(7), 770–791.

Miller, D. (1991). The eight trigrams of the I-Ching. *Qin Journal*, *1*(4), 12–21.

Monferrer, D., Blesa, A., & Ripolles, M. (2015). Born globals through knowledge-based dynamic capabilities and network market orientation. *Business Research Quarterly*, *18*(1), 18–36.

Morrison, A., Pietrobelli, C., & Rabellotti, R. (2008). Global value chains and technological capabilities: a framework to study industrial innovation in developing countries. *Oxford Development Studies*, *36*(1), 39–58.

Motohashia, K., & Yuan, Y. (2010). Productivity impact of technology spillover from multinationals to local firms: comparing China's automobile and electronics industries. *Research Policy*, *39*(6), 790–798.

Moura, G. R. D., Abrams, D., Retter, C., Gunnarsdottir, S., & Ando, K. (2009). Identification as an organizational anchor: how identification and job satisfaction combine to predict turnover intention. *European Journal of Social Psychology*, *39*, 540–557.

Mudambi, R. (2007). Managing global offshoring strategies: a case approach. *Journal of International Business Studies*, *38*(1), 206–210.

Mudambi, R., Piscitello, L., & Rabbiosi, L. (2014). Reverse knowledge transfer in MNEs: subsidiary innovativeness and entry modes. *Long Range Planning*, *47*(1–2), 49–63.

Nadkarni, S., & Herrmann, P. (2010). CEO personality, strategic flexibility, and firm performance: the case of the Indian business process outsourcing industry. *Academy of Management Journal*, *53*(5), 1050–1073.

National Bureau of Statistics of China (2012). *China statistical yearbook-2011*. Beijing: China Statistics Press.

National Bureau of Statistics of China (2017). *China statistical yearbook-2017*. Beijing: China Statistics Press.

Ndubisi, N. O. (2011). Conflict handling, trust and commitment in outsourcing relationship: a Chinese and Indian study. *Industrial Marketing Management*, *40*(1), 109–117.

Ngo, T. W. (2008). Rent-seeking and economic governance in the structural nexus of corruption in China. *Crime, Law and Social Change, 49*(1), 27–44.

Ngo, H. Y., Lau, C. M., & Foley, S. (2008). Strategic human resource management, firm performance, and employee relations climate in China. *Human Resource Management, 47,* 73–90.

Nguyen, H. D., & Yang, J. (2012). Chinese employees' interpersonal conflict management strategies. *International Journal of Conflict Management, 23*(4), 382–412.

North, D. C. (1990). *Institutions, institutional change, and economic performance.* Cambridge, MA: Harvard University Press.

Oetzel, J., Garcia, A., & Ting-Toomey, S. (2008). An analysis of the relationships among face concerns and facework behaviors in perceived conflict situations: a four-culture Investigation. *International Journal of Conflict Management, 19*(4), 382–403.

Opper, S., & Nee, V. (2015). Network effects, cooperation and entrepreneurial innovation in China. *Asian Business and Management, 14*(4), 283–302.

Organ, D. (1988). *Organizational citizenship behavior: The good soldier syndrome.* Lexington, MA: Lexington Books.

Organ, D. W. (1997). Organizational citizenship behavior: its construct clean-up time. *Human Performance, 10,* 85–97.

Organ, D. W., Podsakoff, P. M., & Mackenzie, S. B. (2006). *Organizational citizenship behavior: Its nature, antecedents, and consequences.* Thousand Oaks, CA: Sage.

Oviatt, B. M., & McDougall, P. P. (1994). Toward a theory of international new ventures. *Journal of International Business Studies, 25*(1), 45–64.

Oviatt, B. M., & McDougall, P. P. (2005). Defining international entrepreneurship and modeling the speed of internationalization. *Entrepreneurship: Theory and Practice, 29*(5), 537–553.

Paille, P. (2013). Organizational citizenship behavior and employee retention: how important are turnover cognitions? *The International Journal of Human Resource Management, 24,* 768–790.

Peltokorpi, E., & Vaara, E. (2014). Knowledge transfer in multinational corporations: productive and counterproductive effects of language-sensitive recruitment. *Journal of International Business Studies, 45*(5), 600–622.

Piekkari, R., Welch, D. E., Welch, L. S., Peltonen, J. -P., & Vesa, T. (2013). Translation behavior: an exploratory study within a service multinational. *International Business Review, 22*(5), 771–783.

Pittinsky, T. L., & Shih, M. J. (2004). Knowledge nomads: organizational commitment and worker mobility in positive perspective. *American Behavioral Scientist, 47,* 791–807.

Podsakoff, P., MacKenzie, S., Lee, J., & Podsakoff, N. (2003). Common method biases in behavioral research: a critical review of the literature and recommended remedies. *Journal of Applied Psychology, 88*(5), 879–903. 14516251.

Podsakoff, P. M., MacKenzie, S. B., Paine, J. B., & Bachrach, D. G. (2000). Organizational citizenship behaviors: a critical review of the theoretical and empirical literature and suggestions for future research. *Journal of Management, 26,* 513–563.

Posthuma, R. A. (2011). Conflict management and performance outcomes. *International Journal of Conflict Management, 22*(2), 108–110.

Pun, N. (2007). Gendering the dormitory labor system: production, reproduction, and migrant labor in south China. *Feminist Economics, 13*(3/4), 239–258.

Qian, C. (2010). The culture of China's mediation in regional and international affairs. *Conflict Resolution Quarterly, 28,* 53–65.

Ralston, D. A., Pounder, J., Lo, C. W. H., Wong, Y., Egri, C. P., & Stauffer, J. (2006). Stability and change in managerial work values: a longitudinal study of China, Hong Kong, and the US. *Management and Organization Review, 2,* 67–94.

Randall, D. M. (1993). Cross-cultural research on organizational commitment: a review and application of Hofstede's value survey module. *Journal of Business Research, 26*(1), 91–110.

Rauch, A., Wiklund, J., Lumpkin, G., & Frese, M. (2009). Entrepreneurial orientation and business performance: an assessment of past research and suggestions for the future. *Entrepreneurship: Theory and Practice*, *33*(3), 761–787.

Redding, S. G. (2005). The thick description and comparison of societal systems of capitalism. *Journal of International Business Studies*, *36*, 123–155.

Redding, G. (2016). Impact of China's invisible societal forces on its intended evolution. In A. Y. Lewin, M. Kenny, & J. P. Murmann (Eds.), *China's innovation challenge: Overcoming the middle-income trap*. Cambridge: Cambridge University Press.

Redding, G., & Drew, A. (2016). Dealing with complexity of causes of societal innovativeness: social enabling and disabling mechanisms and the case of China. *Journal of Interdisciplinary Economics*, *28*(2), 1–30.

Rhee, M. (2010). The pursuit of shared wisdom in class: when classical Chinese thinkers meet James March. *Academy of Management Learning & Education*, *9*, 258–279.

Rialp, A., Rialp, J., Urbano, D., & Valiant, Y. (2005). The born–global phenomenon: a comparative case study research. *Journal of International Entrepreneurship*, *3*, 133–171.

Rich, J. L., Lepine, J. A., & Crawford, E. R. (2010). Job engagement: antecedents and effects on job performance. *Academy of Management Journal*, *52*, 617–635.

Richter, A. W., West, M. A., Dick, V. R., & Dawson, J. F. (2006). Boundary spanners' identification, intergroup contact, and effective intergroup relations. *Academy of Management Journal*, *49*(6), 1252–1269.

Riketta, M., & Van Dick, R. (2005). Foci of attachment in organizations: a meta-analytic comparison of the strength and correlates of workgroup vs organizational identification and commitment. *Journal of Vocational Behavior*, *67*(3), 490–510.

Rotundo, M., & Xie, J. L. (2008). Understanding the domain of counterproductive work behavior in China. *The International Journal of Human Resource Management*, *19*, 856–877.

Rowley, C. (1997a). Reassessing HRM's convergence. *Asia Pacific Business Review*, *3*(4), 198–211.

Rowley, C. (1997b). Comparisons and perspectives: on HRM in the Asia Pacific. *Asia Pacific Business Review*, *3*(4), 1–18.

Rowley, C. (2003). *The management of people: HRM in context*: (p. 320). London: Chandos/Spiro.

Rowley, C. (2014). *Relevance and role of interdisciplinarity in Asia Pacific studies and publications*. Working Paper Singapore: HEAD Foundation.

Rowley, C. (2016). The past, the future and rankings. *Journal of Chinese Human Resource Management*, *7*(1), 2–4.

Rowley, C., & Benson, J. (2002). Convergence and divergence in Asian HRM. *California Management Review*, *44*(2), 90–109.

Rowley, C., & Benson, J. (2003). Changes and continuities in Asian HRM. *Asia Pacific Business Review*, *9*(4), 1–14.

Rowley, C., Benson, J., & Warner, M. (2004). Towards an Asian model of HRM: comparative analysis of China, Japan and Korea. *The International Journal of Human Resource Management*, *15*(4–5), 917–933.

Rowley, C., & Bhopal, M. (2002). The state in employment: the case of Malaysian electronics. *The International Journal of Human Resource Management*, *13*(8), 1166–1185.

Rowley, C., & Bhopal, M. (2005). Ethnicity as a management issue and resource: examples from Malaysia. *Asia Pacific Business Review*, *11*(4), 553–574.

Rowley, C., & Bhopal, M. (2006). The ethnic factor in state-labour relations: the case of Malaysia. *Capital & Class*, *30*(1), 87–116.

Rowley, C., & Oh, I. (2016). Business ethics and the role of context: institutionalism, history and comparisons in the Asia Pacific region. *Asia Pacific Business Review*, *22*, 1–13.

Rowley, C., & Poon, I. (2011). In C. Rowley & K. Jackson (Eds.), *HRM: The key concepts in knowledge management* (pp. 142–146). London: Routledge.

Rowley, C., & Ulrich, D. (2012a). Setting the scene for leadership in Asia'. *Asia Pacific Business Review, 18*(4), 451–464.

Rowley, C., & Ulrich, D. (2012b). Lessons learned & insights derived from leadership in Asia. *Asia Pacific Business Review, 18*(4), 675–681.

Rowley, C., & Ulrich, D. (2014). *Leadership in the Asia Pacific.* London: Routledge.

Schmidt, S. W. (2007). The relationship between satisfaction with workplace training and overall job satisfaction. *Human Resource Development Quarterly, 18*, 481–498.

Schmitz, H. (2006). Learning and earning in global garment and footwear chains. *The European Journal of Development Research, 18*(4), 546–571.

Schomaker, M. S., & Zaheer, S. (2014). The role of language in knowledge transfer to geographically dispersed manufacturing operations. *Journal of International Management, 20*(1), 55–72.

Sciascia, S., D'Oria, L., Bruni, M., & Larraneta, B. (2014). Entrepreneurial orientation in low- and medium-tech industries: the need for absorptive capacity to increase performance. *European Management Journal, 32*(5), 761–769.

Semrau, T., & Sigmund, S. (2012). Networking ability and the financial performance of new ventures: a mediation analysis among younger and more mature firms. *Strategic Entrepreneurship Journal, 6*, 335–354.

Seow, V. (2014). The first auto works and the contradictions of connectivity in the early People's Republic of China. *The Journal of Transport History, 35*(2), 145–161.

Shen, J., & Netto, B. D. (2012). Impact of the 2007–09 global economic crisis on human resource management among Chinese export-oriented enterprises. *Asia Pacific Business Review, 18*(1), 45–64.

Sidle, S. D. (2009). Building a committed global workforce: does what employees want depend on culture? *Academy of Management Perspectives, 23*(1), 79–80.

Sobel, M. E. (1988). Direct and indirect effects in linear structural equation models. *Sociological Methods & Research, 6*(12), 155–176.

Sonenshein, S. (2014). How organizations foster the creative use of resources. *Academy of Management Journal, 57*(3), 814–848.

Song, J., Wang, R., & Cavusgil, S. T. (2015). State ownership and market orientation in China's public firms: an agency theory perspective. *International Business Review, 24*(4), 690–699.

Spender, J. -C. (2014). *Business strategy: Managing uncertainty, opportunity and enterprise.* Oxford: Oxford University Press.

Stobbeleir, K. E. M. D., Ashford, S. J., & Buyens, D. (2011). Self-regulation of creativity at work: the role of feedback-seeking behavior in creative performance. *Academy of Management Journal, 54*, 811–831.

Stone, D. L., & Stone-Romero, E. F. (2007). *The influence of culture on human resource management processes and practices.* London: Psychology Press.

Stone-Romero, E. F., & Rosopa, P. J. (2008). The relative validity of inferences about mediation as a function of research design characteristics. *Organizational Research Methods, 11*(2), 326–352.

Su, Z., Peng, J., Shen, H., & Xiao, T. (2012). Technological capability, marketing capability, and firm performance in turbulent conditions. *Management and Organization Review, 9*(1), 115–137.

Sun, P., & Anderson, M. (2010). An examination of the relationship between absorptive capacity and organizational learning, and a proposed integration. *International Journal of Management Reviews, 12*(2), 130.

Sun, L. Y., Aryee, S., & Law, K. S. (2007). High-performance human resource practice, citizenship behavior and organizational performance: a relational perspective. *Academy of Management Journal, 50*, 558–577.

Tang, L., & Fitzsimons, B. (2013). The converging divergence of labor relations in automobile industry: the case of China. *Competitiveness Review: An International Business Journal, 23*(2), 175–188.

Tang, Z., & Tang, J. (2012). Entrepreneurial orientation and SME performance in China's changing environment: the moderating effects of strategies. *Asia Pacific Journal of Management, 29,* 409–431.

Taylor, S. S., & Ladkin, D. (2009). Understanding arts-based methods in managerial development. *Academy of Management Learning & Education, 8*(1), 55–69.

Teagarden, M. B. (2010). The power of context. *Thunderbird International Business Review, 52*(3), 173–174.

Teece, D. J. (2007). Explicating dynamic capabilities: the nature and microfoundations of (sustainable) enterprise performance. *Strategic Management Journal, 28*(13), 1319–1350. https://doi.org/10.1002/smj.640.

Teece, D. J., Pisano, G., & Shuen, A. (1997). Dynamic capabilities and strategic management. *Strategic Management Journal, 18*(7), 509–533.

Teh, J. C., Boerhannoeddin, A., & Ismail, A. (2012). Organizational culture and performance appraisal process: effect on organizational citizenship behavior. *Asian Business & Management, 11,* 471–484.

Thomas, D. (1994). The boundary-spanning role of expatriates in the multinational corporation. *Advances in International Comparative Management, 9*(16), 145–170.

Thomas, R. L., & Kenneth, T. W. (1976). Support for a two-dimensional model of conflict behavior. *Organizational Behavior and Human Performance, 16,* 142–155.

Tian, L. (2007). Does government intervention helps the Chinese automobile industry? A comparison with the Chinese computer industry. *Economic Systems, 31*(4), 364–374.

Tjosvold, D., & Sun, H. (2010). Using power to affect performance in China: effects of employee achievement and social context. *International Journal of Conflict Management, 21*(4), 364–381.

Tjosvold, D., Wu, P., & Chen, Y. F. (2010). The effects of collectivistic and individualistic values on conflict and decision making: an experiment in China. *Journal of Applied Social Psychology, 49,* 2904–2926.

Tolstoy, D. (2014). Differentiation in foreign business relationships: a study on small and medium-sized enterprises after their initial foreign market entry. *International Small Business Journal, 32*(1), 17–35.

Tornikoski, C. (2011). Fostering expatriate affective commitment: a total reward perspective. *Cross Cultural Management: An International Journal, 18*(2), 214–235.

Townsend, J. D., & Calantone, R. J. (2014). Evolution and transformation of innovation in the global automotive industry. *Journal of Product Innovation Management, 31*(1), 4–7.

Tse, E. (2010). The globe: is it too late to enter China? *Harvard Business Review, 88*(4), 96–101.

Tsui, A. S. (2007). From homogenization to pluralism: international management research in the academy and beyond. *Academy of Management Journal, 50,* 1353–1364.

Tsui, A. S., Nifadkar, S. S., & Ou, A. Y. (2007). Cross national, cross-cultural organizational behavior research: advances, gaps, and recommendations. *Journal of Management, 33,* 426–478.

Tung, R. L. (2006). Of arts, leadership, management education, and management research: a commentary on Nancy Adler's "the arts & leadership: now that we can do anything, what will we do?" *Academy of Management Learning & Education, 5,* 505–511.

Tung, R. L. (2008). The cross-cultural research imperative: the need to balance cross-national and intra-national diversity. *Journal of International Business Studies, 39,* 41–46.

Uner, M. M., Kocak, A., Cavusgil, E., & Cavusgil, S. T. (2013). Do barriers to export vary for born globals and across stages of internationalization? An empirical inquiry in the emerging market of Turkey. *International Business Review, 22*(5), 800–813.

Usunier, J. -C. (2011). Language as a resources to assess cross-cultural equivalence in quantitative management research. *Journal of World Business, 46*(7), 314–319.

Van Dyne, L., Graham, J., & Dienesch, R. M. (1994). Organizational citizenship behavior: construct redefinition, measurement and validation. *Academy of Management Journal, 37*, 765–802.

Veitch, R. W. D., & Cooper-Thomas, H. D. (2009). Tit for tat: predictors of temporary agency workers' commitments. *Asia Pacific Journal of Human Resources, 47*(3), 320–339.

Velazquez-Razo, P. N., & Vargas-Hernandez, J. G. (2011). The strategy of de-internationalization of the SMEs of the footwear in the area metropolitana de Guadalajara. *Business Management Dynamics, 1*, 12–23.

Venuti, L. (2008). *The translator's invisibility: A history of translation* (2nd ed.). Abingdon: Routledge.

Von Glinow, M. A., & Teagarden, M. B. (2009). The future of Chinese management research: rigor and relevance revisited. *Management and Organization Review, 5*(1), 75–89.

Wales, W., Gupta, V., & Mousa, F. (2013). Empirical research on entrepreneurial orientation: an assessment and suggestions for future research. *International Small Business Journal, 31*(4), 357–383.

Walumbwa, F. O., Cropanzano, R., & Goldman, B. M. (2011). How leader-member exchange influences effective work behaviors: social exchange and internal-external efficacy perspectives. *Personnel Psychology, 64*, 739–770.

Wang, L. (2011). Perceived equity and unionization propensity in China. *Management Research Review, 34*(6), 678–686.

Wang, L., & Juslin, H. (2009). The impact of Chinese culture on corporate social responsibility: the harmony approach. *Journal of Business Ethics, 88*, 433–451.

Wang, H., & Kimble, C. (2013). Innovation and leapfrogging in the Chinese automobile industry: examples from Geely, BYD, and Shifeng. *Global Business and Organizational Excellence, 32*(6), 6–17.

Wang, Y., & Tanaka, A. (2011). From hierarchy to hybrid: the evolving nature of inter-firm governance in China's automobile groups. *Journal of Business Research, 64*(1), 74–80.

Warner, M. (2014). *Understanding Chinese management: Past, present and future.* London/New York: Routledge.

Warner, M. (2015). Keynes and China: Keynesianism with Chinese characteristics. *Asia Pacific Business Review, 21*(2), 251–263.

Wasti, S. A. (2003). The influence of cultural values on antecedents of organizational commitment: an individual level analysis. *Applied Psychology An International Review, 52*(4), 533–554.

Weerawardena, J., Sullivan Mort, G. M., Liesch, P., & Knight, G. (2007). Conceptualising accelerated internationalization in the born global firm: a dynamic capabilities perspective. *Journal of World Business, 42*(2), 294–306.

Wei, Y., & Liu, X. (2006). Productivity spillovers from R&D, exports and FDI in China's manufacturing sector. *Journal of International Business Studies, 37*(4), 544–557.

Weick, K. E. (2007). Drop your tools: on reconfiguring management education. *Journal of Management Education, 31*(1), 5–16.

Welch, D. E., & Welch, L. S. (2008). The importance of language in international knowledge Transfer. *Management International Review, 48*(3), 339–360.

Westwood, R. (1997). Harmony and patriarchy: the cultural basis for "paternalistic headship" among the overseas Chinese. *Organization Studies, 18*, 445–480.

Whetten, D. A. (2009). An examination of the interface between context and theory applied to the study of Chinese organizations. *Management and Organization Review, 5*(1), 29–55.

Wielemaker, M., & Gedajlovic, E. (2011). Governance and capabilities: Asia's entrepreneurial performance and stock of venture forms. *Asia Pacific Journal of Management, 28*(1), 157–185.

Wiklund, J., & Shepherd, D. (2005). Entrepreneurial orientation and small business performance: a configurational approach. *Journal of Business Venturing, 20,* 71–91.

Wiklund, J., & Shepherd, D. (2011). Where to from here? EO-as-experimentation, failure, and distribution of outcomes. *Entrepreneurship Theory and Practice, 35*(5), 925–946.

Williamson, I. O., Burnett, M. F., & Bartol, K. M. (2009). The interactive effect of collectivism and organizational rewards on affective organizational commitment. *Cross Cultural Management: An International Journal, 16*(1), 28–43.

Woldesenbet, K., Ram, M., & Jones, T. (2012). Supplying large firms: the role of entrepreneurial and dynamic capabilities in small business. *International Small Business Journal, 30*(5), 493–512.

Wrzesniewski, A., & Dutton, J. E. (2001). Crafting a job: revisioning employees as active crafters of their work. *Academy of Management Review, 26*(2), 179–201.

Wu, J., & Chen, X. (2012). Leaders' social ties, knowledge acquisition capability and firm competitive advantage. *Asia Pacific Journal of Management, 29*(2), 331–350. https://doi. org/10.1007/s10490-011-9278-0.

Xiao, Y., & Cooke, F. L. (2012). Work-life balance in China? Social policy, employer strategy and individual coping mechanisms. *Asia Pacific Journal of Human Resources, 50*(1), 6–22.

Xiao, Z. X., & Tsui, A. S. (2007). Where brokers may not work: the culture contingency of social capital. *Administrative Science Quarterly, 51,* 1–31. pii: s10490-011-9278-0.

Yamakawa, Y., Khavul, S., & Peng, M. W. (2013). Venturing from emerging economies. *Strategic Entrepreneurship Journal, 7,* 181–196.

Yan, J., & Sorenson, R. L. (2004). The influence of confucian ideology and conflict in Chinese family business. *International Journal of Cross Cultural Management, 4*(1), 5–17.

Yang, R. O. (2015). Political process and widespread protests in China: the 2010 labor protest. *Journal of Contemporary China, 24*(91).

Yang, D., Chin, T., Liu, R–h., & Yao, Z. (2017). Policy support for own-brand innovation in China's auto industry. *Chinese Management Studies, 11*(1), 107–122.

Yang, Y., & Tang, M. (2014). Do political tensions take a toll? The effect of the Sino-Japan relationship on sales of Japanese-brand cars in China. *Asian Business and Management, 13*(5), 359–378.

Yavas, U., & Bodur, M. (1999). Satisfaction among expatriate managers: correlates and consequences. *Career Development International, 4,* 261–269.

Yen, H. R., Li, E. Y., & Niehoff, B. P. (2008). Do organizational citizenship behaviors lead to information system success? Testing the mediation effects of integration climate and project management. *Information and Management, 45,* 394–402.

Yin, R. K. (Ed.), (2003). *Case study research: Design and methods.* (3rd ed.). Thousand Oaks, CA: Sage Publications.

Yin, R. K. (Ed.), (2009). *Case study research: Design and methods.* (4th ed.). Thousand Oaks, CA: Sage Publications.

Yu, B. B., & Egri, C. P. (2005). Human resource management practices and affective organizational commitment: a comparison of Chinese employees in a state-owned enterprise and a joint venture. *Asia Pacific Journal of Human Resources, 43*(3), 332–360.

Yu, J., & Zaheer, S. (2010). Building a process model of local adaptation of practices: a study of six sigma implementation in Korean and US firms. *Journal of International Business Studies, 41,* 475–499.

Yuan, W. (2010). Conflict management among American and Chinese employees in multinational organizations in China. *Cross Cultural Management: An International Journal, 17,* 299–311.

Zahra, S. A. (2005). A theory of international new ventures: a decade of research. *Journal of International Business Studies, 30,* 20–28.

Zander, L., Mockaitis, A. I., & Harzing, A. -W. (2011). Standardization and contextualization: a study of language and leadership across 17 countries. *Journal of World Business*, *46*(3), 296–304.

Zarankin, T. G. (2008). A new look at conflict styles: goal orientation and outcome preferences. *International Journal of Conflict Management*, *19*(2), 167–184.

Zhang, H., Zhang, T., Cai, H., Li, Y., Wei Huang, W., & Xu, D. (2014). Proposing and validating a five-dimensional scale for measuring entrepreneurial orientation. *Journal of Entrepreneurship in Emerging Economies*, *6*(2), 102–121.

Zhang, J., & Zheng, W. (2009). How does satisfaction translate into performance? An examination of commitment and cultural values. *Human Resource Development Quarterly*, *20*, 331–351.

Zhen, L. (2012). An analytical study on service-oriented manufacturing strategies. *International Journal of Production Economics*, *139*(1), 220–228. https://doi.org/10.1016/j.ijpe.2012.04.010.

Zheng, P. (2014). The contrasting strategies of owner-managed and foreign-engaged joint ventures under market socialism in China. *International Entrepreneurship and Management Journal*, *10*, 539–560.

Zhou, B. (2004). *Zhou Yi Tong Shi*. Beijing: Kunlun [in Chinese].

Zhou, L., Barnes, B. R., & Lu, Y. (2010). Entrepreneurial proclivity, capability upgrading and performance advantage of newness among international new ventures. *Journal of International Business Studies*, *41*(5), 882–905. https://doi.org/10.1057/jibs.2009.87.

Zhou, K., & Wu, F. (2010). Technological capability, strategic flexibility, and product innovation. *Strategic Management Journal*, *31*(5), 547–561.

Zhu, Y. (2004). Workers, unions, and the state: migrant workers in China's labor-intensive foreign enterprises. *Development and Change*, *35*(5), 1011–1036.

Zhu, C. J., Cooper, B. K., Fan, D., & De Cieri, H. (2013). HR practices from the perspective of managers and employees in multinational enterprises in China: alignment issues and implications. *Journal of World Business*, *48*(2), 241–250.

Zhu, C. J., Thomson, S. B., & Cieri, H. D. (2008). A retrospective and prospective analysis of firm research in Chinese firms: implications and directions for future study. *Human Resource Management*, *47*, 133–156.

Zhu, Y., Wittmann, X., & Peng, M. (2012). Institution-based barriers to innovation in SMEs in China. *Asia Pacific Journal of Management*, *29*, 1131–1142.

Zou, H., Chen, X., & Ghauri, P. (2010). Antecedents and consequences of new venture growth strategy: an empirical study in China. *Asia Pacific Journal of Management*, *27*, 393–421.

# INDEX

Note: Page numbers followed by $f$ indicate figures, and $t$ indicate tables.

**A**

Absorptive capabilities
OEMs, 32–33, 38
pattern-matching analysis, 41–42t
Acculturation, 219
ACFTUs. *See* All-China Federation of
Trade Unions (ACFTUs)
Affective commitment (AC), 132–134
art-based *vs.* science-based views, 134–135
common method variance, 143–144
compliance behaviour, 140–141, 143,
146, 149–150
construct validity, 143–144
contributions, 134, 147–149
control variables, 143, 147
degree of harmony, 133–136, 140–147,
149
eight-trigram model, 135–136
implications, 147–149
limitation, 149
organizational commitment, 137–139
results, 144–146, 145t
sample selection, 141–142
sociocultural transformation, 139–140
types of measures, 142–144
Ageing workforce, 219
All-China Federation of Trade Unions
(ACFTUs), 159–160, 162, 183–184
Ambiguity, 199, 214
Analytic hierarchy process (AHP) method,
17
Annual wage
changes, 154f
increasing, 27
of manufacturing employees, 217
Art-based view
east–west cultural differences, 134–135
organizational development and change,
112–113
Yin–Yang dynamics, 115–118

Artificial intelligence (AI), 217, 220
Asian traditional philosophies, 147–148
Asia-originated behavioural theory, 132
Attitude–behaviour compatibility, 120–121,
140
Auto manufacturing, China
development history of, 7–10
employment dilemma, 6–7

**B**

Baseline model
OCB, 126, 128t
reverse internationalization, 77–78, 78t,
102
Blue-collar workers, 153–155
Born globals
context-specific type of, 64
in developed country, 64
from emerging economies, 64–65
international entrepreneurship, 45
knowledge acquisition and strategic
actions, 72
SMEs as, 64
Boundary spanning
abductive process, 203
conceptual model, 200f
dimensions, 194
distribution, 203–204
exchanging knowledge, 207–208
facilitating function, 210–211
higher-level, 210–211, 214
in international settings, 197
intervening function, 211–212
linking function, 209
manipulating function, 209–210
in MNCs, 196–200
performance, 214–215
practical implications, 214
in transferring knowledge, 201
by translators, 206

Bounded rationality, 45–46
Branding
    after 2008 global financial crisis, 61–62
    global start-up OEMs, 69–70
    importance, 70
    in reverse internationalization, 107
British entrepreneurial OEM, 44–58

## C

Case-study methodology, 34–36
CCP. *See* Chinese Communist Party (CCP)
China Automotive Industry Yearbook
    (2014), 16–17
China News Service, 181
China's auto manufacturing
    development history of, 7–10
    employment dilemma, 6–7
China's economic growth
    exports, 115
    lack of skills training, 132–133
    manufacturing FDI and, 25–26, 141
    spectacular industrialization and, 157–158
China's manufacturing industry
    from cross-cultural perspective, 189
    employment *vs.* GDP in, 6*f*
    labour challenges, 5–6, 218–220
    profit margins, 153–155
Chinese Communist Party (CCP), 159, 162,
    217
Chinese management
    measurement, 136–137*t*
    research on, 157
Chinese people
    conflict management, 160, 187–188
    harmonious mentality of, 109–110
    labour conflicts, 160–161
    TECHSAVVY, 51
    win–win resolution, 166
Chinese philosophical ideologies, 113–114,
    163
Chinese Value Survey, 139
Chi-square tests, 78, 101–102
Clash stage, harmonizing process, 164,
    180–182
CMM
    critical disagreements, 54
    cultural differences, 54

decision-making processes, 57
    pricing strategies, disputes on, 55
    product design, 59
    product safety and quality requirements,
        55
    strategic alliance, 57–58
    upgrading to OBM, 53–54
Common method variance (CMV)
    affective commitment, 143–144
    entrepreneurial orientation, 97–98
    reverse internationalization, 71–72, 75
Communication stage, harmonizing process,
    165, 182–183
Compatibility principle, 120–121, 140
Compliance behaviour, 140–141, 143, 146,
    149–150
Compromise stage, harmonizing process,
    165, 183
Confidence Index, 25
Confirmatory factor analysis (CFA)
    construct validity, 124, 124–125*t*
    entrepreneurial orientation, 97*t*
    five-factor model by, 96–98
    multiple regression analyses, 97*t*
    OCB, 124, 124–125*t*
    scale reliability and validity, 74
Conflict, clash, communication,
    compromise, and consensus
    (5C model), 164–166, 178–184,
    179*f*, 186–187
Conflict-coping strategies, 156–157,
    160–161, 187
Conflict stage, harmonizing process, 164,
    179–180
Confucianism, 111–114, 119, 139–140,
    148, 163
Confucian work dynamism, 139
Consensus stage, harmonizing process, 166,
    183–184
Construct validity
    affective commitment, 143–144
    confirmatory factor analysis, 124,
        124–125*t*
    OCB, 124–125
Consumer-oriented industries, 219
Context-effect theories, OCB, 111–112,
    132

Contextualized theories, OCB, 111–112
Control variables
  affective commitment, 143, 147
  entrepreneurial orientation, 96
  OCB, 123
  original-brand manufacturer, 18
  reverse internationalization, 73
Cross-cultural management
  boundary-spanning function, translation and, 196–200
  conceptual model, 200f, 203
  data coding method, 203–205
  data collection, 201–203
  exchanging function, 197, 204t, 207–208, 212–213
  facilitating function, 198, 207t, 210–213
  intervening function, 198, 208t, 211–213
  in knowledge transfer, 194–196, 218
  limitations, 214–215
  linking function, 198, 205t, 209, 212–213
  manipulating function, 199, 206t, 209–210, 212–213
  in manufacturing, 192
  MNCs, 192–194
  results, 206–212
  sample selection, 200–201
  theoretical and practical implications, 213–214
Cultural interference, 199, 214
Customer relationship management (CRM), 39–40

**D**
Data coding method, 203–205
Data collection methods
  cross-cultural management, 201–203
  entrepreneurial orientation, 93–94
  knowledge transfer in MNCs, 201–203
  labour conflicts, 168
  pattern analysis, 35–36
  reverse internationalization, 71–72
  TECHSAVVY, 48–49
Data sources, and informants, 35
Degree of harmony
  affective commitment, 133–136, 140–147, 149

OCB, 116–117, 120, 120b, 122–123, 128–130
Developed economies (DEs)
  after 2008 global financial crisis, 63
  cross-border outsourcing, 47
  entrepreneurial firms, 44
  global value chain, 25–26
  MNCs, 47, 64–65
Digitalization, 217, 220
Direct effect model, OCB, 126, 128
Dragon Multinationals, 29
Dual-concern model, 161
Dui (lake), 116–117t, 136–137t
  Later Heaven sequence, 165–166, 165f
  measurement, 136–137t
  symbolic meaning, 116–117t
Dynamic capability
  FDI OEMs, 42
  and functional upgrading, 30–31
  global start-up firm, 63–64
  reverse internationalization, 67–71

**E**
Eastern Yin–Yang principle, 149–150
East–West cultural differences, 134–135, 147–148
Economic growth, China
  exports, 115
  lack of skills training, 132–133
  manufacturing FDI and, 25–26, 141
  spectacular industrialization and, 157–158
Economic rebalancing concept, 1
Eight-trigram model
  affective commitment, 135–136
  with 5C model, 164–166, 165f
  OCB, 110f, 114–115
  symbolic meaning, 115–117, 116–117t
  Yin–Yang harmony, 156–157
Emerging economies (EEs)
  born globals from, 64–65
  FDI firms in, 27
  globalization, 147
  global start-up OEMs, 27, 44–45
  SMEs in, 61, 92
Empirical findings, 36, 129
Employee behaviours, 118–119

Employment
  auto manufacturing, 6–7
  *vs.* GDP, 6*f*
  of migrant workers, 25
Enterprise resource planning (ERP) system, 37–40
ENTER regression method, 75
Entrepreneurial British OEM, 44–58
Entrepreneurial orientation (EO), 82, 85–86
Entrepreneurial orientation–performance relationships
  characteristics, 85–86
  common method variance, 97–98
  conceptualization and dimensionality, 85–86
  confirmatory factor analysis, 97*t*
  context-sensitive nature, 85
  control variables, 96
  dimensionality, 86
  domestic performance, 94–95
  entrepreneurial orientation, 95
  Europe debt crisis, 2010, 87
  financial crisis, 2008, 87
  hierarchical regression analyses, 100*t*
  hypothesis test, 102*t*, 103
  impact of, 83
  innovativeness, 88–89, 104
  learning advantages of newness theory, 105
  limitations and future research, 106–107
  low-cost production, 87
  measures, 94
  mediation tests, 101–102, 103*f*
  multiple regression analyses, 98–101
  opportunity-seeking tendency, 85
  proactiveness and, 89–90
  reform, 83–84
  reliability and validity of measurement model, 96
  risk-taking, 89, 104
  sample and data collection, 93–94
  social networking, 84
  social network relationships/guanxi, 90–92, 95
  strategic flexibility, 92–93, 95–96
  well-regulated DEs, 84
European sovereign debt crisis 2010, 110–111, 147

Exchanging function, 197, 204*t*, 207–208, 212–213
Explanatory sequential mixed methods design, 167
Export-oriented FDI, 25
Extra-role behaviours, 118–119, 123, 131

**F**
Facilitating function, 198, 207*t*, 210–213
FDI OEMs, 62*f*
  dynamic capabilities for, 42
  global value chain, 65
  low-cost advantages of, 27
  manufacturing, 25–26
  upgrading strategies by, 26–44
FDI spillover effects, 12–13
Financial crisis, 2008, 52–53, 110–111, 147, 156, 219–220
Foreign-owned vehicle manufacturers, 10–11
Full mediation model, 77–78, 102
Functional upgrading
  leadership in, 33
  original equipment manufacturer, 28–31
Fuxi, 114

**G**
Gen (mountain)
  Later Heaven sequence, 165*f*, 166
  measurement, 136–137*t*
  symbolic meaning, 116–117*t*
Global financial crisis, 2008, 25, 38, 61–63, 66
Globalization, 28, 44, 64, 147
Global start-up OEMs
  branding for, 69–70
  developed economies, 44–45
  emerging economies, 44–45
  entrepreneurial orientation
    (*see* Entrepreneurial orientation–performance relationships)
  global value chain, 45–46
  international entrepreneurship, 45–46
  literature review and hypotheses, 64–65
  OEMs, 46–48

reverse internationalization by
    (*see* Reverse internationalization)
TECHSAVVY, 48–49
Global value chain (GVC), 7, 23–24
    analytical framework, 65–66
    design and marketing activities in,
        28–29
    first-tier status, 39–40
    globalization, 28
    global start-up firms, 45–46
    international entrepreneurship and,
        45–46
    prevalence of, 62–63
    technology spillover effects, 32
    upgrading, 24
Grass-roots workers, 162, 170–176,
    185–186
Green technology, 220
Gross domestic product (GDP)
    employment *vs.*, 6*f*
    manufacturing and service industry, 26*f*
    working age population, 219
Grounded Theory approach, 178, 201,
    203–205
*Guanxi*, 90–92, 95, 193

## H

Harmonization process, 109–110, 133
Harmony
    affective commitment, 132–150
    based on *Yijing*, 113–115
    of Chinese people, 109–110
    OCB, 110–132
    scale, 168–170
64-Hexagram system, 115, 118–119
Hierarchical multiple regression (HMR)
    procedure, 18
    affective commitment, 134, 137–139,
        144, 147–148
    Asian traditional philosophies, 148
    cultural variables impact on, 112
    divergence perspectives, 130
    large and novel setting for, 110
    Western theoretical models, 129
Hong Kong Stock Exchange, 5–6
*Hukou* system, 158

## I

Industry 4.0 concept, 1
Informants
    data sources and, 35
    translation tasks, 201, 202*t*
Innovativeness, and performance, 88–89
In-role behaviours, 118–119, 123
Institute of Technical Education (ITE), 40
Institutional Theory, 15–16
Intelligence gathering, 197
International business (IB) literature,
    192–194
International entrepreneurship
    global start-up firms, 45–46
    global value chain, 45–46
Interpersonal harmony, 109–110, 119
Intervening function, 198, 208*t*, 211–213

## J

Japanese auto industries, 21–22
Job satisfaction, 112, 120–121, 123, 129
Joint ventures (JVs), 8–9, 150–151.
    *See also* Sino-foreign JVs

## K

Kan (water)
    Later Heaven sequence, 165*f*, 166
    measurement, 136–137*t*
    symbolic meaning, 116–117*t*
Keyword marketing, 51–52
Knowledge-acquisition capability, 63–66, 73
Knowledge transfer in MNCs, 191–192,
    194–196
    boundary-spanning function,
        translation and, 196–200
    conceptual model, 200*f*, 203
    cross-cultural communication, 192
    data coding method, 203–205
    data collection, 201–203
    limitations, 214–215
    in MNE context, 194–196
    results, 206–212
    sample selection, 200–201
    theoretical and practical implications,
        213–214
Korean auto industries, 21–22

Kun (Earth)
   Later Heaven sequence, 165–166, 165*f*
   measurement, 136–137*t*
   symbolic meaning, 116–117*t*

**L**

Labour challenges, 5–6
Labour conflicts, Yin–Yang harmony,
      156–157
   ACFTUs, 159–160, 162
   characteristics of workers, 170–176,
      185–186
   Chinese *vs.* Westerners people, 160–161
   data analysis, 178
   data collection, 168
   explanatory sequential mixed methods
      design, 167
   5C model, 164–166, 178–184, 179*f*,
      186–187
   instrument, 168–170
   interview data, 177*t*
   least studentized difference approach, 170
   limitations, 187–188
   management, 157–159, 185
   methods, 167
   one-way ANOVA results, 170, 172–175*t*
   participants, 168
   person correlations matrix, 171*t*
   research questions, 166–167
   resolution, 162–164, 186–187
   Western dual-concern model, 161
Labour contract law, 5–6, 159
Labour-related issues, 2, 6–7
Labour strikes, 156–157, 166–167, 186
Lack of equivalence, 199
Later Heaven sequence, 164, 165*f*
Leadership
   in functional upgrading, 33
   pattern-matching analysis, 41–42*t*
Learning advantages of newness (LAN)
      theory, 105
Least studentized difference (LSD) approach,
      170
Li (fire)
   Later Heaven sequence, 164–165, 165*f*
   measurement, 136–137*t*
   symbolic meaning, 116–117*t*

Linear progressive model, 133, 162–163
Linking function, 198, 205*t*, 209, 212–213
Local entrepreneurial OEMs, 62*f*
Low-cost advantages, 27, 36–37, 62–63
LSD approach. *See* Least studentized
      difference (LSD) approach

**M**

*Made in China 2025* initiative, 1
Manipulating function, 199, 206*t*, 209–210,
      212–213
Manufacturing capabilities
   OEMs, 31–32, 38
   pattern-matching analysis, 41–42*t*
Manufacturing industry, China
   from cross-cultural perspective, 189
   employment *vs.* GDP in, 6*f*
   labour challenges, 5–6, 218–220
   profit margins, 153–155
Maoist working-class worker, 158
Market-for-technology policy, 9
Mediating effect
   affective commitment, 144, 146–147
   OCB, 126
   strategic flexibility, 92–93
Methane gas detector (MGD), 54–56
Migrant workers, 142, 158
   ACFTUs, 159
   low-educated, 188–189, 218
   low pay, 156, 158–159
   younger generation, 217
MNE, 191–215
Moderating effect, 90–92
Multilingual environment, 193–195
Multinational corporations (MNCs), 5–6
   boundary spanning, 196–200
   cross-cultural management, 192–194
   data collection methods, 201–203
   developed economies, 47, 64–65
   first-tier status, 39–40
   knowledge transfer (*see* Knowledge
      transfer in MNCs)
Multinational HRs, 219
Multiple regression analyses, 98–101

**N**

Nonmediation model, 78–79, 102, 128

## O

OCB, 110–112
  alternative models, hypothesis test of,
    127–128*t*
  art-based view, 112–113
  assessment of hypotheses, 128–129
  confirmatory factor analysis, 124, 124–125*t*
  construct validity, 124–125
  control variables, 123
  degree of harmony, 116–117, 120, 120*b*,
    122–123, 128–130
  hypothesis, 120–121*b*, 121*f*
  in-role and extra-role behaviours,
    118–119, 123
  job satisfaction, 120–121, 123, 129
  limitation, 130–131
  population and sample, 121–122
  self-report measures, 123, 130–131
  structural equation modelling approach,
    126–129, 128*f*
  theoretical contributions, 129–130
  types of measures, 122
  *Yijing*, 113–115
  Yin–Yang dynamics, 115–118
One-child policy, 132–133
One-way ANOVA, 170, 172–175*t*
Original-brand manufacturer (OBM), 24
  governmental support, 12–16
  industry supporting policy, 10
  methodology
    control variables, 18
    foreign-brand cars, proportion, 18
    policy support, 17
    results, 18–20
    sample selection, 16–17
  own-brand innovation, 12–16
  prosperity of, 10
  Sino-foreign JVs, 12–17
  trade market for technology strategy,
    10–11
  upgrading, 24, 44–58
Original equipment manufacturer (OEM),
    201, 217
  absorptive capabilities, 32–33
  British entrepreneurial, 44–58
  business profiles of two-case companies,
    37*t*

  conceptual framework, 33*f*
  data sources and informants, 35
  dynamic capabilities, 30–31
  empirical findings, 36
  export-led industry, 158–159, 187–188
  foreign-invested, 157–158
  functional upgrading, 28–31
  globalization, 28
  global start-up firms, 46–48
  labour challenges, 5–6, 24
  labour-intensive, 156–159, 187
  leadership in functional upgrading, 33
  limitations and recommendations, 43–44
  manufacturers, increasing, 28–29
  manufacturing capabilities, 31–32
  methodology, 34–36
  pattern-matching analysis, 41, 41–42*t*
  principal of, 158
  sample selection, 34–35
  Singapore/FDI, 26–44
  suppliers, 7, 13
  Taiwan-invested, 167
  technological capabilities, 32
  upgrading, 24
  Yin–Yang harmony framework, 156

## P

Partial mediation model, 78, 126
Pattern-matching approach, 34, 36, 41,
    41–42*t*
Pearl River Delta region, Guangdong
    province, 142
Peasant workers, 158–160
Personal protection equipment (PPE), 53
Person correlations matrix, 171*t*
Point-of-sale (POS) products, 37–38
Predictor–mediator–outcome model,
    75–77, 126
Proactiveness, and performance, 89–90
Public ownership, 14

## Q

Qian (heaven)
  Later Heaven sequence, 165–166, 165*f*
  measurement, 136–137*t*
  symbolic meaning, 116–117*t*

**R**

Research questions (RQs), 166–167,
    200–203
Resource-based view (RBV), 30
Reverse internationalization
    assessment of hypotheses, 79
    branding in, 107
    conceptual framework, 71*f*
    descriptive statistics and correlations, 76*t*
    entrepreneurial orientation
        (*see* Entrepreneurial
        orientation–performance
        relationships)
    factor loadings of perceptual scales, 74*t*
    global financial crisis (2008), impact of, 66
    global value chain, 65–66
    hypothesis test of alternative
        models, 78*t*
    knowledge-acquisition capability, 67–71
    limitations, 82
    literature review and hypotheses, 64–65
    methodology
        common method variance, 75
        conduct of own brand strategy, 73
        control variables, 73
        knowledge-acquisition capability, 73
        measures, 72
        performance, 72–73
        results and analysis, 75–79
        sample and data collection, 71–72
        scale reliability and validity, 74
    regression analysis, 77*t*
Reverse knowledge transfer, 66
Reverse technology transfer, 66
Risk-taking, and performance, 85–86, 89
RMB exchange rate, 5–6
RMB investment plan, 7
RQs. *See* Research questions (RQs)


**S**

Science-based views, 134–135
SEADAQ, 39
Self-report measures, OCB, 123, 130–131
Self-Rescuer (SCSR), 54–56
Service-oriented culture, 153–155
Service-oriented industries, 188–189, 219

Severe acute respiratory syndrome (SARS)
    crisis, 50–51
Shanghai Automotive Industry Corp.
    (SAIC), 8, 16–17
Shenzhen factories, 158
Singapore OEMs
    sample selection, 34–35
    upgrading strategies by, 26–44
Sino-foreign JVs, 12–16
    establishment, 20
    foreign-brand cars on, 19–20, 19*t*
    measures, 17
    mediating effect of, 12
    own-brand products by, 22
    policy incentives, 9, 11–12
    Shanghai Automotive Industry Corp.,
        16–17
    state-controlled, 9
Six-point Likert-type scale, 122, 142
SMEs
    as born globals, 64
    domestic, 71
    in emerging economies, 61, 92
    manufacturers, 61
    OEMs, 65–66
Social Exchange Theory, 118–121
Social network relationships, 90–92, 95
Social psychology, 120–121, 140
Social stability, 198–199, 213
State-owned enterprises (SOEs)
    innovative capabilities, 9
    market for technology, 8
    policy support, 17
    privatization of, 10
Statistical remedial approach, 144
Strategic flexibility, 83–107
Structural equation modelling (SEM)
        approach
    mediation tests, 75–77, 101
    multiple regression analyses, 98
    OCB, 126–129, 128*f*
Sun (wind)
    Later Heaven sequence, 164–165, 165*f*
    measurement, 136–137*t*
    symbolic meaning, 116–117*t*
Supply chain, 38–40
Sustainable career and innovation, 218

## T

Taiwan-invested OEM, 167
Taoism, 113–114, 163
Technological capabilities, 32, 41–42*t*
TECHSAVVY
  background and crippled start-up, 49–56
  cultural differences, 54
  data collection, 48–49
  decision-making processes, 57
  difficulties and challenges, 54–56
  early success, 51
  financial performance, 52*f*
  global financial crisis hit, 52–53
  international entrepreneurship, 56
  keyword marketing, 51–52
  limitations and future research, 58
  pricing strategies, disputes on, 55
  product safety and quality requirements, 55
  severe acute respiratory syndrome crisis,
    50–51
  strategic alliance, 57–58
  upgrading to OBM, 53–54
3D–hierarchical model, 213, 215
Trade Union Constitution 2003, 159
Trade Union Law 2001, 159
Triangulation approach, 35–36

## U

Uncertainties
  macro-level environmental, 197
  postfinancial crisis environment, 132
  variety of, 219–220
Uppsala model, 64, 80
Urbanization, 217

## V

Variance inflation factors (VIFs), 75, 98

## W

WDP. *See* Workforce development
    programmes (WDP)
Western corporate governance systems,
    109–110
Western dual-concern model, 161–162
Westerners, labour conflicts, 160–161
Western ideal of harmony, 162–163
Western organizational behaviour theories,
    117–118

Western society, 113
Workers
  activism, 153–155
  characteristics of, 170–176, 185–186
  goal for, 109–110
Workforce
  commitment, 148–149
  control variables, 123
  diversified and multicultural, 219
  manufacturing, 110
  migrant, 217
  shrinking and ageing, 219
Workforce development programmes
    (WDP), 155
World Trade Organization (WTO), 7

## Y

*Yijing*, 133, 163
  central paradigm, 163
  eight-trigram model, 110*f*, 114–117,
    135–136, 163–164
  harmony based on, 113–115
  perspective, 166–167, 185
Yin–Yang harmony, 114–115
  dynamics, 115–118
  labour conflicts, 156–157
    ACFTUs, 159–160, 162
    characteristics of workers, 170–176,
      185–186
    Chinese *vs.* Westerners people, 160–161
    data analysis, 178
    data collection, 168
    explanatory sequential mixed methods
      design, 167
    5C model, 164–166, 178–184, 179*f*,
      186–187
    instrument, 168–170
    interview data, 177*t*
    least studentized difference approach,
      170
    limitations, 187–188
    management, 157–159, 185
    methods, 167
    one-way ANOVA results, 170,
      172–175*t*
    participants, 168
    person correlations matrix, 171*t*

Yin–Yang harmony *(Continued)*
    research questions, 166–167
    resolution, 162–164, 186–187
    Western dual-concern model, 161
  thinking, 107
Yue Yuan Group, 5–6

**Z**
Zhen (thunder)
    Later Heaven sequence, 164–165, 165*f*
    measurement, 136–137*t*
    symbolic meaning, 116–117*t*
Zhou dynasty, 164